All you need to know™ about the Global Financial Markets 2010/11

Christopher Stoakes

LONGTAIL

in the UK, also known as
All you need to know about the City Part 2

Christopher Stoakes has been a financial markets insider for over 25 years, as a financial journalist, partner in a London law firm and a management consultant.

Chris was a scholar at Worcester College, Oxford where he read law. He qualified as a lawyer at international law firm Freshfields (now Freshfields Bruckhaus Deringer).

He subsequently edited *Global Investor*, *Risk Financier* and *International Financial Law Review* among other finance publications and for eight years wrote the 'Financial Lawyer' column for *Euromoney*. He has been by-lined in more than 30 UK business magazines and in most of the quality nationals.

Chris was also the marketing partner in a London law firm, the head of knowledge management at an international law firm and a founder of Sherwood PSF Consulting Limited. He is a qualified teacher and has held senior visiting positions at Nottingham Law School and the College of Law in the UK. Chris is the author of *All you need to know about the City* and *All you need to know about Commercial Awareness*, also published by Longtail.

Here's the deal. I'm going to take you on a flight around the world to show you the world's financial markets. What we're talking about is money. Who has it, what it looks like. The bricks 'n' clicks.

Who has it is what I call the 'bricks'. The bricks are real. As we look down they'll be what you see on the ground: the international financial centres (IFCs) where the financial institutions and the people who work in them reside – the banks, institutional investors, hedge funds, private equity houses, brokers, the lot. They're the people with the money.

What it looks like – what forms it takes – I call the 'clicks'. These days money is just electronic entries on screens. The clicks are virtual. They're the international financial markets (IFMs), the clouds where all the money floats. What do I mean by money? Currencies and gold for sure. But all those other financial instruments with monetary value too: shares, bonds, derivatives, money market securities and so on. These things used to be traded on the ground, on the trading floors of exchanges. But now the bulk are traded in thin air, in cyberspace, between brokers' screens and over the phone.

That's what I mean by the bricks 'n' clicks.

As we fly through the IFM clouds we're going to get right up close to the weird and wonderful instruments and securities that caused the world's financial meltdown – securitisation, sub-prime lending, structured investment vehicles – all of that credit crunch stuff.

But as we look down we'll see an even bigger picture – the world's economies and how they interact, and how governments stepped in to prevent financial oblivion.

In between we're going to touch down in those IFCs: New York, Tokyo, London, Hong Kong, Shanghai, Singapore, Mumbai, Frankfurt, Dubai – even Chicago, king of derivatives – getting so close we can smell them.

And along the way we'll glide above the island paradises that are the offshore financial centres (OFCs).

By the end you'll know all about the IFMs, IFCs and OFCs which together make up the global financial markets. You'll understand all those confusing acronyms and bits of jargon people in the financial markets like to bandy about. You too will be an expert.

Deal?

Strap yourself in. Time to get airborne.

WARNING

This book is a simple and concise guide to a complex, multifaceted subject that is changing all the time. Given the need to simplify an inherently complex subject, this book is not comprehensive or definitive. Readers must not rely on this book except as a general, schematic overview. Accordingly neither the author, the publisher, their agents, consultants nor employees accept any liability for any loss (direct or indirect; immediate or consequential; contractual or tortious) however caused from use of this book or reliance upon it.

For Eve Stoakes
who for more than thirty years since my father's death
has been the inspiration for so much of what I do
and doesn't realise how clever she is;
in memory (as always) of
Frank Stoakes

Written and edited at Scripto KT and Studio WO
VEJ for all your guidance, support and love

First published January 2010 by Longtail Publishing Limited, UK
Tel: +44 (0)20 7938 1975 Fax: +44 (0)20 7938 3861 Email: info@longtail.eu
Web: www.allyouneedtoknowguides.com

Publisher:	James Piesse	Deputy Editor:	Sheenagh Nixon
Sub-Editor:	Karen Howatson	Assistant Editor:	Sara Jenkin
Assistant Editor:	Josie O'Donoghue	Typesetting:	Louise Downer
Art Director:	Andrew Debens		

ISBN 978-0-9552186-4-4
Printed in the UK by Stones

CONTENTS

fees – hedge funds don't hedge – leverage – prime brokerage – lock-ins – suspended redemptions – closed and soft-closed – prime brokerage – spectacular crashes: LTCM – private equity – venture capital – limited partnership and feeder funds – principal finance – pension funds – demographic time bomb – custody – insurance companies – casualty v life – credit crunch in the insurance markets – AIG – monolines – reinsurance – ART (alternative risk transfer) – sovereign wealth funds – the role of investment banks

Goldsmiths and the origins of lending – banca rotta – bi-lateral lending – common bank lending terms – matched funding – yield protection – security – financial covenants – other events of default – syndicated lending – sovereign lending – acquisition finance – asset finance (finance leasing) – rental – leasing covenants – double dips – finance lease v operating lease – trade finance – project finance – limited recourse financing – who is involved – step-in rights – multilateral agencies – offtake or take-or-pay agreement – Sharia (Islamic) banking – Sharia boards – microfinance – peer-to-peer platforms – pre-bankable – private banking – HNWIs

An alternative IFC geography: the OFCs – the common denominators – capital flight – the role of tax in emerging markets – OECD – trusts in OFCs – the role of regulators in the IFMs – the four areas of regulatory focus – key areas for improvement – of crooks and conmen – macroprudential v microprudential – regulatory arbitrage – principle v rule-based – regulating banks and the banking bonus culture – anatomy of a bank

Governments and the IFMs – the impact of interest rates internationally – supranationals – the World Bank and the IMF – how the world's financial system was saved – how a liquidity crunch became a credit crunch – fiscal stimulus – quantitative easing – bank recapitalisation – deleveraging of financial assets – too big to fail? – the sorry saga of Iceland – the US as the world's biggest borrower – balance of payments – the dollar as the reserve currency – the fear of dollar devaluation – banking flows – a new economic order – emerging markets – BRICs – China

Chapter 1

Getting off the Ground

SPEED-READ SUMMARY

- Money is a fungible store of value that enables people to trade

- There are two types of money: equity (shares) and debt (loans and bonds)

- The term 'capital markets' means the debt and equity markets

- The collective term for shares and bonds is 'securities'

- The international financial markets (IFMs) are a market like any other, with customers (companies and governments), stallholders (banks) and wholesalers (institutional investors)

- In the IFMs, what is bought and sold is the use of money

- Companies need money to expand and for cashflow

- Governments can only borrow (debt) – they can't issue shares

- The buyers of securities are institutional investors (pension funds, insurance companies and investment funds) known as the 'Buy Side'

- Issuers of securities and the banks that advise them are known as the 'Sell Side'

- The biggest banks do everything – they distribute securities (investment banking), lend (commercial banking), manage money (asset management) and provide pension and insurance products (bancassurance)

- In addition to the IFMs there are international financial centres (IFCs)

- New York and Tokyo are the biggest IFCs because they have massive domestic financial markets

- But London is the leading IFC because more of the IFMs are traded there than anywhere else

- There are IFCs that are offshore, called 'offshore financial centres' (OFCs)

Imagine a primitive world without money. You have to barter for what you want. Let's say you grow potatoes but what you want is meat (for a balanced diet). Instead of getting on with growing your crop you have to spend time finding a hunter who not only has meat but wants potatoes in return. This is what economists call a 'double coincidence of wants'. And that's not the end of it. Having found that person, you will only conclude a successful exchange if you can agree a price (how much meat for how many potatoes). One other problem: most activities don't permit the stockpiling of value. With both meat and potatoes, what you can't eat or trade will rot. It will become valueless. You will never be able to build up a store of value to tide you over in retirement, so you won't be able to stop working.

1. WHAT IS MONEY?

As society developed, people used popular commodities such as sheep to pay for whatever they wanted to buy. But sheep are difficult to carry, don't last forever, can't be divided (you can't give a leg of mutton in change as you can three dimes for a buck) and some are bigger and healthier than others. Salt was also used (the word 'salary' comes from the Latin for 'salt money') which had the merit of being transportable, durable, divisible and standard. But it can still get wet, not everyone wants it all the time, and you still need to agree the rate of exchange.

Then people began to use precious metals such as silver and gold as currency. Currency provides a **medium of exchange** (in place of barter), a liquid **store of value** (it doesn't go off, so you can stockpile it for the future), a **unit of account** (whereas sheep don't come in a standard size) and **stability** (it doesn't go out of fashion). It provides, therefore, a standard of **deferred payments** (you can buy now and promise to pay later). But gold isn't that portable and it isn't so divisible.

People entrusted their gold to goldsmiths who gave them a receipt. When a depositor wanted to pay someone else, he wouldn't bother to go and get the gold: he'd simply hand over his receipt to the other for that person to claim the gold off the goldsmith. In practice it was much easier to leave the gold where it was and just exchange receipts. This is how money (paper notes) started. And the goldsmiths, knowing the gold would stay where it was, could 'lend it out' by issuing further notes in respect of it, which is how banking started. (Incidentally, in some parts of Africa salt was worth more than gold.)

Nowadays we use coins and notes over gold because they are portable, uniform (which means that money is **fungible** – when you lend a friend a fiver, you don't expect that identical note back), divisible, acceptable (in the old days, some people didn't want sheep or salt) and durable (you can replace old coins and notes).

In fact the old idea that paper money should be backed by reserves of gold has disappeared. So, when you think about it, we use coins and notes because we have **confidence** in their value, not because they are a substitute for gold. Confidence (the sense that your money has value and you will get it back if you stick it in a bank) is critical to financial markets. Money is a funny thing when you think about it: a confidence trick. And confidence is the oxygen of the financial markets.

Debt v equity

In this book I am going to introduce you to many financial instruments with weird and wonderful names almost expressly designed to be incomprehensible to ordinary people like you and me. So let's get one thing straight. There are only two types of money, whatever anybody says: equity and debt.

Equity is what companies raise when they issue shares. The people who provide that equity become **shareholders** in the company. They are said to invest in the company so they are also known as **investors**. They hope the shares will **appreciate** (go up in value) and, in the meantime, that the company will pay **dividends** to shareholders out of its profits. Shares are traded on stock exchanges which are equity markets (covered in Chapter 2). Although individuals invest, the biggest investors are pension funds, insurance companies, and investment companies, known collectively as **institutional investors** (covered in Chapter 7).

Debt is money that you **borrow**: you borrow money, promise to repay it on an agreed date in the future, and in the meantime pay interest on it. There are two types of debt: **loans** and **bonds**.

Debt: loans v bonds

Loans are what you and I get from a bank. We pay **interest** on the loan and **repay the principal** (the amount borrowed). Generally speaking, we expect the lender to remain the same throughout the life of the loan.

Bonds are like loans but they are **tradable**. A borrower will issue a bond, institutional investors will buy it (so becoming **bondholders**) and they may sell it on in the bond market (which is part of the debt markets). As with a loan, a bond issuer will pay interest on the bond and repay the principal on the bond's maturity, when it expires. But because the bondholder can always sell the bond, the issuer may not necessarily know exactly who the bondholders (lenders) are at any particular moment.

A strange aspect of business life is that companies are much bigger users of debt than individuals (except people who buy virtually everything on credit). This is because the cost of servicing debt (the interest payments) is generally tax deductible as a business expense. This makes debt often cheaper to use than equity (because dividends payable on shares are paid out of taxed income). However, companies only pay dividends when they have enough profit out of which to do so. But they always have to pay interest on their debt.

Apart from companies, the other big borrowers in the international financial markets (using both loans and bonds) are governments. They can only use debt because a government doesn't have shareholders so therefore can't issue shares in itself.

A picture of money

The diagram opposite shows debt and equity in relation to each other and financial transactions and instruments. It will make more sense the further into the book you get. What it does is illustrate how some of the financial instruments and transactions in the international financial markets (IFMs) relate to each other.

At the top is capital – what you and I call money. On the left hand side is equity (shares), set out in the lifecycle of a company, from venture capital (money used to help a start-up survive and expand) to IPO (this is when a private company goes public and lists on the stock exchange – see Chapter 2), to M&A (mergers and acquisitions when public companies take each other over). This may be done by private equity (see Chapter 7) and may lead to sales of unwanted parts of the target through MBOs (management buyouts).

Then on the right side we have debt – the two types. In the left hand column, loan-based funding: syndicated loans, asset finance, project finance (Chapter 8). In the right hand column, different types of bond, by maturity, from short-term commercial paper and other money market instruments through MTNs (medium-term notes) then to long-term bonds and perpetuals (Chapters 3 and 4).

Then we have securitisation (Chapter 5) which turns loans into bonds. It was the securitisation of sub-prime mortgages that caused the credit crunch (also explained in Chapter 5). And at the bottom of the whole picture, straddling both, we have derivatives (Chapter 6) which can be derived from almost anything above and cover both equity and debt instruments. Keep this map by you as we fly deeper into the IFMs.

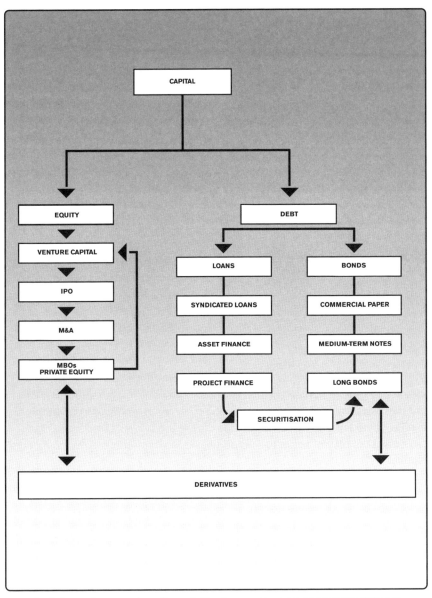

A picture of money: how financial instruments and transactions interact

Why companies and governments need money

Companies use capital (which simply means a pile of cash) for two things. The first is to expand. It's another strange fact of business life that a company that isn't expanding and making more and more profit is going backwards: it risks being overtaken by competitors who are expanding more quickly and generating more profit which they invest back in the business to expand more quickly, and so on.

In this sense money is like petrol in an engine. The more you have, the faster and longer you can go. Companies will borrow money to expand rather than just use existing profit (called 'retained earnings') because they can expand much more quickly than just by using the profit they have generated themselves.

Which brings us on to their second need for money: cashflow. Cashflow is the oil of their business engine. You can have a tank full of petrol and your foot flat on the floor but if you don't have enough oil in the engine it will seize up and break. Cashflow is, at its most simple, the ability of a business (or government for that matter) to pay its creditors (the people it owes money to) on time. If a company cannot pay its suppliers and staff, can't meet its utility bills (electricity, water, heating), or pay for the telephones and technology it uses, or the premises it occupies, it will have to close its doors and cease to trade – no matter how profitable on paper that business is or could have been. Hence the expression 'cash is king'. It's lack of cashflow that caused the global financial meltdown, as we shall see.

Governments are big borrowers in the IFMs because their only other source of money is taxation and at various times their tax receipts aren't enough for what they need to do, such as modernising public services and infrastructure for the long term (schools, hospitals, transport) or meeting the cost of supporting those out of work in a recession. So they borrow in order to pay back later.

So companies and governments are big users of the IFMs to get cash – to meet short-term cashflow gaps and longer-term investment needs. And they turn to banks to help them raise it.

2. WHAT'S A MARKET?

What do you do when you have money? You go and spend it in the market. What does a market look like? If we were airborne over a market – any market, a fruit and veg market, a souk or a bazaar – you'd find it easy to describe: (1) customers coming to buy, (2) stallholders selling to the customers and, behind the stallholders, (3) the wholesalers bringing produce and artefacts from miles around to keep the stalls stocked. Believe it or not, this is a simple picture that works for the world's financial markets. (1) The customers are companies and governments. (2) The stallholders are banks. (3) The wholesalers are institutional investors (pension funds, insurance companies and investment funds). And the only strange thing is that what is being bought and sold is not produce but money or, more accurately, the use of money.

This is done mainly by companies and banks issuing securities, a collective name for shares and bonds (which are explained in the next two chapters). Companies issue both. Governments don't have shareholders so can't issue shares, but they do issue bonds. Companies and governments get banks to help them issue these securities (we'll see what banks do later on). Banks advise them on how to raise the most money at the cheapest cost, and then distribute these securities to institutional investors. It's the institutional investors that buy these securities. They are said to invest in them.

This is how companies and governments get the money they need (see the box for why they need it). Because they do so by selling securities, they and the banks that help them are called the 'Sell Side'. The institutional investors are called the 'Buy Side' (this is where the analogy with a market breaks down − but only a bit).

And where do institutional investors get this money that they invest? From you and me: we pay insurance premiums to get insurance for our house, possessions, car, holiday, sickness and life cover; we pay pension contributions for when we retire; and if we have savings we may put them in a fund. All of this money is invested in the IFMs. IFMs exist to channel this money to those that will make best use of it. At least, this is the old idea of capitalism. The new idea of capitalism is that the IFMs exist to trade risk and speculate − or at least it was until the credit crunch, as this book explains.

3. WHAT'S A BANK?

At the heart of any market are the stallholders. They are the intermediaries between the customers and the wholesalers. Without the stallholders, arguably you wouldn't have a market at all.

So it is with the IFMs. At their core lie banks. So what's a bank?

A bank is, technically, an organisation that has a banking licence. But this definition tells you nothing. Banks are right at the centre of the IFMs. It's thanks to banks that the global economy suffered the recent financial meltdown (more on this in Chapter 5 − the cause; and Chapter 10 − the solution).

The biggest banks these days do four things: (1) they help with the issue of shares and bonds; (2) they manage money; (3) they provide pensions and insurance products (in this sense they act as institutional investors); and − most obvious of all − (4) they lend money. These activities are called

(1) **investment banking**, (2) **asset management**, (3) **bancassurance** and (4) **commercial banking**. Investment banking involves shares and bonds and is explained in Chapters 2, 3 and 4. Asset management, pensions and insurance are explained in Chapter 7. Commercial banking is covered in Chapter 8.

I know what you're thinking: banks are known for lending, so why is he leaving commercial banking until so late in the book? Three reasons: it's easy to understand so can wait till later; it's a bit dull (or can be) compared to other things in the IFMs; and most of it is national not international. But, most important of all, the way banks have switched from lending (commercial banking) to trading (which is part of investment banking – buying and selling those shares and bonds) explains in large part the global financial meltdown: the IFMs moved from being places where capital was channelled to those who could make the best use of it, to casinos where banks and other financial players, like private equity and hedge funds, took large risks with their and others' money.

The diagram below shows what a big bank looks like. It's all summarised in Chapter 9 (commercial banking on the left is in Chapter 8; investment banking in the middle is in Chapter 3; asset management and bancassurance on the right are in Chapter 7).

I've started telling you the book's underlying theme (investing has been subverted by trading) and what's in some of the chapters, so I might as well give you the full picture.

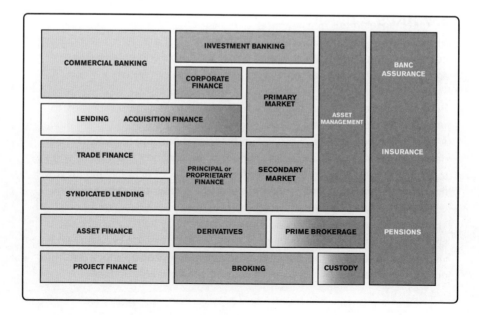

JOURNEY PLANNER: A ROUTE MAP THROUGH THIS BOOK

A big theme of this book is the duality between (a) the IFMs (international financial markets) where instruments such as shares and bonds are traded and which exist mainly in cyberspace and (b) the IFCs (international financial centres) which are territorial and exist on the ground. A sub-set of IFCs are OFCs (offshore financial centres) which are covered in Chapter 9.

So we start with the biggest – but not the most international – IFC: New York. Then we look at a major part of the IFMs: **stock markets** (Chapter 2) because stock exchanges are the physical emanation of a financial centre and the engine-room of corporate growth. They allow companies to raise **equity finance** by **issuing shares**.

Traditionally **share** markets (that is, markets in equities, the shares of public companies) tended to be geographical. Every major country has a stock exchange or *bourse* where local and international companies list their shares to be traded. These markets (in what are often called stocks and shares) compete with each other, as we will see, and, although originally geographical in their coverage, now tend to be interlinked. Many have merged with each other.

So along the way we'll look at how stock markets have changed and how **market-makers** and **brokers**, once found on the floors of stock exchanges, now spend their time at computer monitors and more often than not are part of a **bank**. We'll look at how banks – **investment banks** in particular – have been instrumental in the issue and trading not just of shares, but also of **bonds**. We'll look at the **bond market** (Chapter 3) and the role of investment banks.

Bonds are a type of **tradable debt** (there are only two types of money: equity and debt; and there are only two types of debt: **loans** and bonds). So the bond market is a debt market, where governments and large public companies raise large amounts of debt by issuing corporate promises to pay. The term 'capital market' was originally used to mean the international bond market: bonds issued by governments and companies outside their home country in a currency other than their home country.

Increasingly, large multinational companies issue shares and bonds in the same way so that the term 'the **capital markets**' nowadays embraces both the international bond and equity markets.

Short-term bonds are traded in what are called the **money markets**. The term 'money markets' is used to cover short-term markets in cash, foreign exchange and bonds. It covers everything from overnight deposits to bonds of up to about a year. The money markets are highly susceptible to changes in interest rates, all of which we will look at in Chapter 4.

One very real 'money' or 'cash' market is the **foreign exchange** (aka **forex**) or **currency market**. It's one of the largest single markets in the world and is virtual. There's no single place or trading floor where it happens. Instead, banks, financial institutions, governments and large companies trade foreign exchange with each other.

Why? If you're an international company doing business all over the world, you will need to translate local currencies into your home currency to determine your annual profit, and will need to do the reverse to fund expansion in an overseas market (for instance by setting up a branch or subsidiary or building a factory). Banks are big users of the forex market. Even people like you and me need forex when we go abroad on holiday. So this too is covered in Chapter 4.

Because shares and bonds are both tradable they are referred to as **securities** (the term used to mean a security-printed certificate) and the equity and bond markets are lumped together as the **international capital markets**.

Loans, the other type of debt, weren't historically as tradable as bonds (generally when a bank makes a loan it would keep it till maturity) but a process called **securitisation** (because it turns loans into securities) changed all that. It also caused the sub-prime credit crunch, as we'll see in Chapter 5. All of these trading activities have been made easier – and at times riskier – by **derivatives**, which are financial instruments derived from shares, bonds and commodities, traditionally centred on Chicago in the US. Derivatives, which have been major drivers of the IFMs, are covered in Chapter 6.

A financial centre's users include **hedge funds** (big users of derivatives), **private equity funds** (which take public companies private and turn a profit from breaking them up) and **institutional investors** such as pension funds and insurance companies. All of these buy the shares, bonds, securitisations and derivatives already mentioned. For this reason they are called the 'Buy Side'. They're all covered in Chapter 7, which introduces you to a new set of IFCs which are the heart of investment management.

So far the emphasis is on trading – even private equity investment has turned into a trading activity, as we shall see – but now we turn to **commercial lending** (Chapter 8). The banks we've encountered so far are investment banks, which are involved in the issue and trading of securities.

By contrast, **commercial banks** are less exciting: they take in deposits and lend them out. And the biggest banks are both. Of course, it's commercial banking that did OK in the credit crunch.

This is where, in case you're wondering, we'll touch on **retail finance**. Retail finance is what you and I get from our banks – checking accounts, charge cards, cash. These are necessarily domestic banking operations so don't feature in a book on the international financial markets. The IFMs are about wholesale banking (business-to-business) rather than retail (business-to-consumer). But we will look at two exciting innovations in retail finance that will have global impact: **Sharia** banking (based on **Islamic** principles); and **microfinance** (for the very poor). And in passing we'll touch on **private banking** (for the very rich).

Banks, the sources of this funding, are regulated institutions – they have to be since they take in deposits from the public and are critical to the global economy's wellbeing. So Chapter 9 discusses the role of **governments** and **regulators** in the IFMs. It looks at the structure of banks. But its main topic is OFCs (offshore financial centres), another new topography and which are in Chapter 9 because they tend to be less regulated than onshore markets.

Then Chapter 10 looks at the bigger picture – how economies interact with each other, as they did to avert global financial meltdown. It also looks at **emerging markets** and, in particular, the **BRICs**: Brazil, Russia, India and China – the last two of which in particular will dominate the global economy and the IFMs for decades to come.

THE TOP INTERNATIONAL FINANCIAL CENTRES (IFCs)

Along the way and in between these chapters on markets, we're going to take day trips to the most interesting IFCs, the international financial centres which link the IFMs to the ground. Think of the IFMs as huge dirigibles, floating across the skies, tethered to the IFCs which keep them earthbound. If each IFC – to which the IFMs are attached – were a building, New York would be as high as the Empire State Building (natch), London as big as Big Ben and Tokyo a bit taller than London.

But the rest – well, frankly they are little more than two-storey houses. They include Euronext (a modest-sized department store that includes various European markets including France, Belgium and the Netherlands), then Germany, Canada, Switzerland, Hong Kong and Singapore, with all of the rest as little more than garden sheds.

IFCs: comparative size	
New York	700
Tokyo	200
London	150
Euronext*	80
Germany	50
Canada	40
Hong Kong	25
Switzerland	
Spain	20
Australia	
Taiwan	15
Sweden	10
South Korea	
Finland	

* France, Belgium, Netherlands

This is the shocking thing about the IFCs: the sheer imbalance between the top three and the rest of the world. When people talk about the IFMs they often imply that they are spread evenly around the world. They're not. The IFMs are dominated by New York, Tokyo and London. The rest don't come close.

This book is about *international* financial markets, that is, financial instruments traded internationally. But the fact is that the US and Japan dominate as IFCs just because of the sheer size of their domestic markets.

To give you an example, US municipalities (towns and cities) borrow money by issuing bonds (a bond is a promise to pay back a certain amount on a future date and to pay interest on that amount in the meantime – see Chapter 3). They do this entirely within the US. But the US muni bond market is in its own right one of the largest financial markets in the world. So despite the emergence of China and India, the US is still the single biggest economy in the world. The US has the biggest domestic financial markets in the world and it's their size which gives the US its international dominance too, along with the fact that, as the world's biggest economy, its currency is also the world's reserve currency (it's the currency that international business is conducted in). More financial instruments and

The language of the international financial markets

Whether you talk about the international financial 'market' (in the singular) or 'markets' (in the plural) doesn't matter too much. There is a global financial market in which banks and institutional investors are the key participants. But in fact that market is a series of markets which are either geographical or deal in a certain type of financial instrument. People who work in the financial markets specialise, so although the markets are all about buying and selling (that is, trading) you need a different skillset and expertise if you're trading, say, shares rather than derivatives, or bonds rather than foreign exchange.

So the international financial markets (IFMs) are a bit like a department store: there's one market that comprises lots of different ones; or there are lots of different ones but they are all intimately linked, take place in the same financial centres, and usually involve the same big banks.

Another example of the sort of loose and confusing language you encounter in the IFMs occurs in Chapter 2 which looks at stock markets and stock exchanges ('market' and 'exchange' mean the same thing), meaning the markets for shares. But the term was originally 'stocks and shares' where stocks were generally government bonds. Bonds are certainly listed on stock exchanges (along with some types of derivative) but they are definitely in the minority compared with shares. So 'the stock market' has come to mean the market for shares, even though 'stock' means a bond.

transactions are denominated in US dollars than any other currency: for example, a Malaysian company borrowing from a Japanese bank may well borrow in US dollars.

Japan has massive domestic financial markets too – its Post Office, which is where most ordinary Japanese park their savings, is the single biggest investment institution in the world. But whereas New York is outward-looking, across the rest of the US and the world, Tokyo is inward-looking and reflects Japan's historically introverted and isolated outlook. Tokyo almost rivalled New York in the 1980s. But the Japanese economy fell back in the 1990s and with it so did Tokyo's position as an IFC. It's still up there. But whereas New York reflects like a crystal peak, Tokyo broods like a dark mountain.

Next up on our series of day trips is London, which is actually the most *international* of the IFCs – more of the IFMs take place in London than anywhere else.

By contrast with the US and Japan, the UK has a relatively small domestic financial market (it's not a particularly big country in terms of population, natural resources or manufacturing). In fact the provision of financial services internationally is a significant contributor to the UK economy. It's why the collapse of the world's financial system hit the UK disproportionately hard. The only country to be hit harder was Iceland (population: 300,000). There, financial services dominated the economy to such an extent and had been such a driver of Icelandic acquisitions overseas, funded by debt, that the country's economy has been wrecked (there's more on Iceland in Chapter 10).

Those giants – New York, Tokyo and London – dwarf the others. In the IFCs, size matters: the bigger the market the more likely you will find what you want, the more varieties you will be offered, the greater your order can be, and the lower the unit cost. The biggest markets attract the most customers. It becomes self-perpetuating. Those three are unlikely to be rivalled for at least another decade or two – and then it will be by China. Which is why we turn next to Asia: Hong Kong, the leading Asian IFC after Tokyo; and also Mumbai, one of the up-and-comers.

We pause then to look at Chicago, not a leading IFC but (still) the centre of global derivatives trading which is a key component of the IFMs. Then we visit Frankfurt – the leading European IFC after London, but so far off the pace it's a dot on the horizon. We then look at Singapore, which is becoming a centre for private wealth management; Dubai, which is both an onshore and offshore financial centre that has bootstrapped itself into existence; and finally Shanghai, and its importance in the context of China.

The most interesting thing about all these IFCs is how different they are from each other, how quirky each is in its own right. There's no blueprint for what makes a successful IFC and each has developed in its own way. Maybe Dubai comes closest to what an IFC would look like if you could build it from scratch, because that's exactly what Dubai has been doing (at least, up until recently).

LONDON CALLING

Not surprisingly, given London's position as the most international IFC, the City of London Corporation publishes the Global Financial Centres Index every six months, prepared in conjunction with the Z/Yen Group using a factor assessment model which combines quantitative external indices with qualitative online responses to a questionnaire. What this tries to do is assess what people think of these IFCs in reputational terms, ranging from regulation to culture and places to live in. This is because (thank goodness) you can't have IFMs or IFCs without people and people care about these wider factors too.

London and New York rank first and second but Tokyo merits a lowly 15. Singapore and Hong Kong are top five, Frankfurt top ten. But the others are a mixture of Swiss private banking centres (Geneva and Zurich), European onshore and offshore centres (Luxembourg, Dublin, Guernsey, Jersey and Isle of Man) and centres of asset management (for which see Chapter 7) such as Boston, San Francisco and Edinburgh.

The top five centres in terms of office openings and increased significance include Dubai, Hong Kong, Mumbai, Shanghai and Singapore, all of which we will visit. But our first day trip is to the biggest single financial centre of them all – Wall Street, in Manhattan, in the heart of New York City, New York, USA.

HOW IT ALL CONNECTS

- The rest of this book is a tour around the IFMs, interspersed with day trips to the top and most interesting IFCs

- The cause of the recent global credit crunch was the securitisation of US sub-prime mortgages – which is explained in Chapter 5 – and how the leading economies stopped it getting worse is covered in Chapter 10

- Chapters 2–6 cover the main IFMs where financial instruments are traded (and the role of investment banks), Chapter 7 explains who buys them, Chapter 8 explains the other type of bank (commercial banks), Chapter 9 covers OFCs, and Chapter 10 the wider global economy

- The biggest banks, which straddle the IFMs and are the biggest participants in them, have operations in all the main IFCs – they include JPMorgan Chase, Citigroup and Bank of America Merrill Lynch (all US), Nomura (Japan), Barclays and HSBC (UK), and Deutsche Bank and Commerzbank (Germany). They crop up throughout, as do top investment banks Goldman Sachs and Morgan Stanley

- Investment banking is covered in Chapter 3 and commercial banking in Chapter 8

- Bancassurance (where banks offer insurance and pensions) is covered in Chapter 7

- Warren Buffett, the world's most famous investor, crops up throughout too. He bailed out banks in the credit crunch (Chapter 5), warned against the dangers of derivatives (Chapter 6), is a big investor in insurance companies (Chapters 7 and 9), and bought the first catastrophe bond (also Chapter 7)

DAY TRIP DESTINATIONS

DAY TRIP TO
NEW YORK

As the cliché has it, if capitalism has a capital, then New York is it – although first-time visitors to Wall Street (perched on the southern tip of Manhattan Island) are shocked at the sight of the road that gives its name to, and lies at the heart of, New York's financial district.

For Wall Street itself is a dark, dank, crooked canyon rarely touched by the sun, its road surface pockmarked with a giant's acne, steam rising like a dragon's breath from the subway under ground, the bank buildings sheer on either side casting it in perpetual shadow. It's not Fifth Avenue by any means.

And if you think that's a bit overwritten, that's exactly what New York is: melodramatic, overblown, larger-than-life, self-important, arrogant, aggressive, brash, in a hurry.

So would you be if you had that much of other people's money to play with.

New York is the world's largest and most important financial centre, but that doesn't mean it is the largest international financial centre. That honour falls to London because of the degree of international activity that is carried on there. But New York dominates because of the sheer size and dynamism of its domestic markets. To get an idea of this you have to grasp that, if the US had its own oil, it would have no need whatsoever to trade with the rest of the world while California, if it were a separate country in its own right, would rank within the top ten global economies.

Whereas most financial centres boast one or possibly two exchanges, New York has five.

The biggest one is the **New York Stock Exchange (NYSE)**, roughly $15 trillion in market capitalisation accounting for about two-fifths of the world's entire stock market value and pretty much equalling the other top four altogether (I accept that these are ridiculous, mind-numbing statistics). The most amazing thing about the NYSE is that it still has a trading floor at all. By contrast, the bulk of big stock markets are screen-based. The only other markets which have clung to a floor-based system are the derivatives markets in Chicago, and even there it's changing (see Chicago after Chapter 6). Those who argue in favour of trading floors say that they are much more representative of the way a market is moving than screen-based trading. The latter is antiseptic. The real market conveys immediately, through its atmosphere, noise and volume of tickets (pieces of paper evidencing trades), what is going on (see Chapter 2 for more on this). The NYSE has over 300 members, most of them companies, a quarter of which deal only with each other, and there are roughly 3,000 people in or around the trading floor.

The NYSE was born out of the 1792 Button Wood agreement between 24 stockbrokers and has been tracked by the world's most famous index, the Dow Jones Industrial Average, since 1896. The NYSE has had an extraordinary history and has survived numerous shocks and crashes. The crash of October 1929 which came after six years of unprecedented growth almost destroyed the exchange and by July 1932 the Dow Jones hit rock bottom, having lost 89% of its 1929 peak. Other notable turbulent occasions – aside from the recent global financial meltdown – include the 1997 mini-crash that was prompted by the slump that marked the beginning of the Asian crisis, and the largest single-day plummet in the Dow Jones in the immediate aftermath of the 9/11 attacks (the NYSE closed for six days until 17 September 2001).

An equally important exchange based in New York is **NASDAQ** (National Association of Securities Dealers Automated Quotation system) which is the world's fourth largest exchange by domestic market capitalisation of about $4 trillion. More shares are traded daily on the exchange than any other in the world. When NASDAQ was founded in 1971, it was the world's first electronic stock market and had the limited role of acting as a computerised bulletin board without connecting buyers or sellers. Now, however, it's the largest electronic screen-based equity securities trading market in the US, networked to 3,200 members. NASDAQ, for all its size and establishment, is technically an OTC market which means it's like a street of separate shops rather than a department store (OTC = 'over-the-counter', explained in Chapter 2).

The New York Mercantile Exchange (NYMEX) is the main commodities futures exchange in New York and the world's largest physical commodities futures exchange. NYMEX can be traced back to the Butter and Cheese

Exchange of New York that was set up in 1872 by a group of Manhattan dairy merchants. The organisation changed its name to the current one in 1882 after a more diverse set of commodities began trading on the exchange.

The **New York Board of Trade (NYBOT)** is another commodities exchange in New York and has both the New York Cotton Exchange (NYCE) and the Coffee, Sugar and Cocoa Exchange (CSCE) as its subsidiaries. NYBOT was bought out by the IntercontinentalExchange (ICE) in January 2007. Following the destruction of its offices in the World Trade Center in the 9/11 attacks, NYBOT now uses NYMEX's World Financial Center headquarters and trading facilities. NYBOT is a forerunner in commodities-related innovation. For example, it began trading ethanol futures in 2004 before the energy crisis peaked (for more on futures see Chapter 6).

The **American Stock Exchange (AMEX)** is tiny compared with the NYSE and NASDAQ – it has a market capitalisation of just $100 billion – but has significant niches. These include: (1) acting as a strong junior market for the listing of new businesses (we'll see in the next chapter how tricky it is to keep junior markets going), (2) developing options (a type of derivative useful for equity investors – see more in Chapter 6), and (3) pioneering exchange-traded funds (ETFs – also Chapter 6). ETFs behave like mutual funds (see Chapter 7) but basically mean you can buy one piece of paper that represents an entire index instead of each constituent stock. If NASDAQ is an OTC market, AMEX has its origins as a 'curb market' – in other words, one that started out on the pavement before acquiring its own building – and began in 1842 as an outdoor market for government bonds.

DECLINE IN FORTUNES?

That's a lot of exchanges and a lot of trading. But New York's fortunes as an IFC have dipped since 9/11. Its rate of growth has slowed compared with those of other IFCs and many of the banks headquartered there are seeing faster growth in Europe and Asia and building their presence in other IFCs, most notably London. Of course, New York benefits from the dollar's position as the world's principal reserve currency (that is, more deals and instruments are denominated in dollars than in any other currency, regardless of whether the parties are American), as well as the dominance of its banks and the fact that New York law is used extensively in international financing agreements.

But Michael Bloomberg, mayor of New York and founder of the banking screen-based information service that now rivals Reuters, was so concerned that he commissioned a report from McKinsey, the management consultants. That report said (in 2007, even before the credit crunch) that New York would lose up to 7% in market share over the following five years. That may not sound much, but on the volumes we're talking about, that equates to 60,000 in job losses, and that's excluding the impact of the credit crunch.

The principal reasons identified by McKinsey were legal and regulatory. Sarbanes-Oxley is the name (after the two sponsoring politicians) given to the legislation passed in 2002 in the wake of Enron, WorldCom and the overselling of securities issued by dotcoms (technology companies with business models based on the internet). Known as SOX, it introduced tougher board responsibilities, enhanced financial disclosures and imposed more punitive criminal penalties. It was panned as a business inhibitor. Given (1) US securities legislation, which has always zealously protected individual investors (when in fact most securities are purchased by institutions) and (2) the potentially draconian impact of litigation (much US regulation is in effect the result of class actions brought by groups of disgruntled shareholders), the effect was to put multinational companies off listing on New York exchanges. They chose London and other IFCs instead.

The purpose of SOX was to restore confidence in US capital markets through the improved accuracy and reliability of disclosures which, it was envisaged, would provide greater investor protection. But there has been widespread criticism of its inflexibility and inefficiency. Section 404, which relates to disclosure, is particularly condemned for turning potential foreign companies away from US stock exchanges.

The US Securities and Exchange Commission (SEC – the principal US market watchdog) came in for particular flak, accused of failing to perform rigorous cost–benefit analyses prior to introducing the new regulatory regime. If that's so, it may have underestimated the cost of implementation and failed to recognise the detrimental impact of the regulatory changes.

But in this, the SEC – and the markets – are not helped by the plethora of competing agencies and regulatory bodies which have different responsibilities in respect of different aspects of the markets (for example, derivatives are regulated by the CFTC – a commodities watchdog) which also increases the regulatory costs of doing business in the US.

The US adopted a fortress mentality after 9/11 and this has affected New York as an IFC. Visas are harder to get, potentially putting off some of the best non-US financial minds from plying their trade in Wall Street. Many now view the US as parochial, hostile and unwelcoming and choose to conduct business elsewhere. Islamic finance – a fast-growing and lucrative slice of commercial banking (covered in Chapter 8) – has not found favour in the US, where Islamic finance, Muslim fundamentalism and therefore terrorism are seen popularly as one and the same. By contrast London has majored on welcoming Islamic finance.

NOT ALL DOOM AND GLOOM

However, these drawbacks are temporary blips and are unlikely to affect the world order of IFCs or dent New York's standing as the clear-cut world leader.

New York is headquarters to a tenth of the Fortune 500 companies (the largest 500 in the US) and the foreign companies based in New York employ one in ten of its private sector workforce. It's a byword for financial innovation (the US has six of the world's top ten business schools). The latest fad prior to the credit crunch was hedge funds (see Chapter 7) and New York was the hedge fund capital of the world. More than half of China's 30 largest companies have their regional HQs in the New York metropolitan area in preparation for an eventual listing on the NYSE or NASDAQ. And China – as we shall have seen by the end of this book – is where it's at.

Chapter 2

Stock Markets (Equity)

SPEED-READ SUMMARY

- Stock markets are where equities (shares in public companies) are traded

- Exchanges are regulated markets where members are required to make a continuous market (offer to buy and sell shares at all times)

- OTC (over-the-counter) markets are less regulated where buyers and sellers meet for spot (immediate) payment and delivery

- Junior markets are part of exchanges but are more flexible and are designed for recent start-ups that lack the trading history and size of those listing on the main markets

- New York has the biggest equities markets but London is where the most international trading of equities occurs

- Most stock markets are electronic – even the New York Stock Exchange (NYSE), the biggest exchange in the world, is a hybrid of floor trading and electronic

- Typical exchanges are continuous auction (market makers quote prices at which they will buy and sell, those prices reflecting supply and demand)

- The bid is the price at which the market maker will buy, the offer is the price at which he or she will sell, and the spread is the difference between the two (his or her turn or margin)

- Exchanges provide systems for clearing (the matching of trades) and settlement (payment for delivery of the shares bought)

- Stock markets have been taking each other over to gain economies of scale and offer deeper, more liquid markets

- Big trades are done off-exchange through private networks such as 'dark pools'

Stock exchanges are the oldest and most well-established symbols of the IFMs. After all, a stock exchange is the quintessential trading market. It's what most non-financial people associate with the markets. And it's usually a picture of a stock exchange (the New York Stock Exchange (NYSE) in particular) that is used to illustrate stories in the media about the financial markets. That's why stock markets are a popular proxy for the IFMs. It's certainly the case that any country keen to be seen as a financial centre sets up a stock exchange in short order – witness the various Gulf states that have done so in recent years.

Market	Top index	Index stocks as % of total market	10 largest stocks as % of total market	Daily volume	Market capitalisation
New York	Dow Jones Industrial Average 30	78	12	$150 billion*	$19 trillion**
Tokyo	Nikkei 225	74	15	$16 billion	$3.8 trillion
London	Financial Times Stock Exchange 100	89	36	$9 billion	$2.4 trillion
Total world stock market capitalisation – approx:					$35 trillion

* NYSE: $80 billion; NASDAQ: $70 billion ** NYSE: $15 trillion; NASDAQ: $4 trillion

What the press usually focuses on is the 'index'. Every stock market has an **index**. Charles Dow, whose company published the *Wall Street Journal*, established the Dow Jones for the NYSE by taking the 12 top stocks, adding up their prices and dividing by 12 (it now comprises the top 30). The result is an average figure (he called his index the Dow Jones Industrial Average). If you do that every day (and publish it in your newspaper), readers get an instant sense of how the market is moving compared with, say, yesterday and last week. As some companies become huge, there's a risk that their share price will dominate the index and make it less representative. So indices are **weighted** to avoid becoming driven by just a few dominant stocks.

All sorts of market professionals analyse indices: some, called **technical analysts** or chartists, map out price movements in elaborate charts going back decades to see what these tell us about how markets are likely to move going forward (some people would tell you: not a lot). Economists and commentators look at the way a country's stock market is doing as an indicator of the overall wellbeing of its economy (**bellwether**, a weird word, meaning 'indicator' or 'barometer' or 'yardstick' or 'symbol of'). Why do they do this?

A stock market is simply a place where shares in companies can be bought and sold (see Exchange v OTC box over the page). Professional investors (discussed in Chapter 7) buy on the basis of future expectation. They don't buy shares in a company that is already doing well (the shares have already gone up). They buy shares in a company that may be doing badly but looks as if it may do better. This is the classic strategy of buying low when the shares are cheap and selling high when they've gone up. So if investors are buying (which will drive the market up) economists see this as a good sign for the future. It means companies' prospects are on the rise.

Companies for their part are the lifeblood of any economy. They employ people. This is important to governments because only people in jobs have money to pay taxes, and governments have only two sources of money: tax and borrowing. Companies export to other countries. This creates a trade surplus and profits which can be repatriated to the home economy (how economies function is discussed in Chapter 10).

LISTING, FLOATING, GOING PUBLIC, DOING AN IPO

Companies need to expand to survive: if they do not, faster-growing competitors will steal their customers and markets through greater market impact, economies of scale, lower costs and prices.

A private company (that is, with a small number of shareholders and without a ready market for its shares) will become a public company by having its shares listed on a stock market where they can be bought and sold freely by anyone. This enables the company to raise equity finance readily (equity = shares, see Chapter 1). This is called variously: *listing*, *going public*, *floating*, *flotation*, *admission to listing* or *initial public offering (IPO)* – IPO is the US term. Investors buy the shares if they think the company will do well, in the hope the shares will go up in value and the company will pay dividends (payable out of profits) on them.

However big a public company may be – and some, like the world's biggest oil and telecoms companies, are huge – all companies were start-ups once upon a time. In fact, going public can be an effective **exit route** for a company's initial investors. These are often **venture capital** providers, who make a living by selling their shareholding once a business is big enough and using the profits to reinvest in other start-ups; if a business in which they have a shareholding goes public, this provides them with a means of getting their money out, as their shares are offered to the public as part of the flotation.

Going public has a further benefit. Listed shares have an immediate value –

an immediate price at which they can be sold – which means they are good currency for **takeovers** where the bidder offers shares in itself to the target's shareholders in return for their shares in the target, so making the bidder the target's new owner. This is called **mergers and acquisitions (M&A)** and is generally only open to public companies.

So a stock exchange is a place where companies can list their shares and buyers and sellers can trade them. A stock exchange won't guarantee that a company listed on it is a good investment; only that the company will publish information about its activities and finances on a regular basis. That's part of the *listing agreement* between the company and the exchange and, if the company breaches any of the reporting requirements imposed on it, the exchange can suspend its listing, so no one can trade in its shares.

When a company lists it will issue a *prospectus* setting out its prospects and the statements made in that prospectus have to be vetted by lawyers and accountants in a process called *verification* or *due diligence* (due diligence is also used to describe what a bidder needs to do before buying a target company to make sure the target is as it expects). It will also be required by the exchange to appoint a member broker as a *sponsor*, not in the sense of advertising sponsorship but in the sense of proposing it, like a prospective member of a golf club.

So that's what a stock exchange does, from a company's point of view. Let's go now behind the scenes to see how an exchange actually works.

ANATOMY OF AN EXCHANGE

A stock exchange consists of members, a trading floor (usually nowadays an electronic trading network), a separate function providing clearing and settlement and a regulatory department that ensures the quoted companies abide by the listing rules (in terms of transparency) and that members aren't trading on inside information (see below).

One of the most surprising things is that stock exchanges are businesses in their own right, often listed (bizarrely) on themselves. Historically most started as mutual associations, what you and I would call a club, where the members own the club and decide who they want to admit. Now, however, almost all major exchanges have incorporated (see 'Stock exchange wars' below): London in 1986, Tokyo in 2000 and the NYSE in 2006.

This means they now have shareholders who want a return on their investment, which is one reason exchanges have had to become more efficient.

Exchange v OTC

The term *bourse* which is used widely to describe a stock market is thought to come from Bruges where commodity traders (commodities can be anything from gold to coffee) in the thirteenth century met in the house of Van de Burse. Early exchanges include Antwerp (1631), London (1773), Philadelphia (1790) and New York (1792).

The first joint stock company (i.e. which issued shares) was the Dutch East India Company, founded in 1602, whose shares were traded on the Amsterdam stock exchange which came into existence for that reason around then.

However, not all stock markets are the same. The two principal types are stock exchanges and OTC (over-the-counter) markets. It's not a function of size. NASDAQ (see 'Day Trip to New York') is one of the biggest stock markets in the world but is an OTC market.

A **stock exchange** is a place (a trading floor or cyberspace) where you can always buy and sell shares because the members will always quote you a price (the exchange requires them to). This is called a **continuous market** (in the smallest exchanges trading may only occur at certain times of the day to ensure a concentration of buy and sell orders).

There tends to be quite a high degree of financial disclosure and regulation imposed on companies that list. They tend to be established businesses of a certain size with a trading history (profit or loss) over a number of years. Exchanges also offer other services: they will make sure that your order

matches (that if you bought shares, a member has agreed to sell them – this is called **clearing**) and that when you pay you get the shares you bought (this is called **settlement**). Settlement usually takes a day or two so you don't pay the moment you do the deal, nor do you get the shares on the spot.

By contrast an **OTC market** operates by **matching** buy and sell orders rather than by continuous auction. The companies traded are not subject to the same degree of regulation and so may be younger and therefore riskier businesses. Settlement is immediate: you hand over the money and collect the shares as soon as you do the deal (this is called **spot trading** and is also common to the currencies market – see Chapter 4) .

An OTC market can be very small – some start as a single broker matching buy and sell orders. Because it's that much harder to find matching trades, they may happen less often and the price at which trades are done may vary widely from one day to the next. These markets are therefore said to be **illiquid**, there may be fewer shares to trade and the size of orders may be small, all of which can depress prices. This isn't true of NASDAQ: it has 3,200 members across the US, networked by computer. They post prices at which they will buy or sell.

Then there are **curb** markets which are even more informal. Here, trades are negotiated, so it's like trading with whoever is standing round on a pavement.

An image that works for me is of a stock exchange as a department

⇨ store with different boutiques within it but all under the same roof; an OTC market as a row of shops in the same street; and a curb market as occurring wherever and whenever anyone has something they want to sell or buy.

Stock exchanges are more likely to be government-owned or sponsored in emerging markets, like China and the Middle East. This is for reasons of security (emerging markets don't like the idea of more developed exchanges muscling in, especially if the country itself is new to capitalism) and also support (it can be hard to get a stock market going – as it is for any junior market: see the 'Junior markets' box on p32).

STOCK EXCHANGE MEMBERS

The traditional model is based on a concept called **single capacity**, where you have two types of member – **brokers** and **specialists** (that's the NYSE term) – and each has to stick to his or her assigned role (hence single capacity). In smaller markets they may well be individuals. In larger markets they tend to be firms (partnerships) or companies.

Brokers deal with investors, so if a person or investment institution, such as a pension fund or insurance company, wants to buy or sell shares listed on an exchange, they will contact a broker who is a member of that exchange. Brokers are required to execute trades on behalf of their clients as efficiently and economically as possible. Brokers are their clients' agent and generally are not allowed to buy or sell shares on their own account (for themselves) otherwise that could give them a conflict of interest (they might advise their clients to buy shares because they already own shares in that company and want the price driven up by increased demand; or because they want to offload their shares on to their client). Brokers go on to the floor of the exchange to execute their clients' buy or sell orders.

Specialists deal with brokers. They are required to specialise in a certain number of companies each. For each of the companies assigned to them, specialists must be prepared to 'maintain a fair and orderly market', quoting two-way prices (that is, the price at which they will buy and at which they will sell) throughout the mandatory quote period (that is, the trading day). This ensures there is continuous trading in each listed company's shares. Across the trading floor there are several specialists for each share. The broker's job is to go round all of the specialists dealing in that company's shares to get the lowest price (if the broker's client wants to buy) and the highest price (if the broker's client wants to sell).

The prices specialists quote will depend in part on their inventory – if they

Auction v order driven

Trading in stock markets can be by **auction** or be **order driven**.

Auction is the way you and I would expect a stock market to work, with competing market makers quoting two-way prices (buy and sell) at which they are prepared to trade, usually through a continuously updated electronic board. This is called **quote driven trading**. **Continuous auction** means they are doing this throughout the trading day.

In some markets – smaller ones, where the volume of trades is thinner – a **call auction** system prevails, that is, with orders batched together at certain, specified times during the trading day to concentrate activity and ensure there is a market with sufficient liquidity at all. The market maker then carries out an auction to determine the price at which trades occur. Some markets have short trading days for this reason. When the Mongolian stock market started in 1992 it only had enough volume to open for two hours one day a week. Now it manages to open every day for an hour, achieving daily turnover of $200,000 on a market capitalisation of $60 million. Trading is online. The Rwanda OTC market, which opened in 2008 and has a market capitalisation of under $30 million, is open for three hours a day. You might think it remarkable that Rwanda has a stock market at all.

Where there is a trading floor, it is an **open outcry auction** system (specialists on a trading floor) which can co-exist alongside an **order driven** system (often called an 'order book'). This is based on an electronic order book in which buy and sell orders are entered anonymously. The system pairs up those matching 'buy' and 'sell' orders for the same shares which can be matched, and executes them automatically during continuous trading. Orders that aren't matched lapse or are withdrawn.

Exchanges may use both auction and order driven systems, depending on the size of trades and the liquidity of shares. Order driven is good for high-volume, low-value trades. Auction – especially open outcry – is better at accommodating complex trades in big amounts.

The NYSE is one of the few remaining stock markets that has retained open outcry auction alongside order driven and electronic trading platforms. All stocks are tradable via its electronic hybrid market (launched in 2005) and more than half of all order flow is delivered to the floor electronically. The risk with a hybrid system is that specialists no longer have the full flow of orders and may be bypassed over time, yet they are required to keep prices continuous when volume is low.

don't have many shares in a company they will pay a higher price than if they have too many; if they have too many they will sell at a lower price than if they only have a few. With several specialists making a market in a company's shares, it tends to be an efficient market where the spread (the difference between the buy and sell price) is never that great.

At the NYSE for example, there are ten specialist firms at 17 trading posts making a market in 2,800 stocks. At the start of each day they set a buy and sell price which they modify during the day. They execute limit orders (orders to execute a trade at a certain price or not at all) entrusted to them by brokers. They put buyers and sellers together. They stabilise the market and make it possible to move large orders through. Three-quarters of trades are matched but they will also act as principal, so providing liquidity.

INVESTOR PROTECTION

One of the great advantages of single capacity is implicit investor protection. Because brokers are barred from buying and selling shares for themselves, their clients know they will only act in the client's best interests, including any 'buy' or 'sell' recommendations the broker makes. Single capacity avoids conflicts of interest.

The language of the stock market

The **bid** is the price at which a specialist or market maker will buy a security. The **offer** is the price at which the market maker will sell.

The **bid–offer spread** is the turn (profit) the market maker earns between the two.

The **spread** – the difference between the two – is a measure of how liquid a security is, i.e. how deep the market for it is, and how frequently it is traded. The less liquid a security is, the wider the spread is likely to be.

The **touch** is the best price available (buy and sell) at any particular moment.

Typical trading and broking instructions include:

- Day order = to be done on that day only or else it lapses
- Open order = remains open until done
- Fill-or-kill = do it in its entirety or else it lapses
- Execute or eliminate = do as much of it now as you can and forget the rest
- Limit order = do it at this price or better; don't do it if this price is never reached
- Market order = at best price possible
- Stop order = only do it once this price has been reached, but the trade can then be above or below that price

Institutional investors often want to execute trades in such size that they will have an adverse impact on the price as the trade is being done. To avoid this they may instruct a bank or broker to do a **block trade** or a **program trade** (the latter may be done in instalments, often driven by computer to ascertain the optimal price at which to execute a succession of trades).

Nowadays single capacity is the exception because most exchanges are electronic and members are market makers (sometimes called dealer-brokers) and combine the two roles. This means there has to be a lot of regulation determining when and on what basis they will sell directly to or buy directly from the client using their own inventory.

However, the bulk of investors these days are institutions – pension funds, insurance companies and investment funds (as we will see in Chapter 7) – and they don't need the degree of investor protection that retail investors (individuals) do. In the US, foreign companies issuing shares are exempt from the extensive regulation imposed by the US Securities and Exchange Commission (SEC) if they are selling those shares solely to institutional investors (called 'qualified institutional buyers' or QIBs).

As soon as single capacity is abandoned, there's no need for a trading floor where specialists are concentrated and brokers have to go to find them. Instead, trading switches across to electronic platforms. To ensure a transparent market, members have to notify the exchange as soon as they have done a trade, specifying the company, volume and price at which the trade was done. This is immediately sent to all members' screens. It's why on the trading floors of big banks there is an electronic ticker tape going round the room at a height which all traders can see, updating stock prices with details of the latest trades across the market.

This was most graphically illustrated by the fundamental change the London Stock Exchange underwent in 1986. Under pressure from the UK government to maintain its competitiveness internationally, the exchange abandoned single capacity, opened its members to outside ownership and allowed commissions to be freely negotiable. Within three years the exchange had closed its trading floor. These changes (called 'Big Bang' because they were introduced at the same time) enabled big banks to buy and combine brokers and jobbers (the UK term for specialist). This attracted more capital into the London market so that more and bigger trades could be done at keener prices with smaller bid–offer spreads, making it a more efficient market to trade in, with lower transaction costs. These changes underpin London's leading position as an IFC today.

THE QUEST FOR LIQUIDITY

You will have noticed that I've mentioned the term 'liquidity' from time to time. Liquidity is the ease and economy with which you can execute a trade in the market. All exchanges are competing for liquidity. The problem with stock markets is that they are sensitive to buy and sell orders: a buy order drives up the price and a sell order depresses it (the basic supply and demand of capitalism). The larger and more liquid a market, the less impact individual orders have on it and the greater those orders can be. A large, liquid market is one where buyers and sellers will converge because they know they will be able to trade in their desired stocks at keen prices, the volume of trades means that a continuous price is available, and the bid–offer spread is kept to a minimum. In other words, it is self-perpetuating: the bigger the market, the more business it will attract and the bigger and deeper it will get.

This is why it is so difficult to bootstrap new markets into existence (as the box on junior markets highlights). It's why the NYSE is able to preserve a specialist system. It is so big it can, and this, arguably, offers a more visceral indication of market moves – you can sense it in the air and from the degree and noise of trading activity as members scream orders at each other in times of market stress – than you get just from sitting at a screen and seeing it fill with red (falling prices tend to be in red). Some also argue that specialists enable large orders to be digested by the market with less disruption than through electronic trading.

So liquidity is about how easy it is to buy or sell at a good price. If a share is illiquid that means there aren't many buyers or sellers so you may not find someone to trade with at all or, even if you do, the spread is so wide that the act of buying or selling is itself expensive because you're selling too cheaply or buying too expensively.

It's like any market: the bigger the market, the more buyers and sellers you have, the more trading there will be and the keener the prices will be, whereas if you just have a few people standing around they may not have anything in common that they want to buy or sell at all.

The more liquid a market, the easier it is to buy and sell in bulk. Institutional investors have enormous portfolios (as we shall see in Chapter 7) and they don't want to buy or sell just a few hundred shares at a time. If an investment is going to have any meaningful impact on their portfolio's overall performance, they need to trade in big numbers, and the bigger and deeper the market, the easier it will be for them to do that.

Imagine the markets as oceans where whales – the institutional investors – graze. They want oceans that are deep, where food is plentiful and where they are invisible, not ponds where they can't move without being seen.

STOCK EXCHANGE WARS

Stock exchanges understand the importance of liquidity only too well. This is why over the last ten years there seems to have been as much merger and acquisition activity between exchanges as between the companies

Junior markets

Many exchanges recognise that their requirements are too demanding for young businesses. To list on a main exchange you usually need a trading history of a few years, a certain level of cashflow, a certain amount of new money you want to raise by issuing fresh shares, and a commitment that a percentage of your shares will be available for public trading.

This doesn't suit companies that have no trading history (a biotech company may need a lot of capital for research and development yet not even have a product, let alone a history of selling it); or have lumpy cashflow because of the sector they are in; or the bulk of whose shares will remain in the ownership of the founder and his or her family.

To cater for these companies – which can offer more rapid growth to investors while at the same time being riskier because they can just as easily run out of cash and go bust – exchanges set up junior markets, as they are called (the exchange itself is the senior market). These have much lower regulatory requirements so it is cheaper to list on them. Often the exchange will oversee the junior market and require one of its members to be appointed as a nominated adviser ('nomad') to oversee a company that wants to list.

Junior markets have one big problem: liquidity. By definition, smaller companies will have smaller free-floats of shares. Fewer investors will want to buy and sell them so achieving any kind of matched trade can be difficult. The fewer the trades, the less consistent the price at which those trades take place. And these investments are inherently more risky so attract fewer investors anyway.

So junior markets come and go with surprising frequency. Frankfurt's Neuer Markt looked poised to achieve lasting success, but has closed. Similarly Singapore's Catalist exchange, launched at the end of 2007 to replace its secondary board called Sesdaq, has struggled to attract new listings. The same is true of Hong Kong's Growth Enterprise Market.

Junior markets also suffer from one further drawback: as companies grow they migrate to the senior market because it is bigger, the shares are covered by analysts (see Chapter 7) and it attracts far more weight of investment money. Some don't. NASDAQ in the US, which originally attracted technology start-ups in particular, has been successful in retaining the companies it has nurtured, Microsoft for one.

London has had a succession of them: the USM (Unlisted Securities Market); now AIM (Alternative Investment Market). In 2008 it merged with the Borsa Italiana in Milan expressly to launch AIM Italy. London also has Plus, originally a market run by a single broker that matched trades and acted as a market maker, which became Ofex (itself listed on AIM). Plus is behind Plus-Europe, a European platform intended to compete with AIM Italy. Its companies aren't so small either. Plus has Arsenal football club (market capitalisation about £450 million). Its most successful listing has been Rak Real Estate, a Kuwaiti property company which debuted on Plus ⇨

➡ in early 2009 with a market capitalisation of over £600 million.

China, as in many things, is not far behind. It had a pipeline of 300 companies waiting to list on its junior market, the Growth Enterprise Board, which it launched in 2009 as part of the Shenzhen exchange.

listed on them. With electronic markets, the restrictions on trading are driven more by time zone (when the market is open) than geography (where you happen to be located when you trade). Screen-based trading makes markets virtual.

In 1998, the Stockholm and Copenhagen exchanges merged to form Norex. Three years later the Amsterdam, Brussels, Paris and Lisbon exchanges merged to form Euronext. Euronext and the Deutsche Börse then competed head-to-head to buy the London Stock Exchange (then a public company listed on itself).

In 2006, the NYSE demutualised, ending over two centuries as a mutual, member-owned organisation and bought Archipelago, the US electronic market, in a reverse takeover (that is, the smaller company took over the larger but retained control) to gain the latter's listing. It then bought Euronext for over $10 billion despite a counter-bid at a higher price by the Deutsche Börse. The NYSE Euronext merger was completed in 2007 and created a global equities exchange open 21 hours out of 24, headquartered in New York but with European operations and the trading platform in Paris. Meanwhile the London Stock Exchange merged with Borsa Italiana.

Then in February 2008 NASDAQ bought OMX, the operator of several Nordic and Baltic exchanges (Helsinki, Reykjavik, Riga, Tallinn and Vilnius plus, you guessed it, Norex's original members, Copenhagen and Stockholm). In doing so, NASDAQ bought out Borse Dubai's stake in OMX. Those two now have cross-holdings in each other, NASDAQ OMX owning a third of Borse Dubai which in turn owns just under a fifth of NASDAQ OMX. It has common listing requirements which it hopes will make it attract more new listings than NYSE Euronext which has different requirements in the US and Europe.

This wasn't the first time NASDAQ had merged. Ten years before, it linked up with AMEX (the American Stock Exchange) but that didn't work out and AMEX reacquired independence, remaining mutually owned by its members. Then in January 2008 NYSE Euronext said it would buy AMEX and bought up the Philadelphia and Boston stock exchanges (which with the Pacific stock exchange are the largest US regional markets) for good measure.

Domestic v foreign listings/shares v depository receipts

In terms of IFMs, New York is the world's leading equity market because there are more new listings in the US than anywhere else – but that's because the US is the world's largest economy and more companies go public there than anywhere else. The bulk are domestic listings of US businesses, and this is simply a function of the size of the US as a domestic market.

But the world's biggest companies are often listed on several exchanges – usually because they have international name recognition through being a global brand, which makes it easier and cheaper to raise money wherever they are known. For those companies already listed on their home stock market, London is the top equity IFC. More foreign companies (already listed at home) choose to list in London than anywhere else and more foreign equities are traded in London than anywhere else.

In some markets it is easier to achieve the effects of a listing without going through the time-consuming and expensive formalities of issuing and registering securities that comply with the local law. This is especially true of foreign companies wishing to tap the US capital markets. Instead, they achieve this through **depository receipts**.

Essentially the company deposits shares with a bank in the country where it wants its shares traded. The bank then issues receipts in respect of those shares and investors buy and sell the receipts while the underlying shares are kept in the bank's vaults. This route is especially appealing to companies from emerging markets (which are covered in Chapter 10).

Where a depository receipt programme is set up by the issuer it is said to be **sponsored**. Where a bank does it of its own accord (because it can see a potential market in that company's shares and simply buys them itself) the depository receipts are **unsponsored**.

GDRs (global depository receipts) is the generic term. As markets allow them (as Singapore did in 2007 for example), GDRs become country-specific. Those traded in the US are ADRs (American depository receipts), those in India are IDRs, Russian ones are RDRs and so on.

Tokyo has reacted by listing (2009), having already formed a number of alliances, including a working relationship with the NYSE (2007) to develop trading systems and technology, establish cross-listings (companies listed on both exchanges), discuss regulatory issues and launch exchange-traded funds (see Chapter 6). In 2008 it entered into an alliance with the London Stock Exchange (LSE) to establish a joint venture junior market for Asia (something the LSE has had success in doing with AIM and now in conjunction with the Milan bourse with an Italian version of AIM). Tokyo also bought a 4.99% stake in the Singapore Exchange in 2007. The two exchanges have launched exchange-traded funds (ETFs – which you'll remember AMEX pioneered) and Tokyo should benefit from Singapore's expertise in futures (see Chapter 6) and clearing (see below).

ECONOMIES OF SCALE

In addition to liquidity, mergers between stock markets generate economies of scale. There are various back office functions that have to be carried out behind the scenes in a stock exchange. These include clearing, settlement and regulation. The bigger the market, the greater the volume of trades. This means an exchange can gear up to provide these services in bulk, so the lower the cost-per-trade will be.

Clearing means checking that all the details of a trade match – any trade by definition involves two parties, so clearing is the action of ensuring that each party's record of the trade is the same, otherwise the trade fails and won't clear. Clearing takes place at the end of the trading day for sure, but also intra-day depending on the size and liquidity of the market.

Settlement is when the buyer pays the seller for the shares and the seller transfers title in the shares to the buyer. It may surprise you that settlement does not occur immediately after the trade takes place, but T+3 (three days after) in the larger markets and as much as a week in smaller, less developed markets. This is despite the fact that in the leading markets settlement is now paperless and shares have been *dematerialised* which means they exist now as electronic entries instead of hard-copy share certificates. By contrast the Milan stock exchange became notorious in the 1980s for Monte Titoli, literally 'mountain of share certificates' as trades piled up awaiting physical settlement with actual share certificates changing hands.

The way it works is that when a trade is executed, details of the trade are sent by both parties electronically to the exchange's clearing and settlement systems which match the messages and check there are enough shares in the seller's account. Then, on settlement, they instruct the market maker's bank to make a payment to the seller's account and update their own records with details of the new shareholder.

As with stock markets, so settlement systems in Europe are consolidating. The leaders include **LCH.Clearnet** (LCH was the London Clearing House) and **Eurex**.

SHORT SELLING AND STOCK LENDING

The delay between trade and settlement is what enables **short selling** (selling a share you don't have in the expectation that the price will go

ECNs and dark pools

Electronic communication networks (ECNs) and dark pools are off-exchange markets set up privately among consortia of banks, brokers and institutional investors to bypass exchanges altogether, effectively creating their own.

ECNs work by combing through data posted by traders in order to match buy and sell offers. The leader in Europe is **Chi-X** which launched in 2007. Europe is fertile ground because of MiFID (the EU Markets in Financial Instruments Directive), designed to encourage competition in share trading by establishing different categories of market from full-blown 'regulated markets' to 'multilateral trading facilities'. In the US the leaders are **BATS** and **Direct Edge**. Others include **Instinet**, owned by Reuters, the market data provider, **Pipeline Trading**, **Liquidnet**, **POSIT** and **Turquoise**. Several of these also operate dark pools in the US and Europe.

Dark pools, also called crossing networks, are unofficial markets used to trade large blocks of shares anonymously and off-exchange. By keeping these trades private they don't therefore move markets against those engaged in them (whereas a large buy or sell order on-exchange will drive prices up or down respectively during execution).

Users of these networks say that exchanges no longer have the facility to trade large blocks of shares because electronic trading tends to break packets of shares down into small, executable orders. But these networks risk splintering market liquidity, which is why banks allow each other access to pools to which they belong and have got together to launch 'aggregators' that search across dark pools for matching trades. Stock exchanges see these networks as a threat and are fighting back. The NYSE has merged with ArcEx, a leading ECN. The London Stock Exchange is buying Turquoise and merging it with its own platform, Baikal.

Regulators have also shown an interest: they say that dark pools divert sufficient business from exchanges – about 10% in the US – to distort exchange prices and deprive investors of the best prices.

down). A broker will short sell a share at today's price, borrow it from an institutional investor, deliver it at settlement, then go into the market and buy the share at (what the broker hopes will be) a lower price and give that one back to the institutional investor. This gives the broker a profit if his expectation that the price will go down proves right.

Institutional investors (Chapter 7) will lend out shares in their core, long-term holdings in order to generate additional return. The institutional investor doesn't mind parting with shares for a few days in return for a fee. This is called **stock lending**. It assumes that the shares it gets back, if not identical, are at least **fungible** (that is, their principal terms have the same economic effect).

So the broker borrows the share for a fee and hopes the fall in the share price will more than offset the stock lending fee the broker pays the institutional investor.

Short selling can itself, if done in sufficient volume, drive prices down. This was why in the recent financial crisis short selling, particularly of bank shares, was temporarily banned (permanently, in the US). It can create a false market, which is the reason the authorities can prohibit it.

However, although you and I might not sell something we don't own, in the IFMs this is perfectly acceptable practice: if you think something will go up in price, you buy it (you 'go long' of it); if down, you sell it ('go short' of it or 'short' it). Just because you don't own it is no reason for not acting on your hunch.

VERTICAL INTEGRATION

In all of the M&A activity between exchanges, institutional shareholders have played a pivotal role as both shareholders (who own the exchanges – just another investment like any other) and users (as exchanges' principal customers). Consolidation leading to economies of scale is obviously in their interest if it increases liquidity and drives down costs. But institutional shareholders have been mindful of vertical integration (stock exchanges owning the clearing and settlement systems). They don't want exchanges to achieve dominant market positions and then to drive up the price of clearing and settlement as monopoly providers of these services. In some cases these services have been outsourced, to avoid this degree of vertical integration which some institutional investors dislike.

REGULATION

Stock markets want to attract companies that want to list and investors that want to buy their shares. So they will regulate the market just as much as the authorities will. In particular, stock exchanges are vigilant for *insider dealing* or *insider trading* – that is, buying or selling shares on the basis of market-sensitive information that is not in the public domain. Often before a corporate takeover is announced the target's share price will spike (go up), indicative of insider dealing. Equally, exchanges don't want their market to be manipulated by one or more buyers or sellers who are deliberately trying to corner the market in a company's shares or are trying to control the fair price at which those shares should trade.

So any exchange wants to ensure that (1) companies are transparent about what they are doing and how well they are doing; and (2) investors are operating on a level playing field and aren't trying to gain an unfair advantage over each other. Although these two points are simple to make, in practice they lead to an enormously complex area: the regulation of stock markets. We'll come back to this in Chapter 9 but fortunately, unless you're a financial services lawyer or a compliance officer in a bank, you don't have to worry about the detail.

Talking about heavily regulated markets takes us to Tokyo – still bigger than London, even though the latter has a higher volume of international trading.

HOW IT ALL CONNECTS

- Some stock exchanges also trade bonds (Chapter 3) and derivatives (Chapter 6) – both Deutsche Börse and NASDAQ have bought options exchanges because of the better margins they offer

- Open outcry (the NYSE) has been key to derivatives markets (Chapter 6) but even there it is under threat

- OTC markets occur in other types of instruments – currencies and money markets (Chapter 4) and US government bond markets (Chapter 3)

- The biggest users of stock markets are institutional investors (Chapter 7) which are often shareholders in them – they are just another equity investment

- Hedge funds (Chapter 7) have been big buyers of shares in stock exchanges in the hope of a big payout if stock markets merge

- Analysts publish research on companies and likely market moves (also Chapter 7)

- Market makers are now part of investment banks (Chapter 3)

- Stock markets are sensitive to interest rates (Chapter 4) in that when interest rates go up, stock markets tend to go down because risk-free bank deposits become more attractive in relative terms. The same is true in reverse: when interest rates go down, stock markets tend to go up

- Emerging markets may be too small to create stock markets with the necessary liquidity (Chapter 10)

DAY TRIP TO
TOKYO

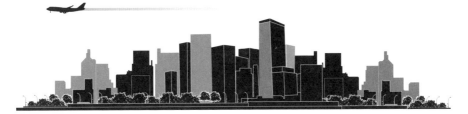

Tokyo is a vast, sprawling metropolis, presenting almost similar vistas in every direction as far as the eye can see. It can be hard to get around. Until twenty years ago, street names weren't in roman script and even now, because of the nature of postal addresses, the nearest a taxi may take you to your destination is to get you to the right block or neighbourhood. After that it's down to you.

So for foreigners the city can be an impenetrable mystery – though so safe that women can walk around almost everywhere unaccompanied at night. For the Japanese it's where salarymen spend their whole careers in one organisation, and even one job.

And that is what the markets feel like: for long stretches they are featureless and directionless, to the bafflement of foreigners.

The truth is that, like Japan until the nineteenth century, Tokyo's financial markets are inward-looking. Tokyo is one of the largest metropolitan economies in the world, it's home to the second largest stock exchange by market capitalisation and the third biggest bond market. But Tokyo is no longer considered a genuinely international financial centre (IFC) in the way that London and New York are, even though, in terms of pure size, Tokyo outstrips London.

Yet it used to be.

In the 1980s, at the height of Japan's economic boom, Tokyo eclipsed London and threatened to rival New York. At year-end 1989 the Nikkei 225 stock index hit an all-time, intra-day high of almost 39,000 and the Tokyo Stock Exchange accounted for a staggering 60% of world stock market capitalisation, making it by far the largest stock exchange in the world. Asset prices – for housing, stocks and bonds – were so high the government issued 100-year bonds. In the Ginza district of Tokyo property cost $1.5 million per square metre.

Then, in 1990, the bubble burst. What followed is known as the Lost Decade. Says it all. The Nikkei eventually hit a low of almost 7,600 in April 2003. By 2004, prime commercial property in Tokyo was less than a hundredth of its peak price and residential property was a tenth of its peak. The combined collapse of the stock and real estate markets are reckoned to have wiped out $20 trillion in paper profits. That's a lot of dough.

The Japanese economy, like the language, is complex, almost impenetrable for outsiders. The size and sluggishness of Japan's financial markets is explained in part by the close ties and extensive cross-holdings between financial institutions and leading manufacturers, creating massive industrial, financial and commercial networkings called *keiretsu*. The constituent companies, which can reach far down into the supply chain, hold shares in each other, making the groups impervious to mergers and acquisitions (M&A activity came late to the Japanese market, in the 1980s, and is still frowned on).

Japan's corporate culture stifles competition: companies that are struggling are supported instead of being allowed to go to the wall; this holds back the better businesses which aren't able to exploit their competitive advantage to maximise profits and invest for greater competitiveness. But I accept that I'm espousing an Anglo-Saxon view of capitalism.

Japanese companies are funded principally through loans from the bank in their industrial network rather than through the more public and demanding capital markets (equities and bonds – see Chapters 2 and 3). This means they have little incentive to change. Banks themselves, until 2009, were not permitted to cross-sell their capital markets services, an area which in any case is dominated by Nomura. This newly introduced liberalisation should encourage companies to access wider types of funding that carry expectations of greater return, so spurring them to greater efficiency and competitiveness.

These close ties between banks and business are reflected in the cosy relations between government bureaucrats and powerful labour-force unions. This explains the tradition of the guarantee of lifetime employment (*shushin koyo*) in large corporations. Then, of course, there is the *Keidanren*, the powerful lobby of the captains of industry who form part of the 'iron triangle' between politicians, bureaucrats and industrialists, determined to protect Japanese industry from foreign companies threatening competition and M&A, which is derided as short-term self-interest at the expense of domestic companies' longer-term safety. These close ties – between the professional elites (the Philippines has the same, between politicians, industrialists and the judiciary), between government and labour, and within the *keiretsu* – served Japan well for almost 50 years after the 1939–45 war. The economy grew at an unprecedented rate: 10% during the 1960s; 5% in the 1970s; 4% in the 1980s.

In this it was dependent on policies designed to encourage the public to save – the Japanese are one of the most frugal nations on earth, which is why the Japanese Post Office, where the tiny amounts saved by millions of individuals aggregate to an institutional tsunami of money, is one of the biggest financial institutions in the world.

These savings provided industry with the necessary capital to expand. The resulting trade surplus enabled Japanese industry to invest further, so improving its competitiveness in export markets. The resulting appreciation in the yen enabled substantial purchases of overseas assets. It was textbook stuff.

But Japan's industry was dependent on high rates of reinvestment to remain competitive and technologically advanced. So the 1990 crash hit the manufacturing sector hard, while the decrease in consumption caused a deflationary spiral.

The Bank of Japan failed to cut interest rates quickly enough to cope with the crash and stimulate demand, and only started to recapitalise its banks almost ten years later. Tax increases in 1997 didn't help either: people spent even less. Since then, the government's efforts to revive a stagnant economy have met with little success, hampered by the dotcom crash in the early 2000s and the more recent credit crunch.

Like Japan itself, Tokyo never really recovered from the 1990 crash and the economic bust that followed. This is reflected in the Tokyo Stock Exchange (TSE). It is the second largest stock market in the world, the market capitalisation of the companies listed on it standing at just under $5 trillion (a quarter of the wealth said to have been wiped out). Yet while it has over 2,000 listed companies, just 30 of them are from overseas. Before 1990, the number of foreign companies listing on the TSE ran to over 100. Now it's just a handful a year, and that's despite the efforts of a dedicated TSE marketing task force. In 2006, initial public offerings on the TSE raised just $10 billion. China doubled that with a single bank listing the same year. The TSE earns about $150 million a year. The Hong Kong stock exchange does that in a quarter.

This sense of sluggishness extends to the bond markets. Japan's bond market is enormous ($9.5 trillion) but less than a tenth is made up of corporate bonds (issued by companies) since companies prefer raising debt funding through bank loans. The bulk are bonds issued by central and local government.

You can begin to see why Japan is such a large economy (second largest GDP in the world after the US) and why Tokyo is the HQ for the world's largest banks and insurance companies; yet why Japan faces year-on-year decline: 2008 saw Japan's sixth successive year of GDP contraction, putting it outside the top ten in the OECD rankings of GDP growth.

Japan is now saving less than the US. This is because the ratio of retired to those in work is now 1: 3 – so savers are now drawing on their money to live in retirement. Thirty years ago that ratio was 1:12. By 2020 it will be 1:1 with each one in work supporting one in retirement – a demographic timebomb worse in Japan than anywhere else in the world. Retiring workers are being replaced by young people on lower salaries who have less to spend in the economy and less to save.

But its export growth remains strong, running at almost 10% a year over the last few years. However, this has not percolated down into the domestic economy through wage increases to encourage domestic demand.

On top of that, government debt runs at 180% of GDP – the worst of any top economy and the cost of successive attempts to stimulate the economy during and since the Lost Decade. Although funded entirely domestically, it depends on Japanese buyers of government bonds continuing to believe they will be repaid or, at least, that the value of their bonds won't be eroded.

Japan can hardly be said to be a first-class economy any more. Massive population, the demographic timebomb, a cripplingly high cost of living, a language barrier that dissuades the brightest foreign brains from coming, and you can see why Tokyo is no longer a leading international financial centre.

At its heart is a protectionist fear of opening up to foreign competition, a fear that runs to the core of the Japanese psyche and has typified the country's isolationist and closed-door history. In January 2007, the top bureaucrat at the Ministry of Economics, Trade and Industry summarised the dominant Japanese mindset when he said that companies should be able to choose their shareholders. The government has categorised a number of sectors as key to national security: buying more than 10%, especially if you are a foreigner, requires government sanction. Cross-shareholdings and M&A preventative tactics (such as poison pills which saddle acquisitive shareholders with extensive liabilities) protect Japanese companies from takeover and restructuring.

It is true that some prominent companies are already foreign-owned, notably car manufacturers Nissan and Mazda, owned by Renault and Ford respectively. But that's more out of necessity from the parlous state of the global auto industry than Japan's embrace of change, competition and foreign investment.

The financial markets' reliance on Japan's large domestic economy has blunted innovation and led to protectionist policies. Japan imposes a high regulatory burden, especially on foreign businesses, for instance requiring all relevant corporate documents to be translated into Japanese and imposing local accounting standards which differ from their international counterparts, both of which add to management time and cost. Regulators are seen as inflexible and unable to keep pace with the increasing complexity of financial products, while regulation itself is often seen as vague and open to interpretation. Japan is shunned by investors. Investment banks avoid locating in Tokyo. Opinion is sharply divided over which way Japan's economy should go (open or closed) but seems to be leaning more towards protectionism and the stability of the old at the expense of competitiveness and future growth.

The TSE itself is a microcosm of this ambivalence towards change. Originally founded in 1878, it combined with ten other stock exchanges in 1943 to form the Japanese Stock Exchange, which was then shut down and reorganised after the Nagasaki bombing. In 1949 it reopened as the Tokyo Stock Exchange once again, this time pursuant to the new Securities Exchange Act which, like much post-war Japanese financial regulation, was modelled on the US equivalent including the distinction between commercial banking and securities.

In 1999, in a bid to end the Lost Decade, the TSE switched to electronic trading then, in 2000, it demutualised and incorporated with a view to going public by the end of the new decade. However, a succession of disasters set that plan back.

In November 2005 a newly installed transaction system crashed and trading was suspended for four and half hours, the worst interruption in the history of the exchange. Just over a month later, in December 2005, a trader at Mizuho Securities input an order to sell shares in listed company J-Com. But the order went in as 610,000 shares at ¥1 each instead of one share at ¥610,000. The resultant pandemonium – it was the trader's mistake but was compounded by the TSE's contradictory response – led to an internationally reported fiasco, a net loss of $347 million and the resignation of the TSE's CEO and two senior executives in what was seen as a TSE systems failure.

Then a little over a month later, in January 2006, the exchange had to close early as trading volumes in an internet company threatened to exceed the computer system's capacity of 4.5 million trades a day (the TSE rapidly increased its order capacity by 0.5 million to 5 million trades per day).

On the optimistic side, there are plans to launch trading in a broader range of financial products built on a platform using state-of-the-art technology designed to attract foreign investors. The TSE is entering into a number of strategic alliances with other exchanges (see Chapter 2). There are plans put forward by the Financial Services Agency (the financial markets' regulatory body) to enhance and promote the financial markets, the first comprehensive reform since 1996. These include measures to: create vibrant markets investors have confidence in; revitalise the financial services industry by promoting competition; improve the regulatory environment; and develop the infrastructure and quality of professional services (such as law, accounting, technology, and management consulting).

The FSA is itself moving from a prescriptive, rules-based regulatory model to one that is principles-based and interpretative (like the UK's) which should make regulation more transparent, more flexible and less oppressive.

Chapter 3
Bonds (Debt)

SPEED-READ SUMMARY

- There are two types of debt: loans and bonds

- A bond is a promise to pay which pays interest (called the 'coupon') during its life and returns the principal amount borrowed on redemption (when it expires)

- Bonds and shares are called collectively 'securities'

- Bonds are issued by companies and governments

- The US government and municipal bond markets are the largest in the world

- The international bond market comprises bonds issued outside the issuer's home country in a currency (usually US dollars) other than its home currency (known collectively as 'eurobonds')

- The terms 'eurodollars' and 'eurocurrency' refer to these 'international' US dollars – the term is historic and has nothing to do with the European currency, the euro

- Primary market activity (aka origination) is the issue of bonds

- Secondary market activity is the trading of bonds already in issue

- Bonds pay a fixed rate of interest (fixed income bonds) or a floating or variable rate of interest (floating rate notes or FRNs)

- Bonds can be of any duration: the shortest (up to one year) are called 'commercial paper'; then there are medium–term note (MTNs) – 'note' and 'bond' mean the same thing – followed by long bonds and perpetuals

- An issue needs a credit rating if it is to attract international investor attention – triple A is the top rating

- Bonds whose rating goes 'below investment grade' can no longer be held by certain types of investor (such as pension funds) – they are called 'junk'

- A bought deal is when a bank agrees to buy an entire issue itself

---

In Chapter 2 we looked at the equity markets. Now we're going to look at their debt equivalent: bonds. Shares and bonds are highly tradable which is why, collectively, they are called 'securities' meaning that originally they were security-printed certificates. Investment banks (which, confusingly, don't invest) play a key role in the issue and trading of securities.

Loans (the other type of debt) are made by commercial banks (an equally confusing name). Loans aren't inherently tradable although securitisation (Chapter 5) and derivatives (Chapter 6) have made them so. Loans and commercial banking are covered in Chapter 8.

WHAT'S A BOND?

A bond in essence is very simple: it is a promise to pay. A company or government borrows, say, $500 million, by issuing a bond. The bond says on its face when it will be redeemed (say in ten years' time) and what rate of interest it will pay in the meantime (say 5% a year).

What we have here is a ten-year bond with a **par** or **face value** of $500 million, and a coupon (see below) of 5%.

Let's examine it in more detail.

Global bond: in the old days bonds used to be security-printed on card. In practice issues are still done by the issuer (borrower) issuing a single global bond or note (the two words are synonymous). But no investor will want to lend $500 million to a single issuer. So in practice the global bond is kept in a bank vault and further, smaller bonds (each of say $10,000) are issued off the back of it, all of which add up to $500 million. This way it's much easier to attract a wide array of investors each of whom is able to participate by buying just $10,000 (or multiples of $10,000) of the issue.

Electronic entries: nowadays, apart from that single global bond or note, bonds aren't issued and traded in hardcopy form. Instead they are electronic entries held by depositaries and clearing houses such as **Euroclear** and **Clearstream** (each of which is owned by a consortium of user banks) in Europe and the **Depository Trust & Clearing Corporation** in the US. They look after clearing and settlement in bond markets since many bonds are not exchange-traded and are therefore traded OTC (over-the-counter – see Chapter 2).

Bearer instruments: despite the fact of electronic entries, bonds are technically bearer instruments, that is, whoever holds the bond is treated in law as the owner. This makes bonds easy to trade since there is no registration administration as there is with shares (with shares, companies have to keep a register of who their shareholders are). This is why the bond markets are among the most international and liquid. This, and their anonymity, makes bonds popular with institutional investors (called 'wholesale investors') and individual investors (called 'retail investors').

Coupon: the coupon is the term used by bond traders to mean the rate of interest a bond pays. Because bonds were bearer instruments and the issuer never knew for sure who its bondholders were (still the case), the bonds were printed with interest **coupons** which the bondholder would present for payment of interest due on the bond (that way the bond itself could be kept safe and only the coupon had to be separated from the bond to be presented). The bulk of bonds have a fixed rate of interest and are known as **fixed income** instruments because they pay the same amount of interest each year. But some bonds are issued with a floating rate of interest and these are called **FRNs** (floating rate notes).

Eurodollars: the amount borrowed is in US dollars. This is because the dollar is – still – the world's reserve currency: it's the most *international* currency and, since we're talking about the international financial markets, it's one that much international fund raising is denominated in. The dollar wasn't always the principal global currency nor will it necessarily remain so (more on this in Chapter 10).

Term: (also called **tenor** or **duration**) is the life of the bond to maturity, in this example ten years. When a bond is issued the investors hand over the money and in return get a promise to pay. Then when the bond expires they get their money back from the issuer. (Note: the issuer may choose to redeem it early before the bond has run its full course. This will happen if interest rates go down in the meantime and the issuer can refinance at a cheaper rate.) The shortest bonds may have a tenor of just one month or less. These are called **commercial paper** and are covered in the next chapter which deals with short-term debt instruments called money market instruments. Traditionally, **medium-term notes** or **MTNs** last about three to five years.

Issuer: if the issuer is a company, any bond issued will be a **corporate bond**; if the issuer is a government, any bond issued will be a **sovereign issue** or bond. The US government and municipal bond markets are the biggest in the world (see separate box on 'munis').

HOW BONDS ARE ISSUED

When a company or government issues a bond it wants to be sure of one

A short history of the eurobond market

Negotiable instruments ('negotiable' simply means tradable and an 'instrument' is evidence of money having changed hands) have been a feature of economic life for centuries.

UK bank Barings famously went bust in the 1890s from holding railroad bonds issued by Latin American borrowers – then repeated the same feat almost exactly a hundred years later but with derivatives (see Chapter 6). Then before the 1939–45 war there were 'foreign bonds', dollar issues by sovereign (country) borrowers such as Australia, New Zealand, some Scandinavian countries and several, yes, Latin American ones too.

But the modern international bond market really dates from 1963 when Autostrade, the Italian state agency that maintains Italy's roads, issued a $15 million bond outside Italy, denominated in dollars, syndicated by an international group of banks.

The term 'eurobond' was adopted for several reasons. Until then, foreign bond issues in dollars had been done in New York through New York banks. But domestic appetite was small (the domestic bond markets were huge: why buy a dollar issue from a foreign borrower you'd never heard of?) and the New York banks creamed off the fees while getting European banks to sell the bonds internationally.

So when, in 1963, the US enacted the Interest Equalisation Tax (to stop US investors from expatriating capital to buy bonds overseas), British merchant bank SG Warburg stepped in, gathered together a syndicate of European banks and launched the Autostrade issue, dubbed the first 'eurobond'.

The European banks were able to see off their US competitors because, since the bonds were bearer, only the European banks knew who the buyers were.

However, it's arguable that the 1961 issue for Portuguese SACOR was the first in that it was in a currency other than the borrower's, it was placed outside the issuer's country using an international syndicate, was listed on several European exchanges, was bearer, and free from Portuguese taxes – conditions typically fulfilled by a eurobond. However, it may be that in future the term 'eurobond' may come to mean a bond denominated in euros.

Luxembourg is the unofficial capital of the eurobond market. London is where bonds are traded. But Luxembourg is where they are listed. Comparable in size with Liechtenstein (see OFCs in Chapter 9), Luxembourg has both a stock market and the Euro MTF ('MTF' stands for 'multilateral trading facility' under the EU Market in Financial Instruments Directive) for issuers that don't need a passport to other European markets (listing on an EU regulated market passports you to the others). In 2008, more than 45,000 securities were listed on Luxembourg's main market, two-thirds of which were bonds, and 5,000 securities were listed on the Euro MTF.

thing: that on the day of issue the bond will be bought. There are various ways of doing this, all involving banks and a certain type of bank in particular, the investment bank.

Investment banks don't invest. They help issuers issue bonds by ensuring those bonds are bought. They do this in a number of ways. First of all, they provide **distribution**. They know the market, in other words the sort of investor that will buy the bond. They will have sounded out potential investors in advance to determine the likely appetite for the bond (how many they'll buy) and therefore the optimal bond **structure** in terms of size, maturity and coupon. They may even **book build**, that is, obtain informal commitments from investors in advance. They may put together a

Different types of bond

Government bonds – are the biggest class of bonds issued. Government bonds issued outside the home country are called sovereign bonds

Municipal bonds – are bonds issued by public bodies

Corporate bonds – are issued by companies

Plain vanilla bonds – are straightforward bonds that pay a fixed or floating rate of interest

FRNs – floating rate notes that pay a variable rate of interest (aka variable-rate bonds)

Zero-coupon bonds – pay no interest but are issued at a discount which effectively rolls the interest up so the redemption figure covers principal and implicit interest. The benefit to the issuer of a zero-coupon bond is that it doesn't pay interest during the life of the bond but effectively at the end when the bond is repaid, which helps its cashflow

Convertible bonds – are corporate bonds that allow the holder to convert the bonds into shares of the issuer

Exchangeable bonds – can be exchanged for equity in a third-party company

Warrants – entitle the holder to buy shares in the issuer at a fixed price

Eurobonds – bonds issued outside the issuer's home country in a currency other than the home currency (usually US dollars)

EMTNs – medium-term notes (MTNs) issued in eurodollars

ECP – commercial paper (CP), that is, short-term bonds of one month or more, issued in eurodollars

Asset-backed debt securities – bonds backed by a pool of assets (these are explained in Chapter 5)

Structured bonds – bonds issued in combination with another instrument, usually a derivative (see Chapter 6)

syndicate of banks that will **underwrite** the issue, that is, agree to take up any part of the issue that is not bought by investors. All of this is called **origination** and takes place in what is called the **primary market**.

If a bond (or shares – see Chapter 2) is distributed to a small number of institutional investors (in other words it's not a public issue and is confined to professional investors) it's called a **private placement** and is subject to less regulation and fewer administrative hurdles than a public issue.

Once the bond is in issue it will be bought and sold in the **secondary market**, which is a sort of second-hand market for pre-owned bonds. Investment banks are crucial players in the secondary markets too.

HOW BONDS ARE TRADED

Bonds can be listed (more are listed in Luxembourg than anywhere else) or can be traded off-exchange in what is called the OTC market (over-the-counter, meaning bank-to-bank). Investment banks are key players in the trading of bonds – they make a market in them and trade them both for their clients and for their own account.

The decision whether to buy a bond is a split-second thing, helped by the fact that the documentation is simpler than for a loan because it's been standardised across the market by ICMA (International Capital Market Association) which is the trade association for investment banks and securities firms. The decision whether to buy is driven predominantly by interest rates and where the bond buyer thinks they are heading, as we shall see in Chapter 4. This means the potential bond buyer doesn't have time to worry about whether the issuer is going to **default** on the bond (fail to pay interest or repay the principal).

This is why all international bond issues have to be **rated** to have any chance of success. These **credit ratings** are provided (for a fee) by specialist **rating agencies**. The top ones are Standard & Poor's, Moody's and Fitch. The best rating is 'triple A' also written as 'AAA'. The rating is, technically, of the issuer's ability to service the bond (pay the coupon during the bond's life) and redeem it on maturity.

If the issuer's credit rating is downgraded during the life of the bond, the bond can end up falling **below investment grade**. This is a serious blow because it means that many institutional investors (Chapter 7) such as pension funds are barred in their constitutional documents (in the case of a pension fund, its trust deed) from buying them. These bonds are called **junk bonds** or – for reasons we will see in Chapter 4 – **high-yield bonds**.

INVESTMENT BANKS

We've seen that investment banks lie at the heart of the bond markets, both in origination (primary market) and in trading (secondary market).

Investment banks are very much a US creation. In origin they were really brokerages, enabling wealthy individuals across the US to invest in the markets by having a network of offices in regional centres (where regional stock exchanges like Boston and Philadelphia were) that advised those investors on what securities to buy and sell. There has always been a strong tradition of private investment in the US (that is, investment by individuals, known as retail investment; investment by institutional investors is called wholesale). For example, until recently US private investors owned as much as half of the shares listed in the US because they are allowed to manage their own personal pension plans and invest them in shares. It was this geographic reach which gave these brokerages the power to **distribute** and, therefore, to **underwrite** issues.

Investment banks don't therefore take in deposits or make loans. That is the role of commercial banks (see Chapter 8). But originally banks could do both. However, the 1929 Crash was caused, or at any rate exacerbated, by banks using depositors' money (commercial banking) to buy and trade equities on the stock market (investment banking/broking). When the stock markets fell, depositors' money was wiped out and banks went bust.

So in the 1930s a piece of US legislation called Glass-Steagall (after the two legislators who initiated it) said a bank could be one or the other but not both. The top US bank at the time, JP Morgan, split into three as a result: **JP Morgan** itself (a commercial bank, now called JPMorgan Chase); **Morgan Stanley** (an investment bank); and **Morgan Guaranty** (a trust bank that looks after securities, among other things).

Over the years, investment and commercial banks encroached on each other's turf. Whenever a bank thought a proposed business initiative might contravene Glass-Steagall, it would write to the SEC (the Securities and Exchange Commission which regulates the US securities markets) seeking approval. The SEC would never say that anything was OK. The most it would say is that it would take 'no action' if such an activity were pursued.

These No Action letters built up into a body of precedent that ripped holes in Glass-Steagall until Glass-Steagall itself was repealed in the 1990s on the basis that, in the modern world of computer-assisted VAR (value-at-risk) models, risk management procedures, instant data aggregating market exposures, and close electronic communication between banks and their

US municipal bonds – the 'muni' market

The US government issues more bonds – they're called Treasuries – than any other country. It's the world's biggest borrower and daily turnover in the US government bond market is about $300 billion. In Japan, nine-tenths of the bond market comprises government bonds.

But the US 'muni' bond market is unique: it's the place where US public bodies of all shapes and sizes, including states, counties, cities (all of these are 'municipalities') as well as utilities, airports, hospitals and affordable housing bodies come to raise money. The great attraction for investors – the bulk of whom are retail (that is, individuals) – is that these bonds are tax-free which means that issuers don't have to offer such competitive rates of return and so can obtain a lower cost of borrowing. For munis to qualify for tax exemption, the money raised has to be spent on capital projects within three to five years.

Muni bonds are serviced and repaid in three different ways:

- **General obligation bonds** aren't tied to a specific source of revenue but are repaid out of the issuer's general receipts – these are the safest and hence the lowest paying

- **Revenue bonds** repay from a source of future income, for example power sold from a power station to be built out of the issue proceeds

- **Assessment bonds** are paid from property taxes gathered in the issuer's area

The market is over $2.5 trillion big and trading is OTC rather than on-exchange. It's harder than in the equity markets to find matching trades in specific issuers' bonds (there are 60,000 issuers but issues can be modest) so to the extent there is any trading it is in **fungible** bonds – buying and selling bonds with similar financial terms and risk profiles rather than seeking identical matches.

The biggest attraction of the muni bond market to issuers and investors alike almost brought it to its knees in the credit crunch. Issuers range from states the size of California to local hospitals. Some are big; some, by comparison, are tiny. How to make sure they all appeal to investors and can raise relatively cheap funding?

The answer is: **monoline insurers**. Monolines specialise in one type of insurance (hence 'mono'). Those serving the muni market effectively guarantee issuers (they charge issuers a fee). This means that the tiniest hospital's bonds can be as attractive as those of the largest state because the credit risk is backstopped by a monoline insurer. Big names in monoline insurance include: Ambac, MBIA, FGIC, FSA, CIFG and XL.

However, for reasons explained in Chapter 7, monoline insurers incurred heavy losses on other financial products they also insured. Their own financial viability was thrown into doubt, so the munis they backstopped were no longer seen as safe. At this point investors had to start worrying about whether that hospital was as strong a borrower as the largest state. ⇨

⇨ The hospital for its part had to start offering higher rates of return for its bonds to remain attractive. The whole market tilted and a third of investors fled.

In particular, two areas of the muni bond market froze up. The first was the $330 billion auction-rate market (ARM). ARM securities are long-term bonds which behave like short-term ones because at regular intervals the interest rate can reset in response to demand from new potential investors. The other was the $500 billion VRDO market (variable rate demand obligation). These are short-term notes (like commercial paper) but can be rolled over far into the future because investors can require issuers to buy them back at regular intervals (this is a form of 'put option' which is a derivative explained in Chapter 6).

Build America Bonds (BABs), launched in 2009 and partly subsidised federally (by the US central government), were designed to stimulate the municipal bond market. In return for longer repayment periods, investors were able to obtain higher rates of interest or a federal tax credit for part of the interest payable.

regulators, these kinds of anti-competitive distinctions were no longer required. Oh, really? Little more than a decade later, banks went bust in the credit crunch. More on this and the credit crunch in Chapters 5 and 9.

BIG BANG AND THE UK MARKET

Now, of course, the biggest banks do both commercial and investment banking. But it's not been easy. When London Stock Exchange members opened up to outside ownership as part of Big Bang in the 1980s (see Chapter 2) it was big commercial banks that swept in and bought brokers and jobbers (the UK term for specialist), hoping to create an investment banking capability in what even then was the world's leading international financial centre.

Many of these experiments failed since commercial bankers are by nature and culture prudential credit-assessors, lending for the long term, while their investment banking cousins are short-term risk-taking traders looking to get in and out of a market for a quick profit.

Even UK commercial banks, operating in their home country, found it tough going. **Barclays**, a retail finance powerhouse, bought broker **de Zoete & Bevan** and jobber (specialist) **Wedd Durlacher** and stuck them together in nascent investment bank **BZW** (**B** = Barclays, **Z** = Zoete, **W** = Wedd).

But it took 20 years and a rebranding to create the global investment-banking behemoth known today as **Barclays Capital**.

CONVERGENCE: EQUITY AND DEBT; LOANS AND BONDS

While this was happening, banking and broking were blurring in another way as investment banks moved into equity origination and trading. A wave of privatisations in the 1980s and 1990s of huge state monopolies like telecoms companies could only be achieved by global IPOs (initial public offerings) with simultaneous listings on several stock exchanges. But the only institutions with sufficient global distribution and underwriting firepower to support such issues were US investment banks, deploying the techniques honed in the international bond markets.

The first of these issues was that of the UK's telecoms monopoly, BT. In 1984 the UK government sold off just over 50% of the business in the first tranche of privatisation. The issue – at £3.9 billion the largest ever seen at that date – was listed in three markets (London, New York and Tokyo) and further prospectuses (the brochure selling the issue) were distributed in Japan and Switzerland, at that time an unprecedented transaction.

Since then the way in which loans and bond issues are made has also converged. The bulk of bond issues by corporate issuers are not stand-alone, one-offs but are part of **programmes**, historically called **medium-term note programmes**, which offer the borrower a variety of ways of raising debt through different types of loans and bonds – another example of convergence between these types of debt raising.

Big loans are called **syndicated loans** (or **jumbo loans**) because they are made by several banks – sometimes as many as 30 or 40 – lending on the terms of one loan agreement to a single borrower. This is because the borrower wants more money than one bank is prepared to lend it (there's more on this in Chapter 8). Although the term 'syndicate' is used here as it is in bond issues, traditionally the mechanics of putting these syndicates together and the underlying legal documentation differed between loans and bonds. No longer. With the biggest banks doing both commercial and investment banking, the way syndication is done in these two markets has converged.

So big loans, bond issues and equity IPOs are increasingly underwritten in the same way. And even that syndication process has become outmoded. Borrowers are prepared to pay a higher fee for a **bought deal** where the bank doesn't put together a syndicate and doesn't even bother to arrange underwriting, but simply buys the whole deal – whether a bond issue or a loan – and then distributes participations in it to other banks. This way the borrower goes to the bank and walks out almost there and then with the money the issue would otherwise have raised.

These bought deals, like the **block trades** banks will do for institutional investors (mentioned in Chapter 2), require a great deal of capital – that is, banks with a lot of money of their own. This is why the biggest banks have got bigger and why the old-style **brokers** which were small businesses (often partnerships) and UK **merchant banks** (the UK equivalent of US investment banks), neither of which had much capital of their own, became obsolete and disappeared.

Finally, even instruments have converged. You get bonds called **convertibles** that allow the holder to turn them into equity in the issuer, **exchangeable bonds** (equity in a third-party company) and **warrants** (to subscribe for shares in the issuer). And, coming the other way, you get **perpetual bonds** (often issued by banks) which are almost like shares. They have no expiry date at all, although the issuer can redeem them if it likes.

Now we need to visit the place where the bulk of these securities, at least when issued internationally, are traded: London.

HOW IT ALL CONNECTS

- Shares (Chapter 2) and bonds used to be issued using different structures and procedures but now investment banks do both

- The biggest banks combine both investment banking and commercial (lending) banking (Chapter 9)

- Acquisition finance (covered in Chapter 8) sometimes involves a bond issue

- Investment banks have market making functions that trade both shares (Chapter 2) and bonds

- As a result of the credit crunch, lending banks haven't had the funds to lend so borrowers may be more tempted to tap the capital markets (that is, issue a bond) instead

- The biggest buyers of bonds are institutional investors (Chapter 7)

- Turning loans into bonds is called securitisation (Chapter 5) because loans become tradable securities

- Through securitisation, sub-prime mortgages in the US were turned into asset-backed securities and caused the credit crunch (Chapter 5)

- Nowadays, most bonds are issued with an interest rate or currency swap attached (these are examples of derivatives – see Chapter 6)

- Short-term bonds are part of the money markets (Chapter 4)

- Government bond markets are watched closely by economists as an indicator of how a country's economy is viewed (Chapter 10)   ⇨

⇨ HOW IT ALL CONNECTS

- Most stock exchanges (Chapter 2) trade government and corporate bonds

- The repo market (Chapter 4) involves repurchase agreements and usually applies to bonds

DAY TRIP TO
LONDON

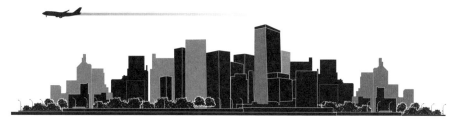

The stats speak for themselves: London is the largest currency market in the world. Its average daily turnover ($500 billion) is greater than that of New York and Tokyo combined. More US dollars are traded in London than New York and more euros than in all of the other European capitals put together.

There are more foreign banks – over 500 – in London than anywhere else in the world (New York, which is second, has just over half that number). For many of these banks, London isn't just their European HQ but the hub of their global operations outside their home market.

More eurobonds (Chapter 3) are traded in London than anywhere else. More derivatives (Chapter 6) are traded OTC (over-the-counter) than anywhere else, accounting for over a third of the global OTC turnover in derivatives.

London is the world's largest centre of fund management (explained in Chapter 7). More money is managed in London than in the next top ten European centres added together. It's where half of Europe's institutional equity capital (worth $5.5 trillion) is managed. More than three-quarters of European hedge funds (Chapter 7) and half of private equity funds (also Chapter 7) are managed in London.

London is home to the world's largest insurance and reinsurance market (Lloyd's of London – see Chapter 9) and, closely related (since over half the risks insured at Lloyd's are maritime), the world's largest shipping market, the Baltic Exchange.

London is also home to some of the world's top commodity markets (these are linked to the financial markets through derivatives – see Chapter 6) such as oil, gold and, through the London Metal Exchange (LME), 95% of the world's trading in aluminium, copper, lead, nickel, silver, tin and zinc (that is, non-ferrous/non-iron metal trading).

The UK is hardly the world's largest economy, yet London is the top IFC. Why?

Answer: history (the past) and innovation (the future).

Economists talk about clusters, the idea that competitors in the same business will congregate in the same location. This way they are more likely, collectively, to attract customers than each individually. More customers collectively means more business for each individually, than being stuck out somewhere on your own. It's why competitors take retail space in the same shopping mall.

So too with London. Walk around the City and history is all around you: Wood Street, Bread Street, Milk Street, Cheapside – clusters dating back to Roman times indicating particular markets. Lombard Street, next to the Bank of England, dates from the influx in medieval times of Lombardy bankers from northern Italy. Even the modern City seems a bit stuck in the past, with Victorian facades, red double-decker buses, black taxi cabs and umbrellas sprouting like spores when it rains (often) – all redolent of a 1950s black-and-white movie.

Don't be deceived.

The mirror-glass office blocks that date from the invasion of US investment banks in the 1980s, the Swiss Re building (known colloquially as 'the gherkin'), the soaring silver towers in the east marking Canary Wharf: all of these show this is an IFC constantly reinventing itself.

London has a higher concentration of banks, brokers, insurance companies, fund managers and supporting services – lawyers, accountants, actuaries, management consultants, property professionals – than its domestic financial hinterland could possibly warrant. This cluster, built on a historic trading empire and a legal system which has been exported all over the world, gives London an edge that only New York matches (New York law is the other legal system used globally for financial transactions). It would be desperately difficult for any other IFC, starting from scratch, to rival London in less than 20 years and it might take 200.

In fact the only danger – which also hit Iceland hard in the credit crunch (see Chapter 10) – is that the UK's financial services sector dwarfs its domestic financial markets. So when the global financial system periodically collapses, the UK is dragged further down than comparable economies. Financial services generate over an eighth of the UK's GDP and employ over a quarter of a million people in London. In the three years preceding the credit crunch, financial services were responsible for a third of overall GDP growth. And this despite the fact that the London Stock Exchange is only the fifth largest in the world by domestic market capitalisation and London itself is only the sixth largest metropolitan economy.

Add to that the time zone (the UK falls nicely between the US and east Asia), the language (only Spanish risks overtaking English as the world's most widely spoken language in the short to medium term), the tax regime (foreigners are taxed so lightly many view the UK as a tax haven) and flexible immigration rules, plus ease of access to the rest of Europe and the fact that most people who come to London like living and working there, and you have a potent mix of attractions. According to recent statistics, more than 10% of City professionals are from countries outside the EU and the US. When you attract the best financial brains from around the world you are going to create the ideal conditions for unparalleled innovation.

Whether it was by luck or judgment, London laid the foundations for its dominance as an IFC in the 1980s. It encouraged foreign banks to sweep in and it deregulated the stock market so they could buy the stock exchange's members.

British merchant banks, the UK equivalent of the US investment banks (called 'merchant banks' because the oldest developed out of merchant houses at the time of Britain's trading empire), were taken over or closed. Morgan Grenfell fell to Deutsche Bank, Kleinwort Benson to Dresdner. Warburg, the bank behind the Autostrade issue in Chapter 3, became part of what is now UBS, Robert Fleming part of JPMorgan Chase, Samuel Montagu part of HSBC (along with top broker James Capel). Hill Samuel was dismembered. Schroders and Kleinwort Benson have shrunk to their fund management core (merchant banks had specialised in trade finance, helping clients export; corporate finance, helping them do IPOs and take each other over; and fund management, investing their profits and managing their pension funds – investment management had been a strength of Flemings, Morgan Grenfell, Warburgs and Schroders). None of this required much capital so these banks were small, lacked capital to compete and were easily swallowed up. Only Lazard and Rothschild maintained their independence and they now style themselves investment banks.

All of this could have meant the end for the City. Instead it had the opposite effect.

The London Stock Exchange (LSE) demutualised, becoming a public company listed on itself, which made it an attractive target for overseas interest as other exchanges pursued global reach and deeper liquidity through consolidation. Its members – the brokers and jobbers (the UK term for specialist) – which had previously been partnerships, incorporated (became companies) and were bought. This deregulation, called Big Bang (because it all happened in one go), enabled members to compete on price, to trade for their own account, and be owned by outsiders. The impact was immediate: the stock exchange became genuinely international and electronic (its trading floor closed and the LSE's new building doesn't have one).

No wonder that, 20 years on, the LSE found itself courted by others. In December 2004, Deutsche Börse bid £1.25 billion to buy it. A week later, Euronext entered the race, initiating a bidding war. The LSE rebuffed them both. A year later, in December 2005, a consortium of European stock exchanges led by Macquarie Bank, the Australian infrastructure investor, offered £1.5 billion. No dice. The bid was withdrawn in February 2006. Three weeks later, NASDAQ bid $4.2 billion. No way. The LSE cited heavy-handed US regulation, to which it might have become subject, as the deal breaker.

Then in June 2007 the LSE found a bride of its own, with a friendly takeover of Borsa Italiana, the user-owned equities, bond and derivatives trading platform. The LSE paid a total of £1 billion for the exchange in cash and shares. The merger has created the leading diversified exchange group in Europe, the foremost market for bonds, ETFs (exchange traded funds) and securitised derivatives (the last two explained in Chapter 6).

It doesn't stop there. In 2007, Borse Dubai secured a 28% share of the LSE by buying OMX shares and selling them to NASDAQ immediately in return for NASDAQ's shareholding in the LSE. The Qatar Investment Authority (QIA), a sovereign wealth fund (see Chapter 7), also acquired a 20% share in the LSE from two hedge fund groups. These shareholdings were diluted after the LSE and Borsa Italiana merger, but they are both still the two biggest shareholders, Borse Dubai with 20% and QIA with 15%. Recent developments include the launch of a new trading system called TradElect in June 2007.

The LSE has pursued other innovations. In 1995 the old Unlisted Securities Market which, like all junior markets, suffered from lack of liquidity, was succeeded by AIM (the Alternative Investment Market) for companies without a trading history or sufficient freefloat of shares or which aren't seeking to raise enough fresh equity capital to list on the LSE's main market. AIM is regulated by the LSE but imposes a lower regulatory burden. LSE is now developing AIM joint ventures with the Milan and Tokyo stock exchanges. The Professional Securities Market was launched in 2005 and is dedicated to the listing and trading of specialist securities including debt, convertibles and depository receipts. As it is aimed at sophisticated professional and institutional investors, it has a less onerous approach to regulation since there is no need to protect lay investors. It offers institutional investors the greater ease of trading listed securities whilst allowing companies to raise capital at a lower cost. The Specialist Fund Market is also a lightly regulated market exclusively for highly sophisticated investors such as large hedge funds and private equity funds.

Plus Markets plc (itself quoted on AIM) is the successor to Ofex which developed out of an OTC market in unlisted securities run by broker J P Jenkins on a matched bargain basis (that is, J P Jenkins would match buy and sell orders without itself making a market in any securities). It was subsequently rebranded Plus Markets in late 2007. Plus runs a primary market (it offers companies the ability to list and raise money) and a secondary market (in which securities are traded). Plus has about 200 companies listed on its primary market (including Arsenal football club) with a total capitalisation of about £2.3 billion. A Plus listing is generally for smaller companies wanting to raise smaller amounts of money.

Outside the LSE, one of London's major successes has been its ability to diversify beyond core equity markets into derivatives (explained in Chapter 6). EDX London (launched in 2003) is dedicated to the trading of international equity derivatives and offers services on two linked derivatives exchanges, OMX in Sweden and the Oslo Børs in Norway. Trading on this market is executed through the world's most advanced automated electronic trading platform, CLICK.

Another major market for derivatives trading is Euronext.liffe. This is the world's leading exchange for euro short-term interest rate derivatives and equity options. The exchange was formed in January 2002 when the London International Financial Futures and Options Exchange merged with Euronext. It is now the international derivatives business of Euronext, which includes the Amsterdam, Brussels, Lisbon and Paris derivatives markets and has merged with the New York Stock Exchange.

There are just two clouds on the horizon, both heading over from the EU. The first is an EU move to impose a withholding tax on bearer bonds. The EU has been trying to do this for years, but it was always vetoed by the UK. The veto system has now ended. London's pre-eminence in bond trading is therefore at risk.

The second is the EU's threat, post credit crunch, to impose a Europe-wide banking regulatory system. London has prided itself on its principles-based approach to regulation. Unfortunately, by splitting responsibility for bank supervision among the Bank of England (the central bank), the Financial Services Authority (the financial markets' regulator) and the Treasury (the government), the UK made a mess of it, with none of the three taking the lead (previously the Bank of England did it successfully on its own). This came to a head with the failure of Northern Rock (see Chapters 5 and 10) which took weeks for the government to rescue. That ruined the UK's reputation for prudential regulation – even though the government subsequently acted swiftly and decisively in nationalising several other major banks (Barclays and HSBC aside). One of those, Royal Bank of Scotland, was described by an EU commissioner in mid-2009 as highly dangerous to the European single market: not a resounding vote of confidence in the UK's bank regulatory system.

The EU is also keen to clamp down on hedge funds and private equity (for both see Chapter 7), seen as the most disreputable elements of 'Le Casino' as the French would have it (for their part, private equity funds were branded 'locusts' by a German government minister).

Worried observers recall that Antwerp's arcaded 'Beurs' was the commercial hub of Europe until, in the seventeenth century, the Spanish and French monarchies restricted repayments on debt to interest only (shades of modern sovereign defaults).

Antwerp was finished within 50 years.

Cluster or not, could the same happen to London?

Chapter 4

Currency and Money Markets

Speed-read summary

- The currency and money markets are the IFMs at the heart of the global economy – both are OTC markets

- The currency markets are dominated by the world's biggest banks

- Money market instruments include commercial paper (issued by companies) and treasury bills (issued by governments)

- Because these instruments are short-term they are treated almost as cash

- Money market investment funds buy much of this short-term paper, offering better returns than bank deposits

- Money market funds replaced bank lending in the run-up to the credit crunch, hence the nickname: the 'shadow banking system'

- Interest rates in the IFMs are quoted in basis points (hundredths of a percent)

- Yield is the interest a bond pays expressed as a percentage of its market value

- The yield curve maps bond maturities against their current yield – the longer the bond, the higher the risk so the higher the yield should be

- The yield curve is said to invert when short-term interest rates are higher than longer-term ones

- Trading activity in the bond markets is driven by traders' views of where interest rates are heading

- Governments use the money markets to change interest rates to control inflation

- The repo (repurchase) market is a key mechanism

- Short selling and arbitrage are trading strategies in the IFMs

In this chapter we get close to the heart of the IFMs. This is where a large slug of the lifeblood of the global economy pumps briefly to the surface before going back down the world's arteries. In fact we're dealing with two pumps or markets: the currency market (or 'currency markets' or 'currencies markets'); and the money market or markets.

The **currency market** (I'm sticking to the singular) is where different countries' currencies are bought and sold. It's also known as the 'foreign exchange' or 'forex' or 'FX' market. Where the deal is done right now for delivery right now we're talking real money: cash, which is known as the **spot market**. Daily volume in the currency market is about $3.5 trillion.

The **money markets** (I'm going to go with the plural, because it feels right) aren't, perversely, as much about real money. True, they include overnight deposits (when you're dealing with hundreds of millions of dollars, what you do with it overnight matters, whereas the loose change in your or my pocket doesn't). But in the main they comprise short-term bonds and other instruments whose durations are so brief they are regarded as almost risk-free and so almost the equivalent of cash. Total size: a bit bigger than currencies, nearing $5 trillion.

These markets are real traders' markets – which is the theme of this book: trading has overtaken investing as the IFMs' principal function. But they are also fascinating for another reason. Both are highly susceptible to interest rates. Interest rates are set by governments. Why and how is what we will explore here. But it's the point at which the IFMs meet macroeconomics (by which I mean finance at a government, country or world level): a kind of swirling vortex, like the one in *Pirates of the Caribbean*; a perfect storm. I stray into macroeconomics in Chapter 10. But in reality it's where this book ends, like the sheer waterfalls on all sides in the cover art of *Close To The Edge* by Yes.

CURRENCIES

All sorts of people need to sell one currency and buy another. You and I do when we go on holiday abroad. Companies do when they earn profits overseas and need to translate them back into their home currency. Institutional investors (Chapter 7) do when they invest overseas and buy the local currency in order to buy shares on the local exchange. You and I don't go to the FX market. We go to a bank. And the biggest users of the FX market – in fact they are the FX market – are the major banks, with an astonishing four-fifths of trading volume concentrated in the hands of just ten banks, the most dominant being the top European and American ones:

Deutsche Bank (Germany), UBS and Credit Suisse (Switzerland), Barclays (UK); and, from the US, Citigroup, JPMorgan Chase and Goldman Sachs. Ten years ago the number was at least double.

The currency market is an OTC market: it exists as trades on the screens of the participants. It's said to follow the sun: banks pass their trading book from one IFC to the next as time zones open and close, from London to Wall Street then across to Tokyo and Singapore, then back to London. Entry to this hallowed market requires one thing: credit standing. The reason why you and I can't trade in the FX markets is because no one knows who we are or whether we are good for the money. Or, looked at differently, anyone can trade – provided they can find someone else to trade with.

This makes the users of the global FX markets an unusually eclectic bunch, from multinational companies, with receipts in local currencies that need to be remitted to HQ in the home currency, to central banks, hedge funds and other institutional investors, specialist FX brokers, retail FX suppliers (otherwise you and I wouldn't be able to go on holiday) and money transfer businesses.

In fact there are different levels to this virtual market. Smaller players command less attractive deals whereas the inner circle of top banks forms an elite trading circle dealing with each other in high volumes on thin margins. For them, what determines how finely priced their trades are is something called the 'line', meaning simply the put-through or volume of trades a bank has – the greater its line the better the prices it will obtain.

This issue of credit standing became a real concern in 1974 when a German bank called Herstatt went bust and the whole FX market ground to a halt as Herstatt couldn't honour its trades which meant, domino-like, no one else could either. There are accepted ways round Herstatt risk. There's simultaneous delivery and payment known as DVP (delivery versus payment). There's netting, which means two counterparties to a series of trades totting them up and one paying a single amount to the other in settlement of them all – this is done at the end of the trading day or even during it (intraday). There's use of a central clearing system (which only works if both counterparties are members) such as Continuous Linked Settlement (CLS), set up in 1997 to provide a global FX settlement system and which now settles over half of all FX transactions.

In terms of what is traded, the US dollar is dominant. The most popular trades are dollar/euro (over 25%), dollar/yen and dollar/sterling (12% each), with dollar/others accounting for a further 20% making the dollar one of the two currencies in more than half of all FX trades. The dollar/sterling trade is known as 'cable' after the transatlantic telegraph cables which enabled the first trades. In terms of where, the UK dominates with over a third of global turnover, followed by the US (16%), then Switzerland and Singapore (about 6% each).

Two other points to note. I talked about the spot market (immediate delivery) earlier. In fact two-thirds of the FX market is for **future delivery**: buying at today's price for delivery, typically, up to six months away. This is done by way of a forward, future or swap – these are all derivatives covered in Chapter 6 and doing this is called **hedging**. If I know I am going to need dollars in six months' time and I think the dollar will appreciate against sterling, I buy dollars now at today's price for delivery in six months' time. I have therefore **hedged my position**: I am no longer affected by vagaries in the FX market. Second, the currency markets are where the so-called **carry trade** can be used successfully – where the return from the invested currency is greater than the cost of borrowing in the sold currency, because interest rates in the invested currency's country are higher.

MONEY MARKETS

Like the currency market, the money markets are also OTC but here the big players are money market funds. These are retail investment funds – that is, individuals put their money into a mutual fund (explained in Chapter 7) which then buys money market instruments.

Investors regard it as risk-free money: the nominal or face value of units in money market funds is $1 and investors do not expect them to trade below that (otherwise they have made a loss on what they regard as a quasi-cash deposit that pays a better return than a bank deposit). If a money market fund's unit price dips below $1 this is called **breaking the buck**. When that happened in the credit crunch, investors deserted the market and the US government had to step in and guarantee the $4 trillion of assets held in money market funds – a massive figure that had almost doubled in a year. Without that guarantee, short-term money would have disappeared.

This highlighted the role that money market funds played in replacing short-term bank lending – banks hadn't been so keen to attract funds by way of deposits in order to lend because, as we shall see in Chapter 5, they weren't making loans, they were securitising them. For this reason money market funds have been dubbed **the shadow banking system**. We will also learn in Chapter 5 how banks were increasingly using short-term money to fund long-term loans, another example of trading supplanting lending.

So if money market funds provide the cash, who uses it? Companies and

Some types of money market instrument

Overnight deposits – a day-long deposit; the shortest term possible

Certificates of deposit – a certificate from a bank confirming a substantial deposit with it: CDs are themselves tradable

Commercial paper – Typically one-month or three-month bonds (can be up to a year) issued by companies to meet cashflow needs

Treasury bills – bills are short-term bonds; treasury means issued by the government

Bankers' acceptances – a bill endorsed (guaranteed) by a bank

Interbank loans – banks fund the loans they make by borrowing short-term in the interbank market (see Chapter 8)

governments, to meet short-term cash needs – for instance a gap in cashflow (remember that from Chapter 1?). Governments issue **bills** (US ones are called T-bills after the US Treasury that issues them). Companies issue **commercial paper** (CP) which can be as short as a day and as long as a year but is typically one-month, 30-day paper. ECP is CP in eurodollars, that is CP denominated in dollars but issued outside the US.

CP doesn't carry a coupon. Instead it's issued at a **discount to face value** (for example CP with a face or nominal value of $100 might be issued at $98 which means the holder is getting $2 for lending for three months which is the equivalent of 8% a year). In this respect CP is similar to a zero-coupon bond. At the end of the three months when a company's CP expires it will often **roll over** the position (replace the expiring CP with fresh CP for a further three months, and so on).

Companies, governments and investors generally also use the money markets to park spare cash they don't need immediately. Funnily enough, the biggest buyers of CP tend to be other companies looking to do just that: put aside short-term money (such as revenue from a subsidiary) which they don't need right now but will soon.

I said at the start that both currencies and money markets are sensitive to interest rates. How?

THE IFMS' KEY EXPRESSION OF RETURN: YIELD

If I sell one currency for another, I'm going to have to do something with the new currency I'm holding. I can't just stick it under the mattress if I'm a bank or an institutional investor. I need it to generate a return. So I need to put it on deposit. If that currency's home country banks are paying a good rate of interest on their deposits this might in fact have prompted me to buy that currency in the first place. Similarly with money market instruments. I will buy those paying the best rate of interest.

Traders and IFM professionals make these comparisons by using something called **yield**. Yield is simply the rate of interest an instrument pays expressed as a percentage in relation to its cost. That's all gobbledygook, so let me use an example to explain.

Say a triple-A company issues a $100 million bond with a term of ten years and a coupon of 5%. We can assume that, when it does this, interest rates are around the 4.5% mark. This 4.5% benchmark is set by the central bank as we shall see later. It's effectively the rate at which the central bank is prepared to borrow. So for a triple A corporate credit to borrow at half-a-per-cent higher is about right to allow for the corporate's credit risk.

The US government is the biggest borrower in the world, issuing Treasuries (longer term bonds) and T-bills. Since the US government borrows at the lowest rates possible (on the basis that if the US defaults, capitalism as we know it is finished) financings are often said to be 'priced off Treasuries'. This government rate is called 'prime' in the US and 'base' in the UK.

So our corporate borrower might be said to be borrowing at **50 basis points** (hundredths of a percent) above or over Treasuries: the IFMs use basis points because in the IFMs even a hundredth of a per cent can be big money: in the case of $100 million, it's $100,000.

Now if interest rates go up to 10% (we'll look at why this might happen later on in the chapter), what happens to the bond?

The bond is now an unattractive investment since investors can get 10% simply by putting their money on deposit at a bank (this is said to be 'risk-free' on the basis that bank deposits will always be guaranteed by governments). Why buy a bond that pays only 5%?

But the bond isn't completely worthless either, because in ten years' time the holder will get $100 million from the issuer when the bond is redeemed. So what is it worth?

I'm about to give you a grossly simple answer that would have most bond traders throwing their arms up in horror. But the underlying principle is OK.

The bond is worth about $50 million. How come?
Remember that the bond is a fixed-income bond which means it will always

pay $5 million (5% of its face value) a year. Now, if interest rates are paying 10%, for $5 million to be a 10% return, the underlying investment must be $50 million. In other words the **market value** of the bond is now $50 million even though its **face value**, also known as **par value** or **nominal value** (from the Latin '*nomen*' meaning 'name' as in its 'named value'), is $100 million. In other words, the bond's **yield** (income, expressed as a function of the price of the bond) is now 10%.

Yield is the single most important aspect of the bond markets. Traders don't talk about bond prices. They talk about bond yields. There are many different types, such as:

Coupon yield: this is the interest a bond pays over its life and does not change. So a bond of $100 that pays interest of 5% has a coupon yield of 5%.

Current yield or interest yield: this is a bond's yield expressed as a function of its market value or price. This does change as the bond's market value fluctuates in response to interest rates.

Gross redemption yield: broadly, this is the expected return the bond will generate (taking both interest and capital value into account) over its remaining life. It's called gross because the effect of tax is ignored.

When I said the bond is now worth $50 million, I was ignoring a number of things including how long it still has to go (known as duration or tenor) before redemption. Obviously if the bond is due to be redeemed tomorrow it is going to be worth a lot more than $50 million since tomorrow I will get back $100 million for it.

But something else that will affect its market value – and this is where things get interesting – is what interest rates are about to do. If I'm a trader thinking of buying this bond at about $50 million, my view of its value is going to be hugely affected by where I think interest rates are heading. If I think rates are going to go higher still, then I may want to pay even less for the bond. But if I think they've peaked and are about to drop, I may be prepared to pay more. That's because if interest rates are poised to fall, then the bond's coupon will be more attractive so its market value will increase and its yield will therefore decline.

This is where we encounter something hugely important in the bond markets: the yield curve.

YIELD CURVE

The shorter a bond's duration, generally speaking the lower the rate of interest it will pay. This is because the perceived risk is lower. If you lend me money for a day, you feel you are more likely to get it back than if you lend it to me for a year: the longer the duration, the higher the risk of me defaulting. So a longer bond should pay a higher rate of interest than a short one, all other things (*viz.* the issuer's credit standing) being equal.

If their respective maturities and yields were plotted on a graph (assuming bonds have the same credit risk) the resulting line connecting them up would be called the yield curve. It's actually more like a straight line going from the bottom left to the top right, with interest rates plotted on the vertical axis and duration on the horizontal one.

This yield curve is said to be positive, meaning that long-term yields are greater than short-term, as you would expect. If short-term yields rise relative to long-term yields, the curve is said to **flatten**. If they fall, it is said to **steepen**.

But if the short-term outlook for interest rates is very uncertain, the yield curve can **invert** (or be **inverse** or **negative**) which means that short-term bonds have higher yields (at least for now) than longer-dated bonds. When the yield curve inverts, it's indicative of short-term uncertainty. It's like an airline flying through clear air turbulence. The skies ahead are blue but for the next few minutes it's going to be a bumpy ride. So the yield curve inverts when the short-term outlook is uncertain or cloudy but the longer-term economic fundamentals are sound.

You can begin to see that this concept of yield is hugely important to the markets because it's a way of comparing bond prices whatever the individual cost of the bond. It's a way of quickly establishing comparisons, because yield is the amount of interest a bond pays expressed as a function of its price. When the bond's price (market value) goes down its yield goes up; and when the price goes up its yield goes down. This is why yield is said to move **inversely** in relation to a bond's market value.

HIGH-YIELD OR JUNK BONDS

Let's say that over the life of this $100 million bond, our issuer loses its triple A credit (because of a greater risk it may default, for instance by going bust). This will impact the yield of the bond, because investors will mark down the value of the bond which will make the yield (the interest rate expressed as a percentage of its market value) increase. This is the increased reward for holding a riskier bond.

If the bond's market value continues to fall further, there comes a point at which some types of investors will no longer hold it (it's no longer of 'investment grade' so pension funds will have to sell it, driving its market value down further and its yield up higher). Bonds like this are called **high-yield bonds**, **fallen angels** or **junk bonds**.

Not all high-yield bonds are junk: a company may issue a short-term high-yield bond, for instance to finance a takeover, with the intention of refinancing it at a lower rate once the takeover is out of the way and things have returned to normal. Because any company involved in making a takeover bid is embarking upon a risky venture it may only be able to raise the necessary funding by offering a bond that is pretty generous to investors in terms of the interest the bond pays. Hence it issues a bond that is high-yield from the start. This is an example of acquisition finance (see Chapter 8).

'IT'S IN THE PRICE'

You can begin to see that the bond market is sensitive to interest rates – where they are and where they are likely to go. In this sense the bond market is a good bellwether of market sentiment as to where interest rates are headed.

Currency markets are also affected because if interest rates in one country go up, putting money on deposit in that country becomes more attractive to the 'hot money' that circles the globe looking for the best home. But to do that I need to convert my cash into that country's currency – which drives up demand for it and, therefore, its price (see more on this in Chapter 10).

This idea that markets are constantly looking ahead is as true of the stock market as the bond market. In the stock market you'll find a company reports fantastic annual earnings – and its share price goes down. Or a company unveils a set of shockingly bad results – and its share price goes up. Weird, huh? Why does this happen?

It's because investors are looking to the future. If a company has done really well they will say: 'It can't go on – things can only get worse from here' – and sell. Whereas if a company is a basket case, they will say: 'Things can only get better' – and buy. The mark of a true investment professional is to buy when markets are rock-bottom and the financial world looks as if it is about to collapse forever, and to sell when markets look incredibly buoyant as if they will keep on going up forever.

So market professionals express this expectation (that interest rates will go up or down or a company will do well or badly) by using the phrase: 'It's in the price' – in other words that the news, whether good or bad, is already **discounted** (allowed for) in the price.

SO WHY DO INTEREST RATES GO UP AND DOWN?

This is where the financial markets, macroeconomics and politics meet. By and large it is governments which control interest rates, usually through their **central bank** (which is an agency of the government) and either directly or – as in the UK – indirectly by setting a rate of **inflation** (usually around 2%) which the central bank then has to deliver against through managing interest rates and money supply as it sees fit. This sounds like gobbledygook. What does it all mean?

First, central banks. Central banks are not what you and I would call a bank. They only lend to the banks they regulate if any of these banks should go bust and need funds – which is why they are often called the 'lender of last resort'. Central banks (like the Federal Reserve in the US) are really part of

What happens when interest rates move

The financial markets are highly sensitive to interest rates. When interest rates go up:
- Bank deposits become more attractive in relative terms – so more investors rush to put their money with banks, which means that:

- The stock market goes down because:

    - Bank deposits are now more attractive because they offer a higher return with lower risk so money is diverted from the stock market and put on deposit instead
    - The cost to companies of borrowing has increased so their profitability goes down so shareholders will get lower dividends so share prices go down

- Bond yields go up, to keep pace with the increase in interest rates, so bond prices go down

The exact reverse happens when interest rates go down:
- Bank deposits become less attractive in relative terms so:

    - Investors put their money in the stock market, which goes up
    - Bond prices go up and bond yields go down as the coupon bonds are paying is relatively more attractive to investors

- The cost of borrowing for companies goes down (since companies will retire old debt at the higher interest rate and refinance it at the new, lower rate) so increasing their profitability, which makes their shares more attractive which also drives the stock market up

A word of warning: this doesn't always happen: if the markets have been expecting an interest rate change it may already be in the price. But mainly it does.

the government and their job, apart from safeguarding the banking system, is to manage monetary policy by controlling the money supply and interest rates. More about this in Chapter 10.

WHAT'S INFLATION?

Inflation is the erosion of the real value of money (what money actually buys). In an **inflationary** economic environment, demand outstrips supply. This is because there is more money around (for instance, because interest rates are low so it is cheap to borrow money) so more people want to buy more things. This demand drives prices up, which means it costs more to buy the same things. So you need more money than you did yesterday, so the money you have is worth less.

In a **deflationary** economy, the opposite happens. Supply outstrips demand. People don't buy things today that they don't need till tomorrow because by tomorrow the price will have gone down – and this becomes self-reinforcing: tomorrow they will postpone buying till the next day when they expect prices to be lower still, and so on: if everyone is doing this, there is less demand for goods and services, which deepens the recession.

A little inflation is probably a good thing because those with assets (such as houses) feel a bit more prosperous (because those assets are slowly going up in value without the owners having to do anything) and so they look benignly on their government.

But a lot of inflation is a bad thing. It means the poor and those on fixed incomes, like the elderly and the retired, have less, in real terms, to live on. And it encourages people to borrow and spend today before prices go up (which itself contributes to inflation) instead of saving for their retirement. The poor, the elderly and those who've failed to save for retirement look to the government to bail them out. And the government can only do that by borrowing (more) or taxing (more), neither of which is an attractive proposition: tax too much and you get voted out of office; borrow too much and you look like an economic incompetent. Neither appeals much to politicians' vanity.

So, to control inflation, the government needs to make sure people have less money to spend, by taxing them more (unattractive) or making the cost of borrowing more expensive (pushing interest rates up). If you make it look as if it's the central bank's decision to put interest rates up, you can even avoid taking the blame. Which appeals greatly to politicians' vanity.

Of course, in a deflationary environment (as you'll remember afflicted Japan in the Lost Decade – see Tokyo) interest rates need to fall to encourage people to borrow and spend and so kick-start the economy back into life. If you, as a senior government official, tell your (quasi-) independent central bank to do just that, it doesn't look like political interference, it looks like strong leadership. Politicians love that.

A WORD OF WARNING

I mentioned earlier that markets are always looking to the future. If politicians and policy makers flag up early enough that interest rates are likely to move and then continue to send out a consistent message, often the market won't move at all.

If a government says that, to keep inflation under control, it will raise interest rates in three months' time and it keeps on repeating this message until, three months later, it does increase interest rates, the markets may not move. That's because the expected interest rate move is already in the price.

Investors in the markets rely on governments to pursue the correct economic policies to promote growth and prosperity. So the markets hate it when economies appear to be out of control and governments don't look as if they know what they're doing: in particular, wild swings in policy that cause markets to oscillate wildly and economies to swing from peaks to troughs, from **boom to bust**, from one extreme to the other, regularly.

This is what market professionals mean by **market confidence**: confidence that policy makers know what they are doing, do it, and that it has the desired consequences.

HOW CENTRAL BANKS CONTROL INTEREST RATES: MONEY MARKET OPERATIONS

Governments implement changes in interest rates through **money market operations**. You'll remember that the money markets comprise short-term bonds such as commercial paper, treasury bills, interbank loans, CDs, overnight deposits, bankers' acceptances and repos (see box).

If a central bank wants to drive interest rates down, it will buy some of these money market instruments (including buying back treasury bills it has previously issued), so introducing liquidity (money) into the market. This additional liquidity means money is more plentiful so it has the effect of driving interest rates down.

To achieve the opposite a central bank will issue treasury bills at an attractive (higher rate) of interest. This will soak up money as investors rush to buy these risk-free bills paying a higher rate of interest, so there will be less money in the system which will drive interest rates up, as will the signal from the central bank that the government is now prepared to borrow at a higher rate which means banks will generally only lend to others at that higher rate.

In this way the money markets are a critical link between the financial markets and those who make economic policy – governments and central banks.

These short-term money market operations are often carried out by specialist **government debt offices** and, in banks and companies, by the **treasury** function which looks after immediate, overnight and short-term cash, money market and currency transactions.

Repo

Repo (pronounced 'ree-po') stands for 'repurchase agreement'. The repo market is part of the money markets and key to how governments control interest rates.

A repurchase agreement is a simple contract under which I sell you a bond for $X and agree to buy it back in three months' time for $Y. Essentially what you are giving me is a secured loan: the purchase price ($X) is the loan, which you will get back when I buy the bond back in three months; and the interest element is $Y less $X (the price I will pay you in three months' time less the amount you paid me). This is called the **repo rate**.

Because it is a genuine sale-and-purchase agreement, you have title to the bond. So if I fail to buy it back you simply sell it in the market, so you are completely covered. In a **reverse repo** the seller is a bank that buys securities in return for providing cash. The amount that you will lend me on the bond is lower than the face value of the bond to cover any fall in its price over the three month period and this difference is known as the **haircut**.

The benefit to you is that you are investing cash risk-free and, if you think the securities will go down in value, you can sell them in the market and buy them back at a lower price just before you need to deliver them back to me.

The repo market is very sensitive to rates and bond prices. It is a critical source of liquidity. Repos are used by institutional investors and banks to gain short-term liquidity by harnessing long-term assets (the bonds in question tend to be government securities with triple A ratings).

In the same way, by buying these instruments central banks introduce money (liquidity) into the market. By selling them, they reduce (soak up) market liquidity. Doing so has a direct impact on the amount of money (liquidity) in the **money supply system** which in turn affects interest rates: tightening liquidity increases interest rates.

TRADING

I hope you can begin to see that the heart of the IFMs is about trading: trading money market instruments, bonds, currencies, shares and even (as we shall see in the next chapter) those most static of financial assets, loans.

They are also about trading instruments that are derived from other instruments (derivatives – see Chapter 6). These include options (an instrument that offers the opportunity to enter into another financial transaction), forwards and futures (the obligation to enter into a financial transaction in the future) and swaps (exchanging one financial transaction or instrument for another). So, for example, currencies are traded for delivery now (in what is called the spot market) or delivery at a specified point in the future (say three or six months away) called the forward market. These derivative transactions now outnumber in volume the transactions they are derived from.

SHORT SELLING AND ARBITRAGE

One major aspect of trading in the IFMs is the ability to **short sell**, mentioned in Chapter 2. Short selling was particularly criticised during the credit crunch when short sellers drove bank shares down, reducing banks' market capitalisation and increasing their need for additional funds (provided by the government) to bolster their balance sheets. In retrospect, as some market commentators have pointed out, maybe short sellers weren't so wicked after all: maybe they were simply telling the rest of the market what a rotten investment banks' shares were (true), and acting on that sentiment.

Arbitrage

Arbitrage is the act of buying in one market and selling in another to exploit price differentials between the two until they are brought into equilibrium.

Let's assume you discover that you can buy a loaf of bread in Paris for €5 and sell it in Berlin for €10. The next day you hire a van, fill it full of French loaves, drive to Berlin and sell the lot for a healthy profit. The next day you do the same again but this time with a truck. Soon a couple of things will happen. Others will start copying you and, as a result, the demand for bread in Paris will rocket.

This increased demand for loaves in Paris will drive the price up, so reducing your profit. At the same time the increased supply in Berlin will drive the price of bread there down, again reducing your profit. Soon loaves in both places will cost the same – €7.5 – so the profit opportunity will dry up and you will have to look for similar opportunities elsewhere.

This is exactly what arbitrage does: it keeps prices in fungible assets in equilibrium by smoothing out differences between markets.

Funnily enough, the market started to self-correct as markets usually do. As the short selling drove down bank prices, the institutional investors who'd made it possible by stock lending the relevant bank shares started to realise that the loss in value of their remaining bank shareholdings was greater than the stock lending fees they were receiving for lending the shares out. So they decided publicly to stop doing it – which would have reduced the flood of stock-lent bank shares to a trickle which in turn would have dried up the short sellers' opportunities to continue to do so. If none of that makes sense, don't worry. It's a point of detail and not important in the big scheme of things.

In the event, short selling was banned in September 2008 during the market meltdown. A bit like the limit on market fluctuations that some stock exchanges and futures markets impose, so that if a market gyrates widely it effectively closes temporarily to restore a degree of calm.

So short selling isn't necessarily bad. It can be used to exploit arbitrage opportunities (see box). Again, if this doesn't make sense, don't worry.

So who would do these things: short selling and arbitrage? Let's call him or her a speculator (in actual fact he or she is probably a bank or broker, trader or hedge fund – hedge funds are covered in Chapter 7). You may not like the term 'speculator'. But in the markets speculators are welcome. They provide liquidity. They make markets. They act as arbitrageurs, scanning the markets looking for price discrepancies which they can then exploit for profit until the price discrepancy has been **arbitraged away**.

This is especially true of the futures markets, which allow market professionals to exploit **pricing anomalies** between the future and the spot (immediate) price. If one is higher or lower than the other, an arbitrageur can exploit the difference by selling the high one and simultaneously buying the low one. The act of doing so brings the two back into line while allowing the arbitrageur to pocket the difference. **Index arbitrage** (betting on anomalies between index prices and futures contracts) is regarded as one of the least risky forms of trading (more on this in Chapter 6). And don't forget that currency markets are amongst the largest in the world. You can make money out of the way interest rates affect exchange rates through what is called *covered interest arbitrage* which involves deciding whether to put money on deposit in, say, euros at the European interest rate or dollars at US interest rates.

Now let's visit an IFC where you can smell cash in the air as soon as you step off the plane, whose very existence is premised on trading and money-making: Hong Kong.

HOW IT ALL CONNECTS

- The money markets comprise short-term bonds (Chapter 3)

- One of the biggest buyers of instruments are money market funds which are part of the Buy Side (Chapter 7)

- Money market funds lost huge amounts of money on bank short-term debt as a result of the credit crunch – specifically investment bank Lehmans going bust (Chapter 5)

- Central banks use the money markets to steer interest rates, key to how governments influence the IFMs (Chapter 10)

- The money markets were a significant source of short-term funding for SIVs and other vehicles that bought securitised US mortgages (Chapter 5)

- Key participants are commercial banks (Chapter 8)

- Currencies can be bought and sold now or for delivery in the future – the latter is a type of derivative as are currency swaps (Chapter 6) which isolate the risk of currency movements

- Short selling and arbitrage are key strategies of hedge funds (Chapter 7)

- Brokers – which also shortsell and arbitrage – are often part of investment banks (Chapter 3)

- Acquisition finance to fund takeovers is often obtained through the issue of high-yield bonds (Chapter 8)

DAY TRIP TO
HONG KONG

The day after China took back Hong Kong (on the expiry of the UK's 99-year lease) in 1997 the Thai baht collapsed, sparking a financial crisis across Asia. Not a good omen.

Hong Kong went into freefall.

The Hang Seng Index (the Hong Kong stock market benchmark) lost a quarter of its value in just three days. Hong Kong's economy contracted by over 5%.

What to do? The Hong Kong Monetary Authority (HKMA) jacked interest rates up. It spent US$1 billion buying HK dollars to keep the currency pegged to the US. It bought US$15 billion worth of shares in locally listed companies (in some cases becoming the dominant shareholder).

Four years later, crisis over, HKMA sold the shares for a tidy profit of US$4 billion.

Typical. Only in Hong Kong would you expect regulators to behave with the street smart of the traders they oversee.

And that's exactly what Hong Kong is about. Step off the plane and you feel it in the air: money, money, money. It's why people come to Hong Kong: to make a mint. In fact in the old days that's how you'd arrive: the plane would dive down vertically to the runway, wingtips brushing the condos on either side, so close you could touch the washing hanging on the balconies. Then the plane would scream to a halt, just short of plunging into the sea. Disaster narrowly averted. Success plucked out of the air. Grins all round.

And that's the way Hong Kong has always been: a headrush.

Of course, it's all different now. There's a swanky new airport and Hong Kong is grown-up and well behaved. It has to be. It's owned by China which, not quite sure what it was getting back, dubbed it a 'special administrative region'. That's like being called a problem child. It means you get special attention.

Like London, Hong Kong is a cluster of financial services and attendant support services which it would be hard to replicate anywhere else in east Asia. Hong Kong is the second Asian IFC after Tokyo with a domestic market capitalisation of US$1.7 trillion and regularly ranks second for international IPOs after London.

Like London, it benefits from having a system of law that is prevalent in local financings (Hong Kong law is based on and is similar to English law).

Like London, it can appear to foreigners to be a low-tax jurisdiction (income and corporate tax are 20% or less and there is no VAT) which has led to the greatest concentration of corporate headquarters in the Asia-Pacific region.

Like London, Hong Kong is open to change. The Stock Exchange of Hong Kong (SEHK) and the Hong Kong Futures Exchange (HKFE) demutualised in 2000 and merged with the Hong Kong Securities Clearing Company Limited (HKSCC) under a single holding company, Hong Kong Exchanges and Clearing Limited (HKEx). HKEx completed the transformation by listing on itself.

But unlike London, Hong Kong is the international gateway to what will be the dominant market in the world this century: China. China has been clever in its handling of Hong Kong in the intervening decade. Hong Kong, for its part, has played ball.

The newly integrated HKEx has had a huge boost from mainland Chinese companies doing dual listings on both the Hong Kong and Shanghai stock markets. In fact in April 2005 the Chinese authorities imposed a year-long moratorium on Shanghai for IPOs (in response to a four-year slump that had halved its market value), which favoured Hong Kong: in 2006 Hong Kong was second only to London for IPOs worldwide.

Hong Kong is a conduit for Chinese retail investment in the outside world. Domestic Chinese investors are only permitted to invest via Qualified Domestic Institutional Investors (QDIIs) and QDIIs can only invest in those markets where the regulator has signed a memorandum of understanding with the Chinese Securities Regulatory Authority. Hong Kong's Securities and Futures Commission has done just that, one of the few to have done so. The

SEHK lists companies incorporated in China. These are known as 'H-share' companies. In 2008, eight of the largest companies listed in Hong Kong were Chinese. The SEHK also lists companies incorporated outside China but controlled by PRC shareholders. These are called 'red chip' companies.

However, there is increasing rivalry between Hong Kong and Shanghai over the city that will become the economic centre for mainland China. Hong Kong has an established reputation as an IFC and east Asian entrepôt, for its strong system of law, economic freedom, financial innovation and expertise. But Shanghai has stronger links to the Chinese central government and a more solid base in manufacturing and technology.

In March 2009 the Chinese government approved a plan to turn Shanghai into a global financial and shipping centre by 2020 – despite the 2005 IPO moratorium. However, it is telling that the London Stock Exchange chose to open its first Asia Pacific representative office in Hong Kong, rather than Shanghai, in October 2004.

Observers raise the possibility of a merger between HKEx and one or both of the mainland Chinese exchanges – Shanghai or Shenzhen. Certainly the largest IPO in the world in 2006 was a joint listing by the Industrial and Commercial Bank of China on the Hong Kong and Shanghai stock markets, raising US$22 billion. Rumours of a possible merger reached a peak when the Hong Kong government increased its stake in HKEx from 4.4% to 5.9% in September 2007, indicating that the increased shares could be used as part of an equity swap.

The official line since December 2007 has been that there are currently no plans for any such merger although nothing has been ruled out. Given the level of consolidation among the world's major stock exchanges, the possibility of such a combination can't be dismissed. If the three merged, their combined market capitalisation would be over $5 trillion compared to Tokyo's $4.5 trillion, putting the combined HK/Chinese market third behind New York and London.

Now there's a thought.

Chapter 5

Securitisation, Sub-prime and the Credit Crunch

SPEED-READ SUMMARY

- Securitisation turns bank loans into tradable securities (hence 'securitisation')

- This enables banks to turn their loan books into bonds in order to continue lending without having to increase their capital cushion

- Securitisation enables loans to be tranched into different bonds

- The first securitisations were of US home loans (mortgage-backed securities)

- Securitisation has been used to turn all sorts of retail loans (credit card debt, auto loans, etc) into bonds

- This attracts capital markets funding into the bank lending market – making cheaper credit more readily available

- The sub-prime credit crunch was caused by originate-to-distribute – the arrangers of US home loans lending to poor-quality borrowers, securitising these loans and selling them off

- These securitised loans were sold all over the world to banks and institutional investors

- Banks couldn't get rid of the worst credits (toxic tranches)

- When the US economy turned, the underlying security (residential property) fell below the value of the debt, leading to massive securitisation losses

- Banks, hit by these losses, stopped lending to conserve cash

- Banks stopped lending to each other causing some to go bust

- Credit dried up, affecting businesses and spreading the financial meltdown into the wider global economy

- This liquidity crunch became a global credit crunch

Around 25 years ago in a suite of offices high above Wall Street, the seeds of the world's recent financial meltdown were sown.

In an investment bank called Salomon Brothers (now part of Citigroup) – at the time one of the top financial institutions in the world – a bunch of the very best banking brains set about creating a financial mechanism that would transform the world's capital markets.

Their mission was simple to express but almost impossible to achieve: in short it was to package up bank loans and sell them to institutional investors. So why were they even trying?

CAPITAL CUSHION

Commercial banking (explored in detail in Chapter 8) is banking as you and I know it. It's about lending. Commercial banks take in deposits (and also borrow from each other on the interbank market, as we shall see) and they use that money to make loans. Central banks do not allow the commercial banks they regulate to lend out all of the money they take in. If a bank did that and a depositor wanted his or her money back, the bank wouldn't have the cash to meet that withdrawal and would technically be insolvent. So bank regulators (mainly central banks) make commercial banks keep a cushion of capital in their vaults (it's not actually real money in vaults but electronic entries in computers).

Banks dislike this **regulatory capital** (see box overleaf). They can't do anything with it and so it represents a cost to them – it's either depositors' money on which they have to pay interest or an interbank loan or loans on which they also have to pay interest.

So regulatory capital acts as a ceiling on what a bank can lend. Once a bank has reached that limit it can't lend any more without increasing its regulatory capital base – which it doesn't want to do. You might not think this matters. If a commercial bank's job is to lend and it can't lend any more, then that's job done: it's feet-on-desk time.

But the interest they receive isn't the only way banks make money from loans. On top of the interest charged they levy big fat fees for all sorts of related activities, especially when lending in the wholesale market (wholesale = business-to-business) to companies and governments: arrangement fees for arranging the loan; commitment fees for agreeing to advance the money; drawdown fees whenever the borrower actually draws down (asks for) the money; early repayment fees; documentation fees; and so on.

Regulatory capital

Basel is the Swiss town where the Bank for International Settlements (BIS) is based. BIS is often described as the central banks' central bank. Central banks aren't what you and I would call a bank. They are part of a government – there's one in each country. Their roles vary from country to country but, apart from borrowing on behalf of the government, typically include (1) supervision of the domestic banking system and (2) control of monetary policy and the money supply (including printing currency). The first is about supervising banks. The second is about using interest rates to keep inflation under control (see Chapters 4 and 10).

Central banks meet through BIS to establish worldwide rules to ensure that the big, international banks are regulated wherever they operate. Part of this involves agreeing the level of regulatory capital banks need to maintain and on what basis. The most recent set of rules – dubbed 'Basel II' – are based on risk analysis: the riskier a bank's exposures in the IFMs the more regulatory capital it needs to maintain.

What this means is that once a bank has lent as much as its cushion of regulatory capital will allow, it can only lend more by increasing the cushion. But the cushion is dead money that carries a cost (interest payable to depositors or lenders) so banks don't like adding to it. The capital cushion can in any case be as much as 3–4% of a bank's balance sheet, that is, the loans it's made.

This is the issue that securitisation solves. It enables banks to turn their loans into bonds and get rid of them, raising fresh money in the process which banks can then lend all over again.

These fees are a good source of revenue but you need to keep on making new loans to earn them. So that's one reason why banks want to make more and more loans. But as we've seen, they can't, not without increasing their regulatory capital – which is money they can't do anything with, so is a cost to the business.

This was the problem Salomons set out to solve. Why? Foolish question: money. If anyone could crack this holy grail of wholesale finance they would be flooded out with business from commercial banks eager to find the way to make more loans.

SELLING OFF THE LOAN BOOK

Even you and I could probably work out that any solution to this conundrum would involve a commercial bank selling off its existing loan book (the collection of loans it's made). You sell it off in return for fresh money that you can lend out all over again. Then sell off that loan book and so on.

The only question is: who out there will buy it? The most obvious answer is the least helpful: other commercial banks. Only they understand what a bank's loan book looks like. But, of course, other banks are the very people faced with the same issue: how to get rid of the loans they've already made. So the last thing they are going to want to do is to buy your loans off you when they've got plenty of their own clogging up their own balance sheets. Result: impasse. Stalemate.

So this is what was keeping those boys at Salomons burning the midnight oil. And what they realised was that they had to find buyers for these loans outside the traditional banking market.

Which is where they had an insight of pure genius. What the brilliant brains from Salomons decided to do was turn loans into bonds.

The bank lending market is big. It consists of all the big banks. But there's an even bigger source of capital which we looked at in Chapter 3: the international bond market, which comprises institutional investors such as insurance companies and pension funds (see Chapter 7) and not just banks. So the trick is to turn bank loans (smaller market) into bonds (bigger market) where there are more buyers. In this way the bank lending market can tap the huge additional capital of the international bond markets.

In those days loans were rather dull things. A bank would make a loan and then basically sit on it till the principal was repaid and the money could be lent out again. In technical accounting language, loans are 'fixed assets' on lending banks' balance sheets, and fixed is very much what they were: stuck.

The challenge lay in how to do it. There were loads of hurdles, obstacles and issues to this cleverly simple idea. It was how Salomons tackled these that makes me take my hat off to them. Here's a sample of those hurdles, obstacles and issues:

- Pension funds and insurance companies have never bought bank loans before. How do you convince them – especially since borrowers sometimes default and fail to repay loans?

- The bank must genuinely sell its loan book in order for the loans to be off its balance sheet (OBS) and it must have nothing further to do with the loans – so what happens to the borrowers?

- How do you convince the bank regulators and accountants that the loan book really is genuinely OBS?

- How do you actually turn a bank loan into a bond?

And this is how they did it (obviously much simplified):

■ The bank sells its loan book to an SPV. An SPV is a Special Purpose Vehicle which basically means it is a company that does nothing except the 'special purpose' it is set up to do, in this case buying the loan book and issuing bonds.

■ In a simultaneous series of transactions, the SPV issues bonds to the value of the loan book, pension funds buy the bonds, their money goes to the SPV which uses the money to buy the loan book from the bank.

■ The bank now has fresh money (in place of the old loan book) which it can go out and lend all over again – using the same capital cushion it had before.

■ The borrowers continue to pay interest and repay their loans but this money is diverted by the bank, acting on instructions from the SPV, so that it goes via the SPV straight to the bondholders.

■ In essence the bank is now out of the picture and the borrowers' interest and repayments go to the pension funds as bondholders.

■ The bonds are effectively backed by the loans, and investors who buy the SPV's bond issue do so because they know the interest and principal they receive will come from the loans the bank has made.

■ As loans mature, the repayments of principal are used to redeem the bonds.

■ Investors can buy and sell the bonds in the capital markets in the usual way.

Result: a static asset (loan) has been 'securitised', that is, turned into a highly tradable security (bond).

This still leaves two problems: what happens if any borrowers default (fail to pay interest and/or repay the loan)? And what happens if borrowers repay early (known as early redemption)?

COPING WITH DEFAULT

Salomons overcame this issue brilliantly by careful choice of which loan books to securitise in order to create this new securitisation market. They chose the sort of loans that people only default on as a last resort: the loan to buy the roof over your head. They also did another clever thing. They chose home loans guaranteed by US housing agencies Fannie Mae and Freddie Mac (make a note of those – we'll come back to them).

This meant these loans were effectively guaranteed by the US federal government and gained triple A credit ratings (see Chapter 3 for credit ratings). This made them particularly appealing to institutional investors and gave early investors confidence in the whole notion of securitisations. In time, securitisations spread to other types of borrowing that weren't necessarily as copper-bottomed – auto loans, credit card receivables, and so on. Even here bondholders would not be amused if there were any hiccup in their receipt of interest or repayment of capital. So this risk of delay or default was covered by **credit enhancement** and **liquidity support** with the cost being passed back to the originating bank (that is, the bank that made the loans in the first place). This is because any delay or default is really the bank's fault – it chose the borrowers when it made the loans in the first place.

Credit enhancement can be provided by a monoline insurer (remember them from the US muni bond market in Chapter 3?) which provides insurance against any default; or by a credit derivative (see Chapter 6).

Liquidity support ensures that there is always cash to pay interest due on the bonds. The four main methods of providing liquidity support are:

- Establishment of a cash deposit which can be drawn upon to fund a delay in payments. The cash deposit would be funded out of either the proceeds of issue of the bonds or money advanced under a separate loan. A bank that agrees to accept the SPV's cash deposits in return for a specified rate does so under a guaranteed investment contract (or 'gic')

- Liquidity facility – i.e. a committed loan facility provided by a suitably rated entity (such as a stand-by credit from another bank)

- A second tranche of bonds subordinated to (i.e. coming behind) the main issue which will receive interest only if and to the extent that there is sufficient liquidity to pay

- Overcollateralisation – e.g. having a pool of loans worth $120 million to support a bond issue of $100 million, allowing for $20 million of defaults.

COPING WITH EARLY REDEMPTION

This second issue may strike you as a bit odd. Being repaid early sounds a good thing. But actually it isn't. It means interest rates have come down so a borrower can refinance its loan at a lower rate. This is bad for bondholders because it means they have to reinvest the money that's been repaid at, by definition, a worse return. So bondholders do not like early redemption. But of course borrowers can always repay early.

The specific issue here was that mortgages are long-term loans that can last anything up to 25 years. But people move house more often than that.

So Salomons couldn't promise investors 25-year bonds if on average people move house every, say, five years.

Again, Salomons overcame this issue brilliantly. They ran computer analyses of mortgage portfolios and worked out the statistical incidence of redemption. This is a gobbledygook way of saying that the computer models showed them what percentage of a loan book would be redeemed when. I don't know what the actual figures were and for this level of explanation it doesn't matter. But let's suppose that a typical loan book worth $1 billion has the following statistically calibrated redemption patterns:

- 35% redeem within five years (people moving house fairly quickly to trade up)

- 25% between six and ten years

- 20% 11–15 years

- 15% 16–20 years

- 5% 21–25 years

What Salomons did was to turn the loan book into slices (called 'tranches' in the financial markets). They split it into $350 million of 5-year bonds (35%), $250 million of ten-year bonds (25%), $200 million of 15-year bonds (20%), $150 million of 20-year bonds (15%), and $50 million of 25-year bonds (5%) – and the percentage after each bond maturity indicates what percentage of the loan book made up that duration or tenor of bond. (This is a fictitious example for illustration only.)

So Salomons could go to the market and offer pension funds whatever bond they wanted: five-year, ten-year, 15-year, 20-year or 25-year (again, I'm making these details up but you get the idea).

Of course, not every mortgage holder likely to redeem within five years will do so right on the last day. In practice what happened was that, as home loans were redeemed, the money was put on deposit and the interest was paid to holders of that bond. Then when the bond matured, the money was taken off deposit and returned to them as part of the repayment of principal.

HOW SECURITISATION HAS DEVELOPED

Nobody had done this before – a brand new instrument and market were being created – so much of the early effort went into persuading investors these bonds were good, in persuading the bank regulators and accountants that the sale by a bank of its loans worked and really took them off its balance sheet, in structuring the transaction so that it didn't incur tax (tax can foul up the cashflow of a deal and make it too costly to do) – all without telling the bank's original borrowers that the bank had sold their loans and washed its hands of them.

From the borrowers' point of view they were still paying interest to the bank only it was now diverting that interest to the SPV and acting as the SPV's collecting agent. In terms of day-to-day administration of the loans, nothing had changed, but legally it had.

The big risk throughout was that if the accountants had said the loans were not OBS or the regulators had continued to insist on the underlying capital cushion, the structure would have failed and the transfer from bank to SPV would have been 'recharacterised', to use the jargon. But in essence it worked.

Once the idea of securitisation became accepted, it had a dramatic impact on the IFMs. Once the financial markets were comfortable with this sort of structure, amazing things happened. Everything that could be securitised was. Why stop at home loans?

Securitisation took off. Once investors got used to the idea, they became more comfortable with the type of loan being securitised. Initially home loans led the way: after all, there is underlying security – a mortgage on the property itself which means the property can be sold if a loan is defaulted. But over time investors were just as happy buying unsecured debt, such as credit card debt or auto loans. Examples of receivables that have been securitised also include hire payments under hire purchase agreements, and rentals under equipment leases (asset finance – see Chapter 8).

In fact you can securitise any income stream into a lump sum, such as the income stream from a business, using the resulting lump sum to buy that business – the target's future income streams are securitised to provide the capital to buy it (this is called **whole business securitisation** and is an example of acquisition finance).

Rock stars, who want the present-day benefit of future royalties that stretch decades into the future long after they are likely to be dead (especially given their rock 'n' roll lifestyle) can turn these future royalties into a present-day capital sum through securitisation.

Football clubs have been able to afford expensive players by securitising the revenue the club will earn from televised games and future gate receipts and using the lump sum to make outrageous bids (and many have found to their cost that by over-mortgaging the future for the present they are actually bust).

CDOs and CLOs

The earliest securitisations were of US household mortgages, called **mortgage-backed securities** (MBSs). Because mortgages are underpinned by the value of the property, MBSs are also called **asset-backed securities** (ABSs). MBSs still dominate the ABS and securitisation market and in their earliest guises were called pass-through certificates. The idea behind any securitisation issue is to package up revenue-producing assets then launch a bond issue off the back of them, using the revenue stream to pay the interest on the bonds.

You can securitise pools of loans and bonds in this way. These are called CDOs (**collateralised debt obligations**): loans or bonds payable by various borrowers are pooled and new securities (CDOs) issued that pay out according to the performance of the pool. The term 'collateralised' simply means the new securities are underpinned by the underlying loans and bonds. Like securitisation in general (of which they are an example), CDOs take loans off commercial banks' balance sheets.

There are different types of credit exposure available through the CDO structure. A **cash** or **cashflow CDO** is where the return to the investor depends on the performance of the interest and principal flows from the portfolio of underlying assets. The **market value CDO** is where the return depends on the market value of the pool of assets. A **synthetic CDO** is where the exposure to the underlying assets is created through use of derivatives – usually credit default swaps (see Chapter 6) – rather than an actual pool.

To give an indication of how the CDO market has grown, 15 years ago there were few. By 2006 there were more than $500 billion, of which almost half were MBSs and, of that half, three-quarters were sub-prime loans. By 2007 banks were holding over a third of those sub-prime MBSs in what they regarded (mistakenly, as we shall see) as super senior tranches.

CDO technology has been extended to the insurance markets where insurance risk is put into the pool. The bonds launched off that pool are then sold to institutional investors, so bringing capital markets' capacity into the insurance market. The first deal of this type was a €95 million CDO issue by Hannover Re in 2008. Previously cash securitisations had been done of insurance risks but this deal was achieved synthetically using derivatives. The trigger events relate to insurance risk, rather than typical credit events like failure to pay or a restructuring of an underlying issuer.

CLOs (**collateralised loan obligations**) are like CDOs and are often taken to mean the same thing and to include sub-prime MBSs (mortgage-backed securities). But they can also mean issues backed by leveraged loans – that is, where the level of borrowing (leverage) is high, such as loans to provide acquisition finance for LBOs – leveraged buyouts (see Chapter 8 for acquisition finance). ⇨

> ⇨ **Structured investment vehicles** (SIVs) were funds (see Chapter 7 for what a fund is) put together by investment banks to buy ABSs. They were, effectively, actively managed CDOs since investors bought participations or units in them, much as an investor would buy part of an ABS or MBS or CDO issue. An SIV would maintain a portfolio of these types of securities and would buy and sell to add to or remove from its portfolio. Although SIVs were separate entities and OBS from the banks that launched them, as the markets turned banks found they couldn't just walk away from them; or if they did their reputation with investors would never recover. So they had to stand behind them. This is what did for Bear Stearns (in its case the funds in question were hedge funds – explained in Chapter 7 – which behaved like SIVs in that they had bought a lot of these sub-prime securities) – as we shall see.

What all of these have in common is an income stream. Essentially what you are doing is taking an income stream and capitalising it – raising a lump sum off the back of the income stream which is used to service it (the way your monthly salary enables you to take out a mortgage to buy a property with a lump sum: the monthly pay check is used to service the interest payments on the lump-sum loan you've borrowed to buy your home).

You'll know from Chapters 2 and 3 that trading is what investment banks do par excellence. It's not what commercial banks traditionally did. But securitisation turned their loans into tradable securities and nowadays loans are routinely structured so that they can be traded.

TRANCHING AND POOLING

Securitisation introduced two further ideas that have had a massive impact on the IFMs.

The first is **tranching**: the idea that you can take an existing income stream (called a **receivable**) and slice it up further. This means you can take any sort of financial instrument and divide it up into smaller tradable instruments each of which carries a different level of risk and return. Securitisations that do this are said to have **multiple-tranche structures**, some of which can be **subordinated tranches** (which means they are inferior in credit quality and rank behind more **super senior tranches**).

This means that investors can specify exactly what credit, yield, maturity and currency characteristics they want (this is called a **reverse inquiry**) rather than wait for the right issue to come along. In fact **credit-default swaps** (a type of derivative examined in Chapter 6) have enabled lending banks to separate out the risk of a borrower defaulting on the loan and parcel off that risk while retaining the loan.

Securitisation also introduced the idea of **pooling** existing securities and launching a new security off the back of them. These are called **collateralised debt obligations (CDOs)**. The term 'collateralised' means there is an underlying security – in this case the original bonds that have been put into the pool.

It's possible for the pool of securities (if they are particularly good ones) to have a better credit rating than the originator (this is called **credit arbitrage**). There's no reason why you can't have a securitisation of a securitisation. These are called **Russian dolls**.

Securitisation pools can be **static** (the instruments and receivables in them remain the same from start to finish) or **dynamic** where securities are put into the pool and others taken out during the life of the securitisation. These latter are said to be **actively managed** (a term used in investment management – see Chapter 7). The risk is that the manager may replace

Toxic tranches and financial alchemy

Securitisations of home loans were originally tranched into bonds of different maturity. But sub-prime lending led to a different kind of tranching: by levels of risk (rather than maturity) with the top slice representing triple A borrowers where risk of default is lowest.

The bottom slice (representing the worst credits in the pool) takes the first losses and for this reason is called (confusingly) the **equity tranche** (since it bears a level of risk closer to equity) or, more colloquially, **toxic waste**.

One problem is that the toxic waste often ends up with the bank selling the securitised issue, because no investors are prepared to buy it, even though the upside is that the toxic waste also carries the potential for the highest return.

On the plus side, stripping out the most senior tranche and bundling it with the senior tranches of other securitisations creates new securities that can be ranked more highly by credit agencies than the generality of sub-prime mortgages. This is because the top slice of sub-prime loans are much less likely to default than the toxic layer. In this way gold (a triple A rating) could be minted from tin (sub-prime mortgages) – the ultimate in financial alchemy?

CDOs also enabled investment banks to package up issues that combined senior debt (which is the top slice, most likely to be repaid) with high-yield debt (remember junk bonds in Chapters 3 and 4?) in such a way that the senior debt might not be paid off (amortised) during the life of the security at all – but only later.

good securities with less good ones (known as **churning** – again, a term common in investment management).

It doesn't matter whether you grasp the detail of this or not. What matters is that you can begin to see how receivables and risk are sliced and diced and sold on. This is called variously **financial engineering** or **structured finance**. You can begin to see now how traditional bank lending (explored later in Chapter 8) came to be replaced by CDOs and how the IFMs went trading crazy as participants played pass the parcel: buying risk, slicing and dicing it, and selling it on. Which is what led to the sub-prime credit crunch. How?

SUB-PRIME AND THE CREDIT CRUNCH

The simple explanation of the sub-prime credit crunch is that banks in the US lent a lot of money to sub-prime (less than good-quality) borrowers to help them buy their homes. These loans were securitised into bonds and sold all over the world from bank to bank. Some were put by banks into special funds set up for the purpose called SIVs **(structured investment vehicles)**. Interests in these funds were sold to institutional investors until, as one commentator strikingly noted, sub-prime securitisations 'marbled' the IFMs like the veins running through blue cheese. If you want to be melodramatic, securitisation acted like a virus, spreading the contagion of sub-prime loans throughout the IFMs.

EMBEDDED SECURITISATION

Now, if you securitise a bunch of mortgages, the collective pool is actually safer than any individual mortgage because if you make a single loan to a borrower and he defaults, you've lost the lot. But if you've bought a bond that is backed by a thousand mortgages and a few of those default, then the percentage impact is minimal.

So the theory behind the securitisation of mortgages is good – that it actually minimises risk. And in the US, securitisation of home loans had become embedded: the US federal government had blessed the use of securitisation to spread mortgage lending by attracting capacity into the market through a number of state agencies (such as Freddie Mac, Sally Mae and Fannie Mae) set up to provide government guarantees of certain types of lending considered socially useful, such as loans to the farmers, students and the poor.

Everybody thought these bonds were safe since they were backed by US real estate loans at a time when US property prices were rising and interest rates were low. And sub-prime represented a huge slice of society that banks hadn't been able to reach before – so this was an untapped new market with a social benefit. For those who cared, it was a way of helping people get on the housing ladder who otherwise couldn't. However, in the goldrush, basic tenets of good lending were overlooked.

Many of these home loans were so far beyond the means of borrowers in general and sub-prime borrowers in particular that they attracted graphic names: so, for example, the **ninja loan** (no income, no job, no assets), the **liar loan** (the borrower self-certifies his or her income without the lender checking), the **stretch loan** (more than half the borrower's pre-tax income will go on mortgage payments), the **piggyback loan** (a second mortgage provides the deposit for the first) and the **teaser loan** (an initial artificially low level of interest to lure the borrower in).

Why were these lenders making such absurd loans?

Partly because with property prices going up – driven in part by this sub-prime lending – it was a no-brainer: if the borrower defaulted, the lender could foreclose and sell the underlying property at a profit that would more than cover the amount outstanding plus interest, fees, etc.

But mainly because these lenders made the loans in order to securitise them and sell them on. This is called an **agency issue**: they don't care because they don't act as principal. It's also an example of **moral hazard** – the structural encouragement of reckless risk-taking.

ORIGINATE-TO-DISTRIBUTE

This is known as originate-to-distribute: you make (originate) the loan in order to distribute (sell on by securitising) it to someone else. And the reason you do that is because the act of making a loan earns you a fee. So in fact your business is based on earning fees from arranging loans rather than the interest received over their life and, frankly, you don't care what happens to the loan. Many of these originators weren't really banks at all but mortgage companies and brokers which came to depend on an increasing flow of these originate-to-distribute loans in order to support their businesses.

The effect of originate-to-distribute was that the securities backed by US sub-prime mortgages spread all over the IFMs on the basis that they paid good returns (loans to sub-prime borrowers carried a risk premium in the rate of interest charged to them) but were as safe as, well, houses – and not just any houses but homes in the US, the biggest financial market in the world where property values were heading inexorably upwards.

This started to feed on itself. The volume of sub-prime home loans started to drive the property market up, so creating more demand as more people wanted to get on to the property ladder and as more lenders saw this as risk-free lending. The last time banks had been in this position was in the 1980s when sovereign lending had been all the rage on the basis that countries never go bust (they do – see Chapter 10). So these US sub-prime mortgage securitisations ended up being bought by banks, pension funds, insurance companies, investment funds, hedge funds, everyone, all over the world.

Housing bubbles are massively inflationary because they drive the rest of the economy. When people move house they buy new white goods (washing machines and fridges). They buy new furnishings. They buy paint for the house and plants for the garden. They give their lives a complete makeover. All of this feeds through into retail spending. So central banks, with a keen eye on inflation, are vigilant when house prices shoot up. In the US the Fed (the US central bank) had relaxed interest rates in the wake of 9/11 in 2001 to keep people spending despite the shock and setback to the economy and the country. Sub-prime securitisations kicked in soon after.

The Fed started raising interest rates to control inflation. The Fed Discount Rate (basically the US base rate) rose 17 times between 2001 and 2006, from 1.75% to 5.25%. Cheap credit got expensive. This put the brakes on the US housing market. It peaked and went into decline. Borrowers started defaulting on their loans, either because they couldn't pay the increased interest rates or because they saw little point in servicing a big debt if the thing it was buying was going down in value. As prices collapsed, they walked away from their mortgages: what was the point in paying interest on a loan funding a declining asset if you hadn't owned a house before and probably wouldn't bother to again?

Lenders, panicked, sold the underlying security (the homes) into a declining market. In the way that demand for houses had chased the market up, now sales of houses into a declining market accelerated that fall, making home loans generally worth less. By then there was over $1 trillion of these securitised home loans out there – not all sub-prime. Some were prime and some in between (called Alt-A).

Banks have always had to **mark-to-market** – that is, record the value of their loans in their accounts at a fair market value. Banks, often left with the toxic tranche, started to write down the value of these sub-prime securitisations. In February 2007 HSBC announced a $10 billion writedown of its US mortgage book – at the time a staggering amount of money for one bank to lose.

Then Century, the largest sub-prime lender in the US, filed for bankruptcy. Moody's, the rating agency, downgraded over 130 asset-backed securities and put 250 bond issues on credit watch. Many of these had to be sold by the pension funds holding them because they were no longer 'investment grade' which is what pension funds are permitted to hold (see Chapter 7).

When US real estate started going sour, everything started going wrong. In particular, banks that had set up the SIVs to buy these securitisations came under enormous pressure to support them. In June 2007, a couple of Bear Stearns funds borrowed money off Merrill Lynch, using CDOs as collateral. When the funds defaulted, Merrill Lynch couldn't find any buyers for the CDOs. Just so you see how it all connects, a lot of the municipalities mentioned in Chapter 3 (muni bond market) had parked their surplus cash in debt issued by SIVs, assuming it was safe. So the sub-prime credit crunch spread that way too.

In July 2007 the rating agencies downgraded more issues and put numerous others on watch. Banks which had securitised the securitisations by taking bonds and packaging them up further into slices or tranches of different risks (the best borrowers in the best tranches) had ended up holding on to the toxic tranches because nobody wanted that level of risk. As the market value of securitisations collapsed, these toxic tranches concentrated losses.

That same month, problems in the RMBS market (**residential mortgage-backed securities** – a subset of MBSs) caused two German banks to go bust: Sachsen and IKB Deutsche Industriebank which specialised in lending to German mid-sized companies – about as far removed from US sub-prime as you can get. Other European banks wondered how many mortgage bombs they were sitting on. Even Macquarie, the Australian infrastructure bank, said it had funds exposed to sub-prime. In August 2007, American Home Mortgage Corp filed for bankruptcy.

By now the IFMs were in freefall. There were two issues. The first was that banks had no idea what value – if any – to put on their RMBS and CDO portfolios. This meant that no one knew how much a bank might be worth. As banks realised their own positions were pretty bad they started to suspect that other banks' positions were just as bad or even worse. It meant the unmentionable could happen: a bank could go bust. If – and this is the second issue – a bank can go bust, no one will lend it – or any bank – money. Remember Herstatt risk (Chapter 4)?

Banks started going under. **Bear Stearns**, which had felt duty bound to stand by its hedge funds (see Chapter 7) to the tune of $1.6 billion, went bust and had to be bought by **JPMorgan Chase**, one of the biggest banks in the world, which is both a commercial and an investment bank. Then came **Lehman Brothers**, another major US investment bank, which went bust owing over $600 billion of which a quarter was held by foreign investors. Japanese bank Nomura took Lehman's European and Middle East businesses and paid $225 million for its Asian operations – considered a bargain and making Nomura the world's largest investment bank. UK bank **Barclays** took over Lehman's US operations.

Merrill Lynch, another major US investment bank, sought safety by being bought – it was Merrill Lynch that was holding CDOs from Bear Stearns that it couldn't sell. **Bank of America** (BofA) took it over. BofA is a commercial bank (remember that securitisation was originally designed by investment bank Salomons to help commercial banks free up their balance sheets?). This is where US commercial banks came into their own: they carry an implicit government guarantee. Deposits are guaranteed by the FDIC (the Federal Deposit Insurance Corporation, a government agency) in order to encourage the public to place their money with banks. So commercial banks have implicit government backing which makes them a safer bet to trade with.

No wonder then that two other top investment banks – **Goldman Sachs** and **Morgan Stanley** – turned themselves into commercial banks (technically, into bank holding companies, which is what commercial banks are in the US) for this very reason, immediately and with the US government's approval. This meant they had government backing so that other banks would continue to deal with them. They also sought external investment. **Mitsubishi UFJ**, Japan's largest commercial bank (it has $1 trillion in deposits), paid $8 billion for a 20% stake in Morgan Stanley. Warren Buffett, the world's most famous investor, put $5 billion into Goldman Sachs. He also put $3 billion into GE, the giant industrial conglomerate, whose problems were caused by its ILC (industrial lending company – as the finance subsidiaries of big manufacturers are called).

Bear Stearns and Lehmans were the last banks allowed to go to the wall. The financial system would not have withstood it. Banks this big, it was now recognised, were too big to be allowed to fail (another example of **moral hazard** – the bigger you are the more reckless you can be since the government is always forced to bail you out; and if your costs of borrowing are reduced by the implicit government guarantee, you're getting an unfair advantage in the market).

So the world over, governments stepped in. First they guaranteed banks' liabilities, then they lent them money, then they took shares in them, then finally they took some over altogether (nationalised them). This is how the US government ended up with 40% of **Citigroup**, injecting $40 billion and guaranteeing more than $300 billion of shaky assets (the guarantee kicks in after the first $30 billion of losses). Citi subsequently agreed to merge its **Smith Barney** broking arm (one of the few bits of the bank doing well) with Morgan Stanley.

ATLANTIC CROSSING

This contagion crossed the Atlantic. **Northern Rock** was a former thrift (savings and loans institution, called building societies in the UK) from Newcastle and the north-east of England. It had demutualised, become a bank and, egged on by senior management whose bonuses were geared to gross lending, turned itself into the biggest home loan provider in the UK. When the sub-prime credit crunch blew across the Atlantic, Northern Rock went bust.

Ironically, it didn't go bust because it was holding US sub-prime securitisations. Nor because it was securitising its own home loans. These were perfectly sound and, besides, it wasn't alone: UK home loan securitisations leapt from around £10 billion in 2000 to over £250 billion by 2006 (40% of the mortgage market).

No, Northern Rock went bust because of cashflow problems (remember the importance of cashflow in Chapter 1?). Having outgrown its humble origins, Northern Rock was no longer funding itself from retail deposits in Newcastle and the north-east but in the wholesale **interbank market**. We will come across this again in Chapter 8 (it's arguably part of the money markets covered in Chapter 4) but basically the interbank market is where banks lend to each other but only for three months at a time. If you want to borrow for longer, you have to roll over (renew) your position every three months. Usually this is fine, no problem.

But with banks extremely wary of each other the interbank market basically closed. And Northern Rock – well known in the UK's north-east but a small and unknown entity in global financial terms – found itself out in the cold: it couldn't roll over its positions. It was funding long-term mortgages with short-term cash and the short-term cash was no longer available. Result: the bank was bust. And the UK government had to step in (how the UK government bungled this is explained in Chapter 10).

It wasn't the only one. The UK government leant on **Lloyds TSB**, one of the UK's top retail banks, to take over **HBOS** (a previous merger between Halifax Building Society and Bank of Scotland). Doing so almost bankrupted Lloyds so the government had to bail it out. Another UK bank

Freddie Mac and Fannie Mae

Freddie Mac (the Federal Home Loan Mortgage Company) and Fannie Mae (the Federal National Mortgage Association) were at the heart of the securitisation crisis. Together they could end up costing the US government $1 trillion.

They had originally been set up by the US government decades before (as government-sponsored enterprises) to buy mortgages from lenders and convert them into mortgage-backed securities (MBSs) that could be sold on to the secondary mortgage market.

Although now privatised, they benefited from implicit government backing to raise cheap finance in the markets. They used this money to buy MBSs paying a higher return. This is called 'carry trade': using cheap finance to buy securities paying a higher return – it's also found in the currency markets (Chapter 4). They also earned fees from guaranteeing 'private label' MBSs – they owned or guaranteed half of the $10 trillion US mortgage market.

Their securities (hybrid debt and equity and regarded as low risk) had been bought by banks which also bought the MBSs they issued – at one point US banks' holdings of Fannie Mae and Freddie Mac MBSs accounted for half of banks' total MBS holdings.

On top of that, banks wrote $20 billion of credit-default swaps (CDSs – explained in Chapter 6) on debt issued by the two agencies. Over a third of their securities were estimated to be held by foreign and central banks – including China's (see Chapter 10).

When they headed towards insolvency (with Freddie Mac $20 billion in debt and Fannie Mae $3 billion) the US government had to step in and take them under federal control, pumping $14 billion into Freddie with estimates that federal aid could top upwards of $50 billion and possibly as much as $120 billion.

As part of the fallout the 12 banks that make up the FHLB (Federal Home Loan Banks), which supports more than 8,000 member banks that provide guaranteed home loans, had to provide more than $1 trillion in support as well as hold over $70 billion of private label MBSs not guaranteed by Fannie and Freddie. Ironically, the FHLB had been thinking of entering the muni market following the monoline insurers' crisis (see Chapter 2) – which just shows how markets interconnect.

considered to be well run was **RBS** (Royal Bank of Scotland) which owned UK retail bank **NatWest** but which, having bought Dutch bank ING, posted the highest UK corporate loss at the time of almost £25 billion. The UK government guaranteed RBS assets up to £300 billion, then had to inject £13 billion and finally ended up owning three-quarters of it.

In Europe, the Belgian, French and Luxembourg governments injected more than €5 billion into **Dexia** which was brought down by providing bond insurance. The Belgian, Dutch and Luxembourg governments bailed out **Fortis**: first all three injected fresh capital into it, then the Dutch nationalised the bit of the bank in the Netherlands, and Belgium and Luxembourg sold their bits to French bank BNP Paribas.

Banks that didn't fall over still found themselves in a terrible position. They started **deleveraging** (getting rid of loans – this is similar to the expression 'a cram down'). They started selling the securitisations they held into a falling market. Doing so depressed the market even further, driving values even lower, forcing them to sell to an even greater extent. So the market collapsed.

Not every country's banking system was afflicted. Spanish banks, such as **Santander**, emerged as heroes. This was because Spain did not allow off-balance sheet (OBS) funding, so securitisations were out. Spain also required fast-expanding banks to make extra capital provision (remember

---

Securitisation: bad or good?

Securitisation may have caused the global credit crunch. But it has also, on the positive side, been the source of much cheap and necessary funding over the last two decades.

Tapping the capital markets via securitisations has made a lot of retail finance (credit extended to individuals) on good terms possible: credit card debt, student loans, small business loans, car loans and so on. Without it, people might not find the financing they want on terms they can afford. In fact, credit card debt almost stopped in its tracks as defaults rose, securitisations stopped, and cheap money was turned off. These types of finance are no longer primarily bank-funded but are funded in the capital markets.

So just at a time when banks have recoiled from continuing to lend to perfectly sound businesses and individuals, preferring to shore up their balance sheets instead, securitisation has become even more critical.

One view is that post credit crunch, securitisations and CDSs will shift from being OTC to exchange-traded. They will become standardised, the margins (profits) much thinner and so therefore less lucrative and attractive to do – and therefore maybe safer.

Even in the housing market sensible securitisation is possible. In Denmark, when a bank lends on mortgage it is required by law to sell a matching bond. But the bank remains responsible for servicing that bond so it has a vested interest in the borrower not defaulting. And borrowers for their part can buy bonds in the market and use them to redeem their mortgage. This becomes a self-correcting mechanism. If bonds go down in price, borrowers will buy them (cheaply) to redeem their (more expensive) mortgage. The more people do this, the more the price will go back up. In this way home loans and the bonds issued to fund them remain in step with each other, in equilibrium. Clever, eh?

that this was the original driver for securitisation). This recognises that a fast-growing business, while appearing superficially successful, is in fact at its most vulnerable – like a plane just leaving the runway – in that it can run out of cash (like Northern Rock) at a critical moment because it is trying to support so much new business from existing income.

And there were individual banks that looked very wise in retrospect. **Standard Chartered**, a UK bank with extensive commercial banking operations in emerging markets in Asia and Africa, seemed every inch the paragon of banking good sense simply by sticking to lending and trade finance (Chapter 8).

Just to show the measure of the credit crunch, banks weren't the only financial institutions caught up in it. **AIG**, the world's top insurer worth $40 billion, was crippled by the credit crunch and had to be bailed out by the US government which embarked upon a plan to break it up.

Soon banks all over the world started going bust too and governments had to step in to stop the entire financial system from imploding. But it didn't stop there. If it had, this would have been a financial crisis and meltdown restricted to the global banking system. But all of these banks started recalling loans they'd made to businesses.

Bank overdrafts to borrowers are typically 'on demand' loans: the bank can simply ask for it back even if the borrower hasn't done anything wrong. So banks, now short of money and needing to shore up their own finances, started calling in loans to businesses even if those businesses were fine and profitable. And those businesses therefore suffered a cashflow crisis and went bust. And that is how the financial meltdown spread to the wider world of business and caused a global recession.

How governments reacted and stopped the financial meltdown is explained in Chapter 10. Before we get there we need to look at another contributor to trading frenzy in the financial markets: derivatives, once likened by the most famous investor in the world (Warren Buffett) to weapons of mass financial destruction.

Just to pile irony upon irony, a major type of derivative is the swap. Nowadays you can achieve a securitisation just by using a swap. Securitisation is an exchange of principal (a book of bank loans) for income (the interest due on them). So with a swap: you can swap future income for a lump sum. So a securitisation can be achieved by a swap, which is an altogether much sleeker and smarter instrument. So you didn't have to know about any of this anyway. That sucks.

HOW IT ALL CONNECTS

- Securitisation is key to retail finance which is part of commercial lending (Chapter 8)

- CDOs have been used in the insurance market (Chapters 7 and 9)

- Banks holding toxic tranches thought they were laying off risk but in fact they were concentrating it − much like Lloyd's of London with the LMX spiral (Chapter 9)

- Marking to market is a feature of the futures markets (Chapter 6)

- The global credit crunch led to concerted government action (Chapter 10)

- The effect of the credit crunch was amplified by credit default derivatives (Chapter 6)

- The SPVs used in securitisations are usually located in OFCs (Chapter 9)

- Interest rate swaps are now typically part of the securitisation structure to prevent fluctuations in interest rates jeopardising the transaction − swaps are derivatives (Chapter 6)

- It is now possible to replicate securitisations entirely using swaps (Chapter 6) which is called a synthetic securitisation

- The collapse of banks provided hedge funds and equity funds with potential opportunities (Chapter 7)

- Counterparty risk wrecked the money markets (Chapter 4) when Lehmans went bust (money market funds had bought Lehman debt assuming it was safe) and $400 billion deserted the money markets

- The reason why Bear Stearns borrowed money off Merrill Lynch, pledging CDOs as security that Merrill then couldn't sell, was because Merrill was its prime broker − prime brokerage is the set of services investment banks provide to hedge funds (Chapter 7)

- The global credit crunch led to 'leaderless credit groups' − swathes of bondholders who have no mechanism for restructuring the debt with the issuer. In Chapter 8 we will see that one advantage of traditional bank lending is that if the borrower gets into trouble it can always talk to the bank and reschedule the loan. This is much harder in the bond market where the issuer never knows who its bondholders are, hence 'leaderless creditor groups'

DAY TRIP TO
MUMBAI

By definition, no one escapes a global financial meltdown. It wouldn't be global if you did. But at least India and other emerging markets weren't seduced by securitisation. Indeed, despite the global recession, India has averaged 8% annual growth since 1991, the year that saw the beginning of India's economic liberalisation.

Come to Mumbai, however, and you'd be forgiven for thinking you'd stepped back a century. Mumbai (formerly Bombay) is India's commercial and financial centre: it generates over 5% of the country's GDP, accounts for two-fifths of its maritime trade, over two-thirds of capital transactions and a third of the country's income tax receipts.

But, with about 15 million people, Mumbai is also the second largest city in the world (after Mexico City) and, like other fast-growing cities in the developing world and India as a whole, it suffers from an infrastructure struggling to cope: the growth in demand for electricity outstrips the growth in supply, there is widespread unemployment, poor healthcare, clogged public transport and insufficient and expensive housing; not to mention rife petty corruption and notoriously inefficient bureaucracy (often referred to as the 'permit raj' – to get a taxi from the airport requires queuing at several different posts and kiosks, and the completion of a complex form which logs details of your luggage's dimensions).

Roads, ports and power supplies, none of which can meet present – let alone future – demand have a direct impact on Mumbai's commercial efficiency. It takes on average 21 days to clear import cargo in India, compared with three in Singapore. The Jawaharlal Nehru Port, which handles two-thirds of India's container traffic, has berths for just nine container vessels, compared with Singapore's main port which has 40.

At times over the past two decades, Mumbai's cost per square foot (India remains rigidly imperial in its measures) has made it the most expensive place on earth: a tiny central Mumbai flat costs the equivalent of half-a-million US dollars. Yet what you get for your money is crumbling facades, birds flying in and out of office buildings' paneless windows, power cables snaking like giant anacondas along office corridors and whole stretches of ceiling supported by scaffolding – and this in one of the most prestigious commercial addresses in the whole of the city.

No wonder office workers dressed neatly in white shirts and pressed suits are as often as not living in shanties (over half of Mumbai's population does) in what is the largest slum city in the world. A third of the world's poor live in India, with three-quarters of the population living on less than $2 a day, which is worse than Sub-Saharan Africa.

India's two main stock exchanges are in Mumbai: the National Stock Exchange of India (NSE) which was incorporated in November 1992; and the Bombay Stock Exchange (BSE) (originally the Native Share & Stock Brokers' Association, founded in 1875, current slogan: 'The edge is efficiency'), which together account for over four-fifths of share transactions in India. Ten years ago there were almost 20 other stock exchanges, located in India's other major cities, but almost all of them are now defunct.

The NSE has a market capitalisation of almost $1 trillion as against the BSE's $750 billion. The NSE's average daily turnover is $4 billion, four times that of the BSE. Its key index is the S&P CNX Nifty 50. The BSE's key index is the BSE Sensitive Index (SENSEX). The Indian financial markets' two principal regulators are in Mumbai: the Reserve Bank of India, the country's central bank; and the Securities and Exchange Board of India (SEBI) which oversees the capital markets.

India's financial sector, although untouched by the sub-prime credit crunch, remains underdeveloped. The corporate debt market (loans and bonds) is severely underdeveloped compared with those of other emerging markets. The same is true of retail customers. Less than half the population use banks. More than half of all Indian household savings are in physical assets such as land, houses, cattle and gold. This is partly because banks are mistrusted, partly because the bulk of the population is rural (agriculture remains the predominant sector in India, accounting for over half of employment) and hard to reach through a branch network, and partly because of alternative sources of finance, such as moneylenders and microfinance institutions (see Chapter 8). Those assets held in cash – about $900 billion – are just a fifth of the equivalent in China.

State-owned banks account for two-thirds of the banking system. The RBI requires them to make available 40% of all credit to primary sectors like agriculture and a quarter of their branches serve rural and semi-urban areas. Foreign banks are kept at arm's length: they represent less than 10% of the country's financial system; Standard Chartered has 90 branches but an offer to double that number (in rural areas) was rebuffed. However, foreign investors can own IDRs (Indian depository receipts – see Chapter 2) in India's private banks. Indian companies for their part raised over $5 billion in ADRs and GDRs (American and Global Depository Receipts) in 2007–08.

Mumbai has fast become a more attractive proposition for foreign direct investment (FDI) since 2005 when restrictions on foreign investment in certain sectors were relaxed. There are now 35 industries in which FDI can be automatically approved (subject to maximum shareholdings that differ between sectors). FDI inflows into India reached a record $20 billion in 2006, almost three times the figure for the previous year and are expected to top $35 billion in 2009, with a third of that going to Mumbai. The chief sources of FDI are Mauritius, the US, the UK, the Netherlands and Singapore. India also has strong trading ties with China, the US, Germany and the UAE. It is one of the BRICS (Brazil, Russia, India, and China), the four top emerging markets (see Chapter 10).

The most attractive areas for foreign investment in India are the Special Economic Zones (SEZs), of which there are about 220, overseen by the Ministry of Commerce and Industry. These are essentially tax-free zones – and there are a lot of taxes in India – that qualify for preferential loans and accelerated bureaucratic approval. A total of $180 billion is invested in SEZs across the country. One of the oldest is the Santacruz Electronics Export Processing Zone (SEEPZ) in Mumbai. SEEPZ was established in 1973 and mainly houses software companies and jewellery exporters: more than 40% of India's jewellery exports come from units within SEEPZ.

India's burgeoning reputation as an outsourcing and offshoring destination explains why the service sector accounts for a quarter of employment India-wide (over four-fifths in Mumbai) and over half of GDP, with industry accounting for about an eighth.

All of this may make Mumbai sound like a city of the past: old, worn-out, antique. Don't be fooled. It's a city of the future.

Chapter 6
Derivatives

SPEED-READ SUMMARY

- There are three types of derivatives: swaps, options and futures (or forwards)

- Derivatives are derived from underlying securities, instruments or transactions (the underlying is also known as the cash market)

- Derivatives can be traded on exchange or in the over-the-counter market – even in the OTC market they tend to be standardised which is why the derivatives markets are deep, liquid and efficient

- Settlement tends to be in cash rather than by physical delivery of the underlying

- A swap is an exchange of assets, liabilities or income streams: for example, an interest rate swap exchanges fixed and floating rates; a currency swap exchanges two currencies

- A swap can achieve the same economic effect as a securitisation

- Credit default swaps (CDSs, aka credit default derivatives or credit derivatives) enable a lending bank to protect itself against the borrower's default

- Other swaps include: asset swaps, equity swaps, total return swaps and property swaps

- Options allow the holder to lock in a maximum price at which to buy or a minimum at which to sell

- Futures are exchange-traded forwards – they are bought on margin and have to be marked to market

- Futures allow exposure to markets without owning the underlying

- Clearing houses remove counterparty risk and require marking-to-market

- Stock index futures are used by institutional investors to obtain synthetic exposure to stock markets

---

If the last chapter on securitisation was a bit tough to grasp, here's the good news: you don't have to. You can achieve the effect of a securitisation with a much simpler instrument called a swap (a swap can exchange an income stream for a principal amount). A swap is a derivative, meaning it is derived from another instrument or transaction. Derivatives have in recent years dominated trading in the IFMs. There are three types: swaps, options and futures (just to complicate things, a swap can in fact be replicated by two futures).

SWAPS

We're going to start with swaps and, in particular, the two most common and simplest: **interest rate** and **currency** swaps. We'll then look at others.

Interest rate swaps

The first swaps were **interest rate swaps**. Let's say I take out a mortgage of $100,000 at a fixed rate of 5%. You too have a mortgage of $100,000 but at a floating rate of interest which is currently also 5%. We each pay $5,000 a year in interest. Why would each have done the opposite of the other? In some markets one form of borrowing is easier or cheaper than the other. Or we may each have had the choice but had different views of where interest rates were heading. Or I was on a low income and wanted to fix my cost of borrowing to give me peace of mind, whereas you were happy with a variable-rate mortgage because you wanted to be sure that you were getting the market rate of interest, however high or low that might have been. No matter, that's what we each did.

Now let's say each of our views or circumstances have changed. I am now earning more so am less concerned to fix the cost of my home loan. I'm now more interested in getting the variable market rate. Or I believe interest rates are heading down for the long term. In your case you think they're going up. Or you now want to fix your cost of borrowing because you have tight cashflow and want that certainty of borrowing cost. Whatever.

How can we each do this?

- Each can pay off the existing home loan by taking out a new loan with the desired interest rate. This is the worst option as it is expensive. Our respective lenders will charge all sorts of fees to let us do this.

- We can each service the other's debt. This is a better option, but our lenders might notice and not like it. Also, each is exposed to the other's credit risk. You may fail to pay my interest one month and cause me to default and my lender to foreclose.

- We can each continue to service our own debt but treat each other as if we have swapped, then every so often settle up between each other as if each were holding the other's debt. This is the best option. This way our respective lenders don't know and we're not dependent on each other paying our own debt.

So what does settling up look like?

Let's say interest rates go up and over the year are 6%. Over the year I pay $5,000 (fixed rate) and you pay $6,000 (floating rate). At the end of the year you have paid $1,000 too much and I have paid $1,000 too little so I pay you $1,000. This means you have paid net $5,000 (as if you were on a fixed rate) and I have paid $6,000 (as if on a floating rate). Simple.

An observer might say that you did a good deal and I did a bad one. But that's not so. I got what I wanted, although I paid $1,000 more than I would otherwise have done. And if I enter into the swap for a number of years then some years I'll do well and others not so, depending on interest rates. But the point is I got what I wanted: a floating rate of interest. You can begin to see that in fact I have a **synthetic** position: a floating rate achieved through a derivative, in this case an interest rate swap.

In real life, you and I wouldn't deal directly with each other, for two reasons: first, counterparty risk – neither knows whether the other will be good for the money at the end of the year; second, what are the chances of our finding each other, with each of us providing what the other wants in relation to home loans of exactly the same amount? Answer: nil. So for these two reasons each of us would in fact deal with a bank (assuming they are less risky than we are: when they are not, banks are said to be **disintermediated**).

Initially banks would have only entered into matching trades (they would only enter into a swap if they could find an exactly off-setting one to enter into as well). But swaps are now so tradable, because of the degree of standardisation, and the market is now so deep, that banks don't need to trouble to keep a square book (where deals offset each other).

Interest rate swaps make up by far the biggest segment of the swaps market. Next come currency swaps.

Currency swaps

A currency swap enables a company to raise funding in one currency (such as its home currency where, because it is known, the cost of funding may be lower) and then swap the proceeds into another currency which it wants to use (for instance to expand into another territory such as an export market).

So with a currency swap there is (1) an agreement for an initial exchange of currencies at the current spot (cash market) rate and (2) a simultaneous agreement to reverse the swap at a later date but at the same currency rate, regardless of intervening currency rate changes. Unlike an interest rate swap, the principal amount in a currency swap does pass between the parties (because each wants the actual use of the other currency) and then back again on termination. The benefit is that any intervening movements in the currencies' respective values are neutralised. As with interest rate swaps, banks usually stand in the middle or act as counterparty in a currency swap. At the end of the deal, the principal is swapped back.

Under both types of swap and in order to reduce counterparty risk, the companies simply make a periodic net settlement: each continues to service its own debt, then they periodically tot up who would have been worse or better off under the swap structure, and the loser pays the amount of the difference across to the winner. The important point is that although there is a winner and a loser, each is getting (synthetically) what it wants: the other's position.

What companies are doing when they use a swap is **hedging**, which means protecting themselves against the risk of an unwanted market movement, in this last example against adverse currency rate movements.

Whether or not you follow the detail of these examples doesn't matter. All that matters is that two parties are able through a single transaction to swap one underlying position for another. Almost every bond issue (Chapter 3) these days is made with a view to swapping the proceeds so the issuer gets what it wants (straightforward bond issues are called **plain vanilla**; a bond with an exotic derivative attached is said to have **bells and whistles**).

Credit default swaps

We've begun to see that a swap enables you to swap one thing for another: one interest rate for another; a currency for another; indeed, in securitisations, a lump sum for an income stream or the other way round.

Now you know how swaps work, I want to move on to a more recent type of swap that contributed to the sub-prime credit crunch from Chapter 5 (for example it brought down insurer AIG): the **credit default swap (CDS)** also often called **credit default derivative** or **credit derivative**.

CDSs enable lenders to separate a loan from the credit risk of the borrower so that a bank can remove part or all of a borrower's credit risk (the risk that the borrower may default on the loan). Let's say I am Bank A and I've made a loan to a Borrower B. Let's say I like the loan but Borrower B's credit rating falls or I am overexposed to B (I've felt obliged to lend more than I really want to). I enter into a CDS with insurer C. I pay C a premium and in return get protection if B defaults. Under the CDS, if Borrower B defaults, I can require insurer C to make good my loss. In other words, the CDS will pay me by **reference** to B. B's default is the **credit event** that triggers the payment from insurer C to me under the CDS. This means I have got rid of my exposure to B while retaining the loan.

Why is it called a CDS? Well, it's to do with a loan (credit) going wrong (default) and is a transaction where I swap a premium for protection against B defaulting (for this reason C is called the **protection-seller**). It's a derivative because it is derived from the underlying loan I made to B.

Note, it's possible to calibrate a CDS so that it isn't just an actual default that triggers the CDS (which, short of insolvency, is the most extreme situation) but, say, a deterioration in B's credit standing (a downgrade in its credit rating). In other words you can slice up the risks involved in making that loan. So far we've looked at the reference point as being B. But it could be by reference to other things: a fall in an index, for example. You can begin to see, I hope, how flexible a CDS can be.

Two further things: first, what I have bought from C is basically a 'put' option – that is, if the loan goes bad I can 'put' it (transfer it) to C or, at least in economic terms, be treated as if C were now the loan maker (options are explained later on); second, a protection-seller (C) may hedge its position by – oddly – buying protection from the Borrower B itself which thus, strangely enough, earns a fee for not defaulting. This is called a **self-referenced credit default swap**.

There are **credit-linked notes** which combine a CDS with a bond (i.e. they have a coupon, maturity and redemption) and are used by investment managers (see Chapter 7) to hedge against rating downgrades or defaults (this is an example of **structured finance**). Don't worry if this is all hard to grasp. The point is simply to show how risk can be sliced and diced and passed on – which is what stoked the trading frenzy in the IFMs.

CDSs are sometimes said to provide 'insurance'. This isn't strictly true: insurance is a different product and market (some would say it isn't part of the IFMs, although it is covered in Chapter 9) and is regulated differently. In fact the CDS market goes to some lengths to ensure it is **not** categorised as insurance (for which you need an insurance licence). However, the debate has been clouded by the fact that big insurers have stepped into the CDS market – AIG sold almost $500 billion of CDS protection on CDOs (collateralised debt obligations – see Chapter 5) which is why in my example I said C was an insurer. Of course, CDSs are available on banks themselves. The spreads – the difference between the buy and sell prices – on these CDSs widen as banks' credit-standing shrinks. So the spread reflects the cost of 'insuring' debt against the risk of default. A widening spread reflects the increased cost. Just before Bear Stearns went bust, the five-year spread on its CDSs went to just under 750 basis points (7.5%) meaning that $100 million of its debt cost $7.5 million to insure; while the CDS spread on Icelandic bank Glitnir (now 75% owned by the Icelandic government) touched 1500 basis points (15% to you and me). These are big spreads.

Other types of swap

Swaps aren't limited to exchanging liabilities. There are also **asset swaps** where parties exchange the return on different types of assets (e.g. an unlisted equity into a bond), **equity swaps** (where returns on portfolios are exchanged, for instance for cash), **total return swaps** (where all the cashflows such as interest or dividends are paid to the holder as if it held the bond or share directly) and even **property swaps**.

Property swaps help to overcome a drawback of real estate investment: it is extremely illiquid; buying and selling commercial property can take weeks or months rather than minutes or hours. Property swaps achieve exposure to the property market without transferring the physical property assets.

The party that wants to reduce its property exposure (a long-term property investor such as an institutional investor – see Chapter 7) pays part of its return from a particular property or portfolio (rent or an amount tied to a property index) to a party that wants to increase its immediate exposure. This might be a property developer that doesn't want to waste months going through long-winded property purchases and which, in return, simply pays across annual interest on the notional value of the assets swapped.

The developer is betting that property returns will increase at a higher rate than it could get from a bank. Each has avoided the usual property costs (legal, tax and agents' fees) while acting on their view of the market much more quickly than if trying to complete an actual property transaction. This is where swaps and other derivatives start to converge because they simply create a different, synthetic position.

There are now plenty of other swaps such as **basis swaps**, **pay-fixed swaps**, **forward starting swaps**, **yield curve swaps** and so on. There are even **tax rate swaps** (locking in a current tax rate while the other party takes the risk of a rate change).

Swaps: role model for an OTC market

You'll recall that in the equity markets (see Chapter 2) a distinction is drawn between on-exchange and OTC (over-the-counter) trading. So, too, in derivatives. Originally, when they started in the 1980s, a swap was a one-off deal between a bank and a company. A company would go to a bank for an interest rate or currency swap and the bank would try to find an offsetting trade with another company or bank.

But swaps are now so standardised that there is a huge, deep and liquid secondary market for 'second-hand' swaps even though, like NASDAQ for shares, it is technically an OTC market (there is no exchange as such). This means that banks no longer bother to find an off-setting swap for each one they enter into – instead they manage their overall portfolio and make sure that over time they keep a square book (the swaps in their portfolio balance each other out). Swaps were originally dominated by – interestingly enough – commercial banks (traditional lending banks, which we'll explore in Chapter 8). Now all banks – investment and commercial – are active in the swaps market.

Of the other types of derivative, options can be OTC or exchange-traded (the latter tend to be options on individual company shares), futures are exchange-traded (on futures exchanges, although these now cater for a much wider array of derivatives) and forwards are OTC (a forward is actually an OTC future). In the OTC market many types of derivatives (like swaps) are standardised, but others

may not be: the original meaning of OTC was a market where you could buy customised, one-off products from a bank to meet a particular need.

If that need becomes widespread and the product standardised, then you have an OTC market that is like an exchange except for the comparative lack of regulation (which doesn't matter because most OTC markets are wholesale, not retail markets – that is, they are business-to-business, not business-to-person).

Swaps became standardised – and, hence, highly tradable – thanks to ISDA which started in 1985 as the International Swap Dealers Association and introduced standardised documentation to the market. This was so successful that its remit was widened and ISDA now stands for the International Swaps and Derivatives Association.

ISDA devised standard documentation that allowed banks to enter into master agreements with each other. This had two effects. First, it sped up the market because, prior to ISDA, it often took weeks to document a deal. Second, it allowed banks to **net off** their exposures: remember Herstatt risk (Chapter 4)? Well, under ISDA, if two banks do a succession of deals with each other, those deals are automatically netted (the deals are aggregated and the amounts owed cancelled out until there is a single amount owing from one to another) which reduces their exposure to each other (the counterparty risk) to a minimum.

Apart from netting, a more recent innovation is **trade compression.**

➡ This is a service provided by third parties who will analyse a trading book and replace offsetting agreements with new ones that reflect a netted position. It was work by compression vendors on behalf of dealers in credit-default swaps (explained in this chapter) that got the CDS market down from almost $60 trillion to almost $40 trillion over the second half of 2008.

Swaps can also be combined with other derivatives: a **swaption** (option on a swap) allows the holder to enter into an interest rate swap and is used to swap fixed-rate cashflows that are irregular where one party doesn't want to do the swap unless some market condition (risk) happens. Swaptions are themselves traded.

Daily volume in swaps is over $5 trillion and is growing at an annual compound rate of 20% which puts it ahead of exchange-traded derivatives. The majority of swaps are interest rate swaps. Currency swaps and CDSs account for well over $500 billion each. Half of all swaps trading occurs in London.

FORWARDS AND FUTURES

The final types of derivative are forwards and futures. A **forward** (short for 'forward contract') is simply a *contract to take delivery* of something at a *fixed date* in the future for an *agreed price*. Because it's a contract that is delivered and paid for at some point ahead of the present, no actual cash changes hands until maturity. The critical point about a forward is that it is an obligation to make payment and take delivery whereas an option gives you the right but not the obligation. Forwards are traded in the OTC market.

Origins in commodities

Forwards have their origins in the **commodity** and currency markets and go back 3,000 years. Originally they were a way for producers (of foodstuffs such as wheat, sugar, cocoa, coffee, tea and so on) to sell their crops forward, so guaranteeing a return on planting, nurturing and harvesting their crop. For consumers it was a way of locking in a price in advance. The effect was to smooth out peaks and troughs in natural production (if the harvest is too good, producers suffer because the price they get goes down; if the harvest is poor, consumers have to pay a lot more). It means, for example, that a cocoa farmer can lock-in a sale at a price that will return a profit; and makers of chocolate can keep prices constant to the consumer without supermarkets having to alter prices from week to week.

This explains why the biggest futures markets in the world started in Chicago (the agricultural crossroads of the US) in the 1850s in response to a series of bad grain harvests. Although the majority of instruments traded there now are financial derivatives, they have their origins in agricultural produce which is why stock markets and banks are still keen on commodity contracts. It's why NASDAQ bought Agora X, an institutional trading platform for OTC commodity contracts, and why in mid-2009 a platform called Source, backed by banks such as Goldman Sachs, Morgan Stanley and Bank of America Merrill Lynch, was launched to trade commodity-related products (such as commodity-linked certificates) in conjunction with the Deutsche Börse. Daily trading volumes in the US are $90 billion and in Europe only $2 billion. Source hopes to bridge that gap.

In the **currency** markets, trades are either immediate (for settlement now, called the **spot market**) or for **forward delivery** at some point in the future (known as the **forward market**). Since currency markets are amongst the biggest in the world (Chapter 4) so are their associated forward markets as companies hedge multiple-currency revenue streams and banks and brokers exploit arbitrage and trading opportunities. (cont. p117)

Options

Of the three types of derivatives – swaps, futures and options – options are the easiest to understand and the most benign.

An option is exactly what it says: it gives you the *option* to buy something but *not the obligation* – in other words, you don't have to. Let's say shares in X Corp (a fictitious oil company) are trading at $3 each. They may go up or down but if they go up – because of the discovery of a new oil field – I want to make sure I don't completely miss the boat. Instead of buying shares, I buy options. Each option allows me to buy a share in X Corp at $3.30 and costs ten cents. Options usually last three months.

If over that time X Corp's share price goes above $3.30 the option is *in-the-money* and I will exercise it. If not, it is *out-of-the-money* and I'll walk away (if the shares are, say, at $3.25 and I want them I'll simply buy them in the open market rather than exercise the option because under that I have to pay $3.30). $3.30 is the *strike price*. Some options can be exercised at any time (*American*), some only on expiry (*European*) and some only on specified dates (*Bermudan*) – these terms have nothing to do with geography; they are just market labels. Now, certain things flow from this option trade.

I always know at any point what my worst possible loss is (ten cents per option).

I will only make a profit once the cost of the option is factored in (that is, if I exercise the option above $3.40 which is my *break-even*).

The option itself has an intrinsic value that will go up as the underlying shares do (as soon as the share price goes above $3.40, the option itself will start to rise in value) which means I ⇨

can sell the option itself for a gain (depending on how long it has to go before expiry – once expired it is worthless). Many options are created principally to be traded over their lives: these are called **traded options** and tend to be exchange traded, for example on the stock market where the underlying equity is listed.

The option (this one is called a **call option** because it entitles me to 'call' for the share) locks in a *maximum* I will have to pay to buy the share – however high X Corp shares go I will have locked in any gain above $3.30.

I can do the opposite – buy a **put option** that entitles me to sell X Corp shares at the strike price, which means the strike price is a *minimum* below which, however badly X Corp shares do, the price I get for them will not fall.

I have *synthetic* exposure to X Corp – that is, I do not own the shares but I can participate in any upside as if I did.

Options give me **gearing**: let's say that instead of buying an X Corp share at $3, I buy 30 options at ten cents each with a strike of $3.30 and the shares go to $3.45. If I buy the X Corp share, my gain will be 45 cents. If I exercise the options my gain will be $1.50, that is 30 options x $3.45 market price minus $3.30 strike = 15 cents, less the cost of the option (15 minus ten) = 5 cents = 30 x 5 = $1.50. Again, don't worry about the maths: the point is that by using options I made a profit of almost four times what I would have done by owning the underlying share. True, if X Corp had stayed the same and I therefore didn't exercise the

options and they expired unexercised, my loss would have been $3 (the cost of all 30 options). But if I had owned 30 shares in X Corp I would have had to have invested $90 (not $3). And I would have made a paper loss of $90 if they had gone down just 30 cents to $2.70. Instead I had $87 to invest elsewhere in the meantime.

Options like many derivatives are not always *physically settled* (I don't ask the option seller for the X Corp share). Instead he pays me what I would have made if I had exercised the option, he had delivered the share and I had then sold it in the market – this is called *cash settlement*.

By dealing in the options market I avoid transaction costs in the physical or underlying market (also confusingly called the cash market) such as stamp duty (tax on share trades) – by and large the derivatives market is more liquid and efficient (cheaper to deal in) than the cash market.

Option sellers
Who would sell me such an option? Answer: institutional investors (the same people who stock lend to allow short selling) – see Chapter 7. If I'm a big pension fund and will always hold X Corp shares because they give me sectoral exposure to a key market (oil) then I can afford to write options because some are exercised (so I hand over shares) and some aren't (so I don't) and provided more expire than are exercised I will be earning useful premium income from my portfolio of X Corp shares. If I write options where I hold the underlying shares the options are **covered options**. If I

⇨ don't and I would have to go into the market to buy the shares to deliver them, I am writing **naked options** and am a naked option writer. A **covered warrant** is a short-term exchange traded option (call or put) aimed at retail investors.

Convertibles and warrants

You can now see that a convertible (a bond which allows the holder to switch into the issuer's equity at a pre-set price) and a warrant (a bond that entitles the holder to buy shares in the issuer or another company) are really just bonds with an option **embedded** in them to buy equity at a certain price. So each is a bond with an **embedded equity option**. A convertible pays investors a lower rate than an equivalent bond, because it gives them the right to convert it into shares if the issuer's share price rises above a certain point. The benefit to the issuer is a lower rate of interest with the possibility of redeeming the bond through issuing shares – which costs it nothing.

Trading strategies

Options lend themselves to use in combinations. For example:

Straddle = simultaneously buying or selling both a call option and a put option with the same strike price. The purpose is to exploit expected market volatility

Strangle = straddle with different strike prices for each option

Strap = a combination of two call and one put option

Bull spread = buying and selling an option at different prices: used where the trader expects only a modest increase in the underlying so gives up part of the potential upside to recoup part of the premium

Bear spread = opposite of a bull spread: used where the trader expects a fall in the underlying but caps the downside risk

Cylinder = buying an option while selling (writing) one at a different strike price – the effect is to offset the two premiums, reducing the cost while reducing the upside

All-or-nothing option = the option holder receives a fixed price if the underlying reaches the strike or goes above it

Butterfly or alligator spread = combination of a bull and bear spread where the premium receipts and payments cancel each other out, so (in theory) it costs nothing

Condor spread or top hat spread = a trading strategy that limits the downside and upside – through buying and selling calls at increasing strike prices. A variation is the *Christmas tree spread*

I hope you can see that options are versatile instruments that provide great flexibility and are relatively risk-free (in that the maximum loss is the premium and is always known, right from the outset) compared with futures.

A **future** is simply a standardised forward that is traded on-exchange in a futures or derivatives market. As soon as a contract is for a specific amount of cocoa (say 500 kilos) of a certain quality (say drinking chocolate quality) for a set time you have a standardised contract that can be traded on an exchange. This is a **future**. They tend to be three-month contracts. The terms 'futures exchange' and 'derivatives exchange' are synonymous now since most futures markets have expanded to embrace other types of financial derivatives such as exchange-traded options.

Futures go up and down in value depending on (1) what is happening in the underlying commodity market (called the **underlying** and also, confusingly, the **cash market**) and (2) how long the future has to go to expiry. These contracts (like traded options) therefore take on a life and value of their own and are heavily traded. **Locals** are futures exchange members who trade for their own account. They act as speculators, brokers and arbitrageurs, buying and selling contracts all the time, which makes futures markets liquid and efficient.

Cash settlement v physical delivery

Let's say I am a local (speculator) and you are a drinking-chocolate manufacturer. You want to lock in a *ceiling* for the price of cocoa, to cap the price you'll have to pay for it so that you don't have to increase the cost of the packs of drinking chocolate that you sell to consumers. You buy 500 cocoa contracts (where each contract is a sack of standard weight and quality of cocoa) from me for delivery in three months' time at $100 per contract.

In three months' time the price of cocoa in the underlying or cash market is $120.

In theory a future can be settled by **physical delivery** but in practice they are **cash settled**. So instead of actually giving you the cocoa (which I could buy in the underlying commodity market at $120 and deliver to you), I pay you 500 x ($120−100) = $10,000. You now buy cocoa in the cash market at $120 a sack. But the $10,000 I hand over to you compensates you for the fact that you are having to pay $20 more per sack than you had wanted: indeed, as a result of the $10,000 the *effective cost* to you is still $100 per sack, just as we had bargained. So you're happy.

What about me? The chances are that I have entered into an *offsetting* trade. A producer, worried that he might not get buyers for his cocoa if there is a glut, sold futures contracts to me at $90. In this way he locked in a *floor* below which the price he would get for his crop would not drop. In the event the cash price is $120 (this is what he is able to sell his crop for in the underlying market). So, of that cash he receives, he hands over $30 per contract to me ($120–$90). He has forgone that 'super-profit' on his crop but has had the peace of mind of knowing that he would get $90 for his crop whatever the market price. If in fact the price of cocoa had fallen below $90, I would have had to pay him the difference. So for him the futures trade has provided peace of mind.

You can begin to see that futures enable producers and manufacturers to smooth out spikes in demand and supply. They also enable speculators (locals) to bet on the likely future moves in supply and demand. Locals can enter into a variety of offsetting trades to cover their positions. These are called *trading strategies*. They can be very complex.

In the above example, the loss on my trade with you was $10,000. But it could have been much higher. If the cash price had risen to $150, then it would have been 500 x ($150 – 100) = $25,000 in relation to a contract price of just $50,000 (500 x $100). This is one of the downsides of futures: they can lead to huge losses relative to the price paid. We'll return to this in a moment.

Margin and marking-to-market

Of course the one risk in all of this when you are dealing with contracts that are only settled in three months' time is our old friend **counterparty risk**: how can you be sure the other person will still be around in three months' time and will honour his or her side of the trade, especially if it goes against them and in your favour?

Futures exchanges tackle this issue through their **clearing houses**. As soon as you do a deal with another trader, it's cleared through the clearing house. The clearing house steps in as the counterparty to each side of the trade: so your counterparty is now the clearing house, not the other trader; and the other trader's counterparty is the clearing house, not you.

(Just as an aside, in contrast to futures, CDSs are OTC instruments: when big banks started going bust, counterparties to CDS trades with them worried about default; commentators suggested that CDSs should move on-exchange or at least be cleared by a central clearing house. But with several exchanges – including NYSE Euronext and CME Group – vying for this business, there is a risk of global netting between banks across all types of financial instrument being harder to achieve.)

What the clearing house requires you to do is to put up **margin**, that is, a deposit. To avoid any nasty surprises at the end of the contract, the clearing house requires each participant to keep that margin topped up if the price of the contract moves against him. If your position deteriorates over the three month period you are required to **mark-to-market**, that is to make good that loss by increasing your margin.

This is what happened to Nick Leeson who famously blew up Barings, the UK merchant bank, in 1995. He ran out of margin and so was unable to mark-to-market. Leeson was holding futures contracts on the Nikkei 225 (the Japanese stock market index) which he was buying through Simex, the Singapore futures market. He was doing it because an options straddle on the Nikkei had gone wrong. Leeson predicted that the market would stabilise and took a position to reflect this.

An earthquake that hit Kobe and Osaka in January 1995 depressed the Nikkei 225 to such an extent that it was trading well below the straddle's range and the bank's options position was badly out-of-the-money. By buying the future, Leeson was hoping the Nikkei would recover and – possibly – that his activity in the future would have a positive impact on the cash market.

When the Japanese market continued to fall, Leeson's futures contracts exposed him to that fall without any get-out (unlike options from which you can walk away on expiry). He had to mark-to-market but his futures positions were so big and so in debt that when Barings ran out of cash to meet the margin calls, the Simex clearing house had to step in and close out his positions. Barings was bust. In fact, if Leeson had been able to hold on, his trades would actually have come right in the end.

Regular users of futures markets maintain accounts with the clearing house. As futures fluctuate in value, **margin calls** are made. If my futures positions gain in value, margin is credited to my account and I can withdraw some of it. If my positions fall in value I have to top it up. Major participants (e.g. banks) are allowed to **crossmargin** between accounts held on different futures exchanges.

Liquidity, efficiency and synthetic positions

Gearing is one benefit of futures (see box over the page). The other is exposure to a market without – in the terminology of derivatives – 'owning the underlying'. What does this mean?

Take another look at that property example (in the gearing box). That contract on the fictitious Manhattan prime real estate index gives you the same exposure as if owning the underlying (the condo) but without actually doing so. Why is this such an advantage? Two major reasons.

The gearing effect of futures

The ability to **trade on margin** is what gives futures their dramatic **gearing or leverage effect** (similar to the gearing effect of options). Margin is what you put up by way of deposit when you enter into a futures trade. Buying a futures contract is a bit like buying a house with a mortgage: you put up a deposit and borrow the rest.

Say you have $100,000. Let's say you buy a house for $100,000 and over a year it increases in value by 10%. You sell it and you've made $10,000. Not bad. Could do better.

Supposing instead you use $10,000 of that as a 10% deposit and borrow the other $90,000. Ignoring the interest you have to pay on the loan (this example is merely to show the impact of gearing) your deposit would have produced a gain of the same amount ($10,000). Good. But could do better.

Instead, you use all $100,000 as a 10% deposit and borrow $900,000 and buy a house for $1 million. After a year you'd have a gain not of $10,000 but of $100,000. Excellent.

But since you don't actually want the house (you're going to sell it after a year) you could enter into a contract that is the equivalent of owning the house and which says: 'This contract is worth $1 million of residential real estate. It expires in a year's time. If by then real estate has increased in value the seller will pay you the gain; if real estate has declined in value, you pay the seller the loss.' This means it is **cash settled** rather than settled by **physical delivery** of the underlying (a house).

This is in fact a forward or, if bought on an exchange, a future. And it can be valued by reference to a residential real estate index (say, an index of Manhattan prime real estate). Now you're a futures trader.

This gearing effect echoes that of options. It means that by using a derivative you can achieve a much bigger position in the market than if you bought the underlying (as the transaction from which it is derived is called): by buying the derivative on margin, you in effect just need to put up a deposit rather than the full price.

It's this amplification effect that makes derivatives so powerful (and potentially dangerous – when you enter into a futures contract you don't know what your downside might be). Derivative amounts are now so great that they dwarf the underlying or cash market as it is called; in other words, the market value of derivatives is greater than that of the underlying to which they relate – to the extent that on occasion the derivatives market drives the underlying, rather than the other way round.

This is one reason why financial markets have been so volatile and why the highs and lows have been so extreme. It's also why Warren Buffett, probably the most famous investor in the world, once described derivatives as 'financial weapons of mass destruction'. It's also what brought down Nick Leeson and Barings (see main text).

First, **transaction costs**. When you buy the condo you will have agents', lawyers' and surveyors' fees, plus any local taxes to pay. To sell the condo you'd need agents and lawyers again. In the meantime, you'd have to repair it and pay local municipal charges. A single bit of paper is much easier.

Second, **liquidity**. Once you've bought the condo it's a fairly illiquid asset – you can't sell it there and then and get your money out immediately. But that contract on the index, especially if it's a standardised exchange-traded contract and valued by reference to an accepted index, can be sold readily.

This is why taking a position in the derivatives markets can be preferable to holding the underlying – a **synthetic** (artificial) position, although market professionals use the term to mean a combination of derivatives to achieve a particular position.

In fact derivatives take on a life of their own – become an edifice in their own right, piled on top of each other (for instance options on futures) – separate from the underlying but with their own intrinsic value driven in part by what is happening to the underlying in its market. It is this versatility combined with liquidity and low transaction costs that have given derivatives markets such volume – and worry people like Warren Buffett who believe that real markets should be driven by economic fundamentals.

Instead you can get enormous market volatility. Like bonds, whose market value converges with their face value as they reach redemption, futures converge with the underlying as they reach expiry. But such is their volume that they can drive the price of the underlying. This means there can be twitchy times in the markets when futures, options and options-on-futures are surging towards a common expiry date as their prices and those of the cash market converge, with arbitrageurs working all three (underlying, futures and options). This can send the markets into spikes and freefalls – so much so at times that the point at which these things occasionally come together has been dubbed in Chicago the **triple witching hour.** It can be like landing a plane in a storm – a bumpy ride with massive market gyrations before the plane finally touches down in one piece (so far).

CONTRACTS FOR DIFFERENCE

Futures are also known as **contracts for difference** (CFDs) and in their retail guise – where they are sold to individual investors rather than institutional buyers – that is often what they are called. The investor and broker agree to exchange the difference between the price of an asset at the beginning and end of the contract.

The property example (in the box describing the gearing effect of futures) is not quite as fanciful as it may seem. There are brokers offering property-related hedges or 'hedgelets' as one broker calls them. These are based on another retail-oriented derivative trade: **spread betting**.

The broker quotes a range or 'spread' for the future price of an index (such as a stock or property index). The investor bets on whether it will end up higher or lower than the spread suggests. For each point that the index moves in the investor's favour, his profit is multiplied by his stake. For each point it moves against, the loss is multiplied by the stake.

Say a broker quotes a spread of 5000 to 5100 on the Emerald 100 (a fictitious index; in real life it would be on an actual one) and the investor bets $10 for every point above 5100. If the Emerald 100 moves to 5200, the investor's return is $10 x 100 = $1000. The investor can also bet the market will fall (shorting it).

Returning to property, if you own a house, betting that the market may fall may offset some of the gain you'd make if property prices rose, but will protect you if the market does fall. In this sense, any property owner (whether he or she knows it or not) is betting on property prices going up by being *long* of property: this is called naked risk (unconscious risk). Far better, these brokers argue, that you take that risk consciously and hedge against it.

STOCK INDEX FUTURES

Nowadays you find futures in all sorts of markets: bond futures, currency futures, commodity futures. In oil, for example, oil companies use them to protect against falls in the price of oil and airlines to protect against increases. However, in the IFMs, the most exciting futures are on financial instruments and transactions, such as **stock index futures** (SIFs).

In Chapter 7 we'll be looking at institutional investors, the big buyers in the IFMs of all of the types of instruments we've looked at so far. SIFs were a conscious effort by futures exchanges to develop new financial derivatives products that would appeal to them. SIFs provide institutional investors with great flexibility in the management of their equity portfolios.

A SIF is a single contract that represents an underlying index. If I want to invest in the Nikkei 225, I can buy each and every share. Or I can buy a Nikkei 225 futures contract on a futures exchange by paying margin. Now, on the face of it, the future will give me each of the underlying shares at the end of three months. In practice I simply receive money if the underlying index (the cash market) has gone up or pay the difference if the Nikkei 225 has over that time gone down. I can then *roll over* my position: take out a new stock index future for another three months. If I keep on doing this, I have a position in the Nikkei 225 without actually owning any of the underlying. This is an artificial position created for me by the future. In short I have a *synthetic* position.

Used prudently, SIFs enable institutional investors to:
- Reduce their exposure to a stock market – without having to sell the shares in their portfolio

- Gain rapid exposure to a stock market – without having to buy the underlying shares

Moving in and out of stock markets is cumbersome, and the mechanics can wipe out the projected benefits. Commissions or spreads in the futures market are significantly lower than in the underlying market and the futures market is more liquid so there is less risk of moving prices against you when you trade. A money manager's nightmare is wanting to gain exposure to a market – knowing it is likely to move up – but finding the physical act of investing is too slow and inefficient to execute the strategy quickly – meaning that he or she is out of the market just when they want exposure to it. SIFs allow an investor to gain market exposure more rapidly – through a single trade rather than individual trades in scores of stocks in the underlying (cash) market (i.e. on an exchange).

On the other hand, SIFs also enable an investor that holds a substantial share portfolio to keep it while exploiting short-term market declines by selling the future: there's no need to exit the cash market just because you think it may go down, if you need to be invested in that market over the long term (e.g. a UK pension fund investing in UK equities which it will hold for years).

This may explain why some of the most popular SIFs are on stock indices from emerging markets. Equity products (including equity options) account for over half of all derivatives. SIFs on indices of the Johannesburg Stock Exchange and the National Stock Exchange of India (NSE) have seen the highest increase in volumes of any derivatives contracts. The NSE launched derivatives trading in 2000 and in its first year saw trading volumes of $200 million, which just seven years later had shot up to over $3 billion. The KOSPI 200 Option (Korean Stock Exchange) has the highest annual volume of any single exchange-traded derivative (over 2 billion contracts traded a year).

Some money managers maintain global market exposure completely synthetically – simply by trading in the relevant SIFs and altering their holdings to reflect their asset allocation decisions (asset allocation has a greater impact on investment returns than individual stock selection; what matters is choosing between particular markets rather than particular shares – as we shall see in Chapter 7).

ETFs (exchange traded funds) are, like SIFs, based on stock indices. They are funds (see Chapter 7 for what a fund is) in which investors buy units – with each security representing an entire stock index or portfolio of shares. They are themselves exchange-listed and traded (pioneered by the American Stock Exchange) so carry a continuous quote. They were first introduced in 1993 and within ten years had an underlying asset value of $100 billion on the AMEX alone.

DYNAMIC HEDGING

A pension fund that wants to divest itself of a share portfolio (for instance to meet pension liabilities) but fears the market is falling can sell the SIF to fix the value of the portfolio at the current market price, buying itself time to unwind its cash positions at an orderly rate. This – and the act of using SIFs to fine-tune investment performance – is called dynamic hedging. One example of dynamic hedging is portfolio insurance.

PORTFOLIO INSURANCE

By using SIFs, an institutional investor can constantly adjust its asset allocation by adjusting the stock/cash mix of its portfolio in line with movements in the market to give the portfolio maximum exposure to equities (which, historically, give the best return) without taking on the attendant risk. As the equity market rises, assets are switched out of cash (the risk-free or reserve asset class, usually money market instruments) into equities (the risky or active asset) and as the market falls the reverse is done.

If the market keeps falling there comes a point when the portfolio is entirely in cash – which is why this technique is called portfolio insurance (which has nothing to do with real insurance) or **portfolio protection**. This point can be set in advance as a floor below which the portfolio will not fall (even if the market does) because the portfolio no longer has any equity exposure – hence the term insurance. The 'premium' the investor pays is the loss of upside gain when the market rises because the portfolio is progressively switched into equities in response to the market's upswing and not in anticipation of it, so missing out on that initial increase. But this is the great attraction: it does not require any market judgment or forecasting. Just to be complicated, the result is like being fully invested in shares while having a put option whose strike price is the same as the pre-set floor.

ISOLATING RISK

The use of currency futures also helps isolate the risk a money manager is running. So, for example, let's say a money manager has an expert stock selector in the Japanese market. So the actual individual Japanese stocks (shares) in the portfolio are good. But if the money manager likes the US market, it can sell the Nikkei 225 future (so keeping the Japanese stock selection without the Japanese market's systemic risk) then go into the US market by selling the yen currency future for dollars to get the US cash to buy the S&P 500 future (the largest, most liquid future on the US stock market). This way the money manager gets the best stock return (Japan) plus the best market and currency return (US).

WHO BUYS ALL OF THESE INSTRUMENTS?

So far we've looked at shares (Chapter 2), bonds (Chapter 3), the money markets (Chapter 4), securitisation (Chapter 5) and derivatives (this chapter) and have ended by looking at some of the ways in which derivatives are used for investment management. Now we need to meet those investment managers – the people who buy, use and trade all of these instruments and securities on behalf of the pension funds, insurance companies and funds that make up the universe of institutional investors.

But first let's visit Chicago, home of what we've just been discussing – the world's biggest futures markets.

HOW IT ALL CONNECTS

- A swap can achieve the same economic effect as a securitisation (Chapter 5)

- Traded options are available on leading shares, and stock index futures on stock market indices (Chapter 2)

- Bond futures are available on sovereign bond issues (Chapter 3)

- Hedge funds (Chapter 7) are big users of derivatives

- Stock index futures are used by institutional investors (Chapter 7) to gain exposure to equity markets – some of the highest volumes occur in emerging markets (Chapter 10)

- Commercial banks (Chapter 8) have always dominated the swaps market for interest rate and currency swaps

- Stock exchanges (Chapter 2) are keen to offer derivatives contracts and this, too, has prompted some of the M&A activity and alliances between them

- CDSs (credit default swaps) exacerbated the effects of the credit crunch (Chapter 5) as protection sellers such as banks and insurers were no longer trusted as counterparties

- Volumes in derivatives markets can dwarf those of the underlying stock and bond markets (Chapters 2 and 3)

DAY TRIP TO
CHICAGO

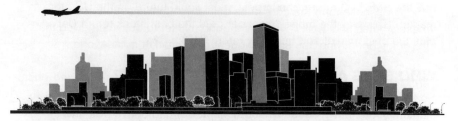

Chicago is the capital of the world's derivatives markets. True, it's not an IFC in the accepted sense, although a 2007 survey by *Trader Monthly***, the industry magazine, put it first, ahead of New York and London. But derivatives have been at the epicentre of the trading frenzy that has gripped the IFMs for a decade or more and two massive mergers – between Chicago's two futures markets, the Chicago Mercantile Exchange (CME) and the Chicago Board of Trade (CBOT) to form CME Group in 2007; and then between CME Group and NYMEX (the New York Mercantile Exchange) in 2008 – have ensured that for the time being Chicago retains its crown as the king of derivatives exchanges.**

When open outcry (aka floor trading) was at its zenith, Chicago's trading pits were as loud as a rock concert and the trading floors big enough to take a 747 jumbo jet with room to spare. That's how loud and big. No wonder, then, that futures traders are considered to be the brash wideboys of the IFMs, lying somewhere between outright sharks and human computers. After all, Chicago is the city that on the one hand spawned Al Capone but on the other hosts the business school whose academics invented the famous Black-Scholes options pricing model. That's how street smart Chicago is.

Originally the crossroads for the US grain trade, hence its tag as 'the land of grain and pork bellies', Chicago launched a futures market in 1848 (CBOT) in order to smooth out spikes in supply and demand. It meant farmers could sell their crops forward (so guaranteeing them an acceptable price when they came to harvest) and manufacturers could buy grain supplies in advance (so guaranteeing a pipeline of produce, enabling them to maintain constant prices to consumers). These agrarian futures were the bedrock of the market and, until the merger with CME, three-quarters of CBOT's 1400 seats (the term for a membership of a futures exchange) were still in its grain-trading room.

CBOT began trading its first non-grain related commodity with futures contracts in the late 1960s. It set up Chicago Board Options Exchange in 1973. Then two years later, it created the first interest rate future (allowing interest rate hedging). In 1982, it launched its first future on US government bonds and these form the core of its derivatives business (futures on Treasury notes and T-bills) which is a good market to dominate given the size of the underlying, the single biggest bond market in the world.

For its part, the CME (formed in 1898) was the first of the two to move into financial derivatives, with the launch of the world's first financial futures contract, offering contracts on foreign currencies in 1972, the first cash-settled futures contract (the Eurodollar future) in 1981 and the first successful stock index futures contract, S&P 500, in 1982. Currency futures and stock index futures remain the core of CME's business.

Since launching the original CME FX futures contracts, CME has become the largest financial derivatives exchange in the US and the most diversified in the world. In 1971, before the development of financial futures, CME's annual transaction volume was just over 3 million contracts (all in agriculture) – which is now what it trades in a single day. Just over 30 years later, its annual trading volume had reached almost 650 million contracts (of which almost all were financial derivatives) making it the biggest derivatives exchange in the world. CME's currency market is the world's largest *regulated* marketplace for foreign exchange trading – almost all trading occurs there or the Brazilian Exchange in Sao Paulo (note: here we're talking regulated; London is the top IFC for unregulated OTC forex trading).

Prior to 2007, tentative moves towards a merger between CME and CBOT had been going on for the best part of a decade and had to overcome entrenched rivalries. CME demutualised in 2000 and was the first US exchange to go public when it listed on the New York Stock Exchange (NYSE) in 2002. Then in 2003 it entered into a cooperation agreement with CBOT for its clearing corporation to handle CBOT's trades (CBOT lacked its own electronic trading platform and risked losing business to other futures exchanges which offered cheaper and faster electronic processing).

CME approached CBOT in 2005 with a merger proposal. This was rejected, but it prompted CBOT to follow suit: it too demutualised and listed on the NYSE (with a value of $6 billion). In 2006 a merger was announced valuing CBOT at $8 billion. This prompted an anti-trust investigation by the Department of Justice. Then, in March 2007, Intercontinental Exchange (ICE) trumped CME's offer with a bid for CBOT valuing it at $10 billion. ICE needed the deal which would have taken its and CBOT's combined market share of global commodity futures trading to just over a third. But in July 2007 CME came back with an offer of $11 billion which 95% of CBOT's shareholders accepted.

Now rebranded the CME Group, the combined CME and CBOT took over NYMEX in March 2008, also for $11 billion. NYMEX is the main commodities futures exchange in New York and the world's largest physical commodities futures exchange. Prior to the merger, NYMEX held just under a quarter of global market share in exchange-traded commodity futures and CBOT just over an eighth. Together they have just under 40% of that market and 95% of the US futures market.

The combined CME Group is the world's largest financial exchange in notional (that is, underlying) value traded, at $5 trillion a day (compared to just over half that at NYSE Euronext) and market capitalisation ($40 billion, almost double NYSE Euronext). It is also now the world's largest derivatives clearing house, clearing 85% of the US exchange-traded derivatives market.

The merger between CME and CBOT, and CBOT's historical strength in the commodity markets, have pointed up a peculiarity in the way US derivatives markets are regulated. The Securities and Exchange Commission (SEC) oversees the securities markets and could naturally expect to see its remit extend to related derivatives. But the Commodity Futures Trading Commission (CFTC) has traditionally regulated commodities and the exchange-traded derivatives that relate to them. The CFTC has tried and failed in the past to extend its remit to OTC derivatives markets. Expect these turf wars to continue.

One of the unusual features of the NYMEX deal is that NYMEX is one of only a handful of exchanges that has continued to use open outcry – a system championed by CME and CBOT. Most others have closed their trading floors and have moved over fully to electronic platforms.

Futures exchanges have traditionally been open outcry with locals and brokers (often in brightly coloured coats) yelling, and using market-accepted hand signals that new recruits are taught, to telegraph buy and sell orders to each other in pits. These are the various designated areas on a trading floor (in reality ovals with two or three tiers round the outside providing elevated standing room so everyone can see everyone), each pit dedicated to one or a few instruments.

Open outcry has several advantages over electronic trading, as purists will argue. It is immediate and visceral: since all orders have to be channelled to the pit for execution, all members have the chance to see all orders, their size and price from the hand signs and screams from the traders standing on the low steps tiered around each pit. This means everyone can see and sense simultaneously the mood of the market from the noise, the signs, the tension and so on. The effect is to make trading more immediate, sharper and quicker, with increased liquidity, narrower spreads, more accurate pricing and rapid execution.

But open outcry has one huge disadvantage: it is limited by time zone and geography. By contrast, electronic markets are virtual and happen anywhere. Members simply have to inform the centre of their trades and the details are then beamed out to all other members. CME has fought back as it has found other derivatives exchanges around the world competing in its markets and the demand for 24/7 global trading in its contracts too great to meet. CME pioneered electronic futures trading with the development of the CME Globex platform which started in 1987 and saw its first electronic trades in 1992. Globex now has alliances with derivatives exchanges all over the world. About a quarter of CME trading volume is electronic rather than open outcry.

In 2008, CME migrated electronically-traded CBOT products to the CME Globex platform and moved its pit-traded products over to CBOT's trading floor, so consolidating the two trading floors. Although CME Group estimated the expected cost savings at $125 million a year, this could spell the end for open outcry.

Speaking of open outcry, a near-neighbour, the Chicago Stock Exchange (CHX) trades more stocks – almost 4,000 – than any other *floor trading* US exchange. In 1982, it became one of the first stock exchanges to provide fully automated order execution by implementing the MAX system. In 2005, it demutualised and, backed by shareholders such as Bank of America Merrill Lynch, Bear Stearns (before it went bust) and Goldman Sachs has introduced further platform changes. Electronic seems the way to go.

One of the most successful futures contracts pioneered by the CME is the stock index future (SIF) which is of particular use to institutional investors (next chapter) allowing them to move in and out of equity markets far more efficiently than by trading in the underlying index. Prior to the mergers, CME had 40% of SIF trading, but the next two competing exchanges had almost 30% between them: Eurex (the combined Swiss and German futures exchanges), which has always been an electronic exchange; and Euronext.liffe, the London international financial futures exchange which merged with FOX, the London options exchange, and closed its pits in 1999. These three are the largest futures exchanges in the world. Fourth in terms of SIFs volume is the National Stock Exchange of India – mentioned in Chapter 6 – with just over 5% as global investors seek to get exposure to the Indian market.

Chapter 7
The Buy Side

SPEED-READ SUMMARY

- The Buy Side comprises institutional investors (pension funds, insurance companies and fund managers)

- Fund managers are people who invest money – they are variously called asset managers, investment managers, money managers, portfolio managers and wealth managers (all mean the same thing)

- Their performance is measured against market indices

- Research analysts are employed by banks and brokers to produce research reports that encourage institutional investors to buy and sell securities, so generating commission for the bank or broker

- Passive management is about tracking an index and can be computerised

- Active management is about picking individual company shares and is more expensive and less predictable

- Hedge funds pursue risky trading strategies such as short selling and leverage through derivatives to generate absolute (positive) returns

- Private equity funds raise money (equity) from institutional investors and use it to buy large companies, take them private and break them up or improve their performance

- Some insurers, like AIG and the monolines, suffered heavy losses on credit default swaps

- ART (alternative risk transfer) enables the insurance industry to tap the greater capital available in the bond markets

You're familiar now with the IFMs, their instruments and securities, and the IFCs – New York, Tokyo, London and the rest – where those instruments and securities are traded.

Now I want to introduce you to an alternative IFC geography. This one embraces Greenwich and Hartford in Connecticut, USA; Edinburgh in Scotland; Luxembourg in Europe; Zurich and Geneva in Switzerland; Singapore in Asia; and, in London, not just the City, but Mayfair which is in the capital's West End.

What all these places have in common is that they are centres of fund management, also known as asset management, investment management, money management, portfolio management or wealth management – take your pick.

This is where all the money that is used to buy the instruments and securities we've looked at in preceding chapters comes from – which is why the insurance companies, pension funds and investment funds that buy these instruments are known collectively as the Buy Side (issuers of shares and bonds, and the banks which help them distribute and place those securities, are known as the Sell Side).

Thirty years ago, three-quarters of the US equity markets was held by individual private investors; 20 years ago two-thirds; ten years ago half; now under a third. Their place has been taken by institutional investors – funds investing on their behalf, pension funds and insurance companies. So this chapter is about these institutional investors that invest money on our behalf.

Some of these institutions are vast, such as the Japanese Post Office, which is the biggest savings institution in the world and takes small retail deposits from tens of millions of savers and aggregates them into a mountain of money which it invests. One of the largest institutional investors in Europe is – possibly surprisingly – the Dutch Post Office pension fund. One of the most active in the world is CalPERS, the California Public Employee Retirement System, which is responsible for providing the pensions for all public sector employees (except teachers – they have their own) in the state of California. California would be a top ten global economy if it were a country in its own right so CalPERS is correspondingly huge with $150 billion in **assets under management** (a.u.m.).

They all get their money from us, whether as contributions to our future pensions or as premiums we pay to take out insurance or as savings we set aside for a rainy day. Each of us, like the savers with the Japanese Post

Office, contributes to the mountain of money these institutions invest. So it's as well to know what they do with it on our behalf.

1. FUNDS AND FUND MANAGERS

The term **fund** crops up all the time in the context of investment management. A fund manager is simply a generic term for someone who manages a fund of money (such as a pension fund). But 'fund' also means **mutual fund** which is more or less the basis for most retail funds offered to the investing public, as well as hedge funds and private equity funds which we'll encounter later.

Let's say you have 20 clients. They each give give you $1. You now have $20 a.u.m. You invest this $20 in the market. You invest well. After a year you've turned it into $40. Leaving aside your fees for a moment, you have made each of them $2 out of the $1 they entrusted to you.

Now, let's say that when they gave you that $1 each, you gave each of them in return a sort of receipt, a bit of paper saying 'You own one unit in my fund'. If any of them wants to *redeem* (cash in) their unit at any time, they give that unit back to you, you cancel it and you give them 1/20th of the fund's net assets (net means after taking into account your fees, other expenses, borrowings, etc) which, to keep it simple, we will say is 1/20th of $40 which is $2.

Now if at that point a new investor wants to join the fund, they can. But they need to pay $2 for a unit because that is what a unit in your fund is currently worth. In fact there's no limit to the number of units you can issue provided that the cost of each one is the same as the value of an existing unit in the fund. So currently I have 20 customers and a fund worth $40. If another ten turn up they can each buy a unit for $2 so my fund will now have $60 a.u.m. (of which $20 is in recently-received cash which I need to set about investing) and I have 30 unit holders or investors in my fund.

The whole point of funds is diversification: with my $1 I'd be lucky to be able to afford one share in one company. But putting all of my portfolio (especially given how small it is) in one company is concentrating risk, not diversifying it. By contrast, investing my $1 in a fund gives me exposure to all of the underlying companies the fund invests in.

Types of fund

A fund like this is called a **mutual fund** or **unit trust**. These types of fund are **open-ended** funds – that is, there is no limit to the number of units they can issue, provided of course they receive in return the cash that represents the value of the units they are issuing in relation to the rest of the fund.

There are also **investment companies** (sometimes called **investment trusts**) which are simply listed companies that invest in other companies. They are **closed-ended** in that at any one time there are a limited number of shares in issue and investors invest in these companies by buying their shares on the stock market rather than units from the fund manager.

Then there are funds that are a cross between the two: like investment trusts, they are companies, but like mutual funds they are open-ended. They have names like **companies with variable capital** and OEICs (**open-ended investment companies**). Some funds are set up as **limited liability partnerships** (LLPs) for tax reasons and because some pension funds are restricted in the types of fund they can invest in. But the principle remains roughly similar.

The umbrella term for all of these types of fund is **collective investment scheme** (the relevant EU regulation is a directive called UCITS, Undertakings for Collective Investment in Transferable Securities, and enables funds to be marketed across Europe which is one reason why Luxembourg is the centre for eligible UCITS funds). IOSCO (the International Organisation of Securities Commissions) defines a fund as 'an open-ended collective investment scheme that issues redeemable units and invests primarily in transferable securities or money market instruments'.

Retail funds

The bulk of these funds are *retail funds*, that is, they are marketed to the man in the street, the individual investor. Financial services regulation, designed to protect ordinary investors, means that these types of funds are usually only marketed within national boundaries (or across the EU) since the regulations differ between countries.

In the US and UK, *equity funds* are the most popular. In Europe, *bond funds* are the most popular. There is less of a cult of equity investment in markets like Germany, partly because companies there have been used to funding themselves in the bank loan market (see Chapter 8), partly because retail investors are used to buying government and corporate bonds (see Chapter 3). In fact the hypothetical bond market retail investor is known as the *Belgian dentist*, the cliché of the European white-collar professional, who invests his wealth in bonds.

The people who manage these funds will often build up a business (an *asset management business*) which can be sold in its own right. The most well-known are independent like Fidelity and Vanguard in the US but most big banks and insurers have asset management arms that run mutual funds.

Key aspects of investment management

Fund managers specialise according to the type of asset they invest in and know about (see box on **asset classes**). Whether they are running their own retail fund or are managing money on behalf of a pension fund or insurance company or are working in-house as a member of an insurance company's or pension fund's investment team, there are certain things they all have in common (hedge funds and private equity funds are different as we'll see later).

They generally claim to be investing for the long term (in the case of a pension fund to meet liabilities to future pensioners as far out as 30 years) but their performance is generally measured against short-term benchmarks: typically, a fund manager investing in equities is measured against a stock market index like the Dow Jones or Nikkei 225 or FTSE; so their performance is assessed **relative to the benchmark**. Those that are in the top 25% are said to be **upper quartile** which is the place you want to be.

The biggest insurance companies and pension funds have their own in-house money managers but they also appoint external fund managers to run at least a part of their portfolio (for instance to get specialist expertise in certain asset classes and to keep their own fund managers on their toes). They have **chief investment officers** (CIOs) whose principal job is to get the **asset allocation** right: if your fund is $150 billion, as CalPERS's is, what matters is not whether you invest $10 million in Microsoft or Apple, but how much of your fund you decide to invest in (or allocate to) equities. Fund managers generally charge **annual fees** that are usually calculated as **a percentage of assets under management** ranging from 0.25% up to say 2%.

Equity investment styles

One of the largest asset classes is equities and here fund managers tend to specialise by country, by type of investment and by size of company they invest in. In the equity markets there are **active investors** (known colloquially as **stock pickers**) who research and invest in individual companies. Within active investment there are at least two further styles. Some go in for **growth stocks**, often fast-growing companies (for instance, fairly new businesses) that won't pay much by way of dividends (any surplus cash is reinvested in the business) but whose growth will be rewarded by an increasing share price.

Asset classes

The two most important factors in successful investing are **timing** (when to be in and out of particular markets) and **asset allocation** (what percentage of your portfolio to have in what types of investments). Studies of historic market data have shown that calling the market right (saying when it has peaked in time to sell, when it has bottomed in time to buy) has a massive effect on performance, as does asset allocation. Here's a selection of typical assets, activities and events that insurance companies and pension funds are involved with:

- **Cash** (including currencies)

- **Equities** (shares) including: venture capital (start ups and small cap stocks); IPOs; private equity; M&A; MBOs; stock indices (e.g. through stock index futures and exchange traded funds); passive/index-tracking; funds (mutual and open-ended investment companies); equity derivatives (traded equity options); stock lending (which generates additional fee income)

- **Debt**: money market instruments (commercial paper, CDs); fixed-income bonds; FRNs; convertibles; government bonds and securities; repos; securitisations (ABSs, CDOs, MBSs, whole business); acquisition finance

- **Derivatives**: swaps (interest, currency, credit default); currency forwards and futures; bond futures; traded options; credit default derivatives

- **Commercial property/real estate** through: direct investment (buying actual buildings); indirect investment such as REITs (real estate investment trusts), which are mutual funds that own buildings

- **Infrastructure**: investment in ports, airports, roads, bridges, utilities – an investment class pioneered by Australian bank Macquarie

- **Hedge funds**

- **Alternative risk transfer** (catastrophe bonds)

- **Alternative investments** such as art (including old masters paintings), wine and even race horses (yes, really)

The three most important are equities, debt and commercial property/real estate. Real estate is a massive asset class for institutional investors (most shopping malls and office blocks are owned by insurance companies or pension funds). So a typical institutional portfolio will look like the illustration below (illustrative only – much will depend on its location and size, and the size and incidence of its liabilities).

Asset class	Allocation
Equities (domestic, private equity and international)	40%
Bonds (CP, fixed income, FRNs and government)	30%
Commercial real estate	20%
Hedge funds, derivatives, cash, currencies, other	10%

By contrast, some investors – notably pension funds which need the income to distribute to pensioners and the elderly who need the income to live off – go for **income stocks** that pay relatively high dividends but are in mature industries where the possibility of growth is more restricted so there is limited upside. The irony is that demand for income stocks can drive their value higher so that they behave like growth stocks (increasing value) but pay good dividends (good income).

Possibly the most successful style in recent years has been **value investing**. The idea is to find companies that are undervalued on their **fundamentals** (good product or service, good management, good brand, good markets with great potential; none of which is reflected in the current share price but all of which will underpin a company's long-term success) then to buy shares in them and hold them for a long time. One exponent of this approach was Peter Lynch who ran Fidelity's flagship Magellan Fund. Another was Sir John Templeton who, with colleague Mark Mobius, specialised in emerging markets. Another is Warren Buffett, who is possibly the most famous investor in the world. He runs Berkshire Hathaway, an investment fund, that has made many of its investors millionaires. Buffett is based in Omaha, Nebraska and is known colloquially as the 'Sage of Omaha' for his erudite views on investment.

Active v passive investment

However, active investors do not always outperform the market and since the index is what they are measured against, many pension funds have opted instead to invest in portfolios that mimic the index, either by owning all the shares in the index or by sampling or by using stock index futures or exchange-traded funds (see Chapter 6). That's why this style of investment is called **index-tracking** or – because it can be done by computer and simply follows the market – **passive investment**. It costs only a fraction of the fees charged by active investors.

Incidentally, the same issue – of trying to pick funds that consistently outperform – explains why **fund-of-funds** and **multi-manager** structures are popular. A fund-of-funds is a fund that simply invests in other funds, choosing those doing the best. Multi-manager is what some pension funds choose in order to get the benefit of an array of fund managers' complementary investment styles.

Predicting the markets

Investment is about **maximising return** while **minimising risk**. There are different types of risk. **Systemic risk** is general **market risk**, as opposed

Research analysis

Armies of analysts employed by brokers and banks spend their days trying to work out where markets are heading. If they use complex computer programs to model markets they are called **quants** (**quantitative analysts**). If they plot previous market patterns on charts to map long-term market movements in shares they are called **chartists** (also known as **technical analysts**). They use this historic data (such as moving averages and trend lines) to predict future price movements on the basis that if you know where a share is coming from in terms of price, it is easier to predict where it is likely to go.

All analysts tend to look at the way in which markets have behaved historically and try to use this as a basis for predicting the future. They try to identify **trends** and **correlations** – a correlation being a relationship between two things. So, for example, some shares behave historically just like the index of which they are a part; when the market moves up, they do; when it falls, they do. This is a correlation between the share price and market. How closely a share correlates to the index is called its **beta**. If a share has a beta of precisely one, then it correlates perfectly to the index – it moves exactly up and down with the market.

Deltas and **gammas** are to do with options pricing (options are derivatives, covered in Chapter 6). Delta is the ratio of the movement of the price of an option to the movement in the price of the underlying share. Gammas are used in the valuation of options and measure the rate of change of delta in relation to a movement in the underlying share. So now you know.

Banks and brokers employ these **research analysts** to publish reports to encourage institutional investors to buy and sell securities through them, which earns the bank or broker **commission**. In the early 2000s, there was a scandal in New York when research analysts were found to be writing favourably about dotcom issues simply because their bank was the lead underwriter. This has led to the separation of broking and research through **chinese walls** (functional separation) monitored by **compliance officers**.

to the **specific risk** of a particular bond or share. Systemic risk affects the whole market. Factors include interest rate rises, weakness in a particular currency, the price of oil, the collapse of a government, the outbreak of war. These are **macroeconomic** variables – they affect the big picture. We'll come back to these in Chapter 10.

Markets were once famously likened to a **random walk** (no one knows where they are heading). More recently, **efficient market theory** (which says that markets respond rationally to information which is uniformly available) prevailed but has been called into question, especially in the light of the credit crunch. Instead, people are turning to **chaos theory** and

imperfect knowledge economics, which owe as much to fractal geometry and the mathematical analysis of chaos and complex systems as to traditional economics. These disciplines highlight false beliefs among investors that create self-reinforcing boom-and-bust cycles. Imperfect knowledge economics takes the same tools as conventional economics but turns the conventional outcomes on their head, acknowledging that the future is inherently unknowable however much statistical analysis you try to subject it to.

In short, markets are driven less by what markets should do and more by what everyone thinks they will do, which is called **market sentiment**: if everyone thinks the market is going up, they will buy and it will go up – a self-fulfilling prophecy leading to **market momentum**. There are **momentum investors** who try to spot market moves that reflect underlying sentiment then jump aboard the market bandwagon – and jump off it again before it changes direction. There are people called **day traders** (or intra-day traders) who trade from home over the internet and who buy and sell several times a day on this basis, hoping to make lots of small gains. Then there are **contrarians** who do the opposite of what they believe everyone else is doing.

Markets react to expectations. They are forward-looking. They are said to **discount the future** – in other words to reflect in today's price expectations of what is likely to happen in the future. Again, market professionals say that what matters is not whether a share or a bond is a good investment but whether you can find someone prepared to buy it from you in the future at a higher price than you paid.

Economists also talk about **secular trends**. These are big, but long-term, currents that lie under the surface in markets. For example, between the 1960s and 1980s economies experienced high rates of inflation and, therefore, high interest rates – known as the boom-and-bust era. Then in the 1990s through to the recent credit crunch, the global economy experienced low inflation with correspondingly low interest rates. This change from a high-inflation to a low-inflation environment is called a secular trend.

Traditionally, investment management has always been about investing for the long term, riding these trends, taking the highs with the lows. **Hedge funds** and **private equity** have turned this on its head. They are asset classes in their own right since insurance companies and pension funds allocate small portions of their portfolios to them. But they are very different in their approach from long-term institutional investors and have been a key contributor to the trading frenzy that seized the IFMs in the run-up to the credit crunch.

2. HEDGE FUNDS

Hedge funds are a type of mutual fund. But they don't hedge. Hedging means using derivatives (Chapter 6) to protect against financial risk – a rise in interest rates or a currency, for example. Hedge funds do use derivatives (they are one of the market's biggest users of derivatives) but they use them to speculate (not hedge), making particular use of the leverage that derivatives provide (explained in Chapter 6).

To give a measure of their impact on the IFMs, hedge fund assets were under $50 billion 20 years ago. In 2007, prior to the recession, they stood at roughly $2 trillion and almost a hundred of those hedge funds based in London had assets of more than $1 billion each.

The barriers to entry are low: you can set up a hedge fund in your back bedroom. But you need a profile in order to attract investors. So you need some star quality, which is why a lot of hedge funds are established by ex-investment bankers with a following: fellows who can set up in their back bedroom (or a serviced address in Mayfair or Monaco) and persuade half-a-dozen pension funds that they have the key that has eluded investors the world over for so long: infallible investment expertise. After all, the world and his dog like a good investment story. We all believe there's a pot of gold round the corner.

New York is the hedge fund capital of the world, with $950 billion (just under half) of global hedge fund assets and over 250 of the world's top 400 hedge fund managers. A lot of mystique attaches to hedge funds and those who run them. In good times individual stellar names routinely pocketed $100–200 million a year. As a result of the recession many hedge funds have folded, but others have exploited the opportunities of unwanted and undervalued assets that any market collapse throws up.

Absolute returns

Most investment managers measure their performance against a benchmark – usually a stock market like the Nikkei 225, the Dow Jones or the FTSE. Hedge fund managers don't. They offer **absolute returns**, that is, positive returns regardless of what the markets are doing.

This is significant in an industry that is measured against benchmark indices. If an index declines by −10% but you manage a decline of −5% you have done better than the market average (which is what an index is) and are said to have **outperformed** the market or index even though you have made a loss. Hedge funds aren't like that: they promise positive returns, regardless of market conditions. In fact, up till the credit crunch, hedge funds made out that they didn't correlate to the main stock markets, which made them good countercyclical investments: if markets went down they went up. But in practice this didn't happen.

They claim to be able to generate absolute returns by taking greater risks than the average fund and by selecting from a wider array of (risky) instruments to do so. They tend to over-concentrate their investments with a small number of huge, dominant holdings, whereas conventional investment wisdom says you should diversify across different asset classes so your eggs aren't all in one basket. They are big users of derivatives, because of the leverage effects, the ease of moving in and out of markets, and the ability to trade on margin (Chapter 6). They also short sell (Chapter 4) – in fact they are the biggest short sellers in the market. They play the currency markets. They borrow, again to get the amplification effect of leverage.

Some are **global macro** funds that make massive investments in any asset class anywhere in the world if there is a 'directional' opportunity, that is, a strong sense that it will move in a particular direction.

Some specialise in buying **distressed securities** such as junk bonds (these funds are sometimes called **vulture funds** because they then hold issuers to ransom and only back off if they get a disproportionate pay-off for their holdings).

Some go in for **merger arbitrage** – exploiting M&A activity by buying the target's shares and selling the bidder's (bidders' shares always go down when a bid is announced because of the additional costs and uncertain benefits that result from taking another company over; while the shares of the target, or suspected target, always go up if a bid is suspected since those shares will be in demand).

Some are **event driven** and aim to profit from corporate announcements such as deals and restructurings.

Some are **activist investors** in that they buy shares in public companies then boss the boards about how to improve their companies, including encouraging them to sell out to, or merge with, other companies.

Some go in for **relative value arbitrage** – they exploit 'relative' mispricings between fungible assets (different instruments or types of instruments that have the same economic effect), independently of which way markets may move.

Some pursue **long-short strategies** (buying shares they consider undervalued and shorting those they think overvalued), and so on.

In general, hedge funds do not see themselves as 'long' funds – that is, buying and holding assets. A long fund is what you and I would describe as a normal fund: it invests in securities that it hopes will increase in value; and avoids those that it thinks won't.

But – as explained in Chapter 4 – short sellers don't see the IFMs in that way. And neither do hedge funds. If they take a negative view on an instrument or market they will short it. This is why they aim to make positive returns regardless of what the IFMs are doing. Provided there is **volatility** – that is, markets are moving up or down – they aim to make money. Only if markets are flat are they impotent. Hedge funds also make **illiquid investments** – taking bets on investments which they may not be able to exit easily or quickly.

Lock-ins

It's for these reasons that hedge funds often impose **lock-ins**: preventing investors from withdrawing their money for a period of as much as five years. This is because hedge funds can generate huge positive returns one year and lose that gain the following year. They don't want investors pulling out and wanting their cash back otherwise, in order to meet that redemption, the hedge fund would have to sell assets at a time when they are either rock bottom in price or otherwise illiquid. Because of the lock-up, they don't need liquidity to meet redemptions so they can take big, risky positions in illiquid markets. At times of market stress they will **suspend redemptions.**

Leverage

Hedge funds are highly leveraged. This means they take on a large amount of debt. When credit was cheap, hedge funds did well: if you raise $5 million, borrow $95 million and achieve performance of 30%, you've made $30 million out of $5 million, which makes you a hero. However, as credit has tightened and markets have correlated (in other words they start to behave like each other, as they tend to do in a downturn) it's been much harder for hedge funds to make stratospheric returns or any returns at all. Some critics say cheap money flattered mediocre investment performance. Certainly when cheap credit dried up, so did many hedge funds: 350 closed in the first half of 2008 alone.

Leverage is also embedded, in that hedge funds are big users of derivatives. We saw in the last chapter the dramatic gearing effect of derivatives: they can give you an exposure to the underlying that is far greater than if you were invested in the underlying itself. Hedge funds exploit this to maximise the positions they take in backing their market bets. In addition they borrow and are highly-leveraged, again for the gearing effect. As a result, at the height of the bull market hedge funds were reportedly behind the huge growth in currency volumes with daily turnover of almost $2 trillion. At times hedge funds account for half of all daily trading activity on the New York Stock Exchange.

Spectacular crashes

One of the most surprising things about the global credit crunch was that it was caused by banks going bust, not hedge funds. Hedge funds are by definition rollercoaster rides and the history of hedge funds is littered with spectacular collapses.

Long-Term Capital Management (LTCM) wasn't quite as institutional or established as its name suggested. In fact it was short-term and speculative and went spectacularly bust in 1998. It had on board some of the brightest financial brains in the business. It was the complete opposite of its name: it majored on short-term speculative trading. Its total losses were more than $4.5 billion.

When it imploded it had equity of just under $5 billion, borrowings of $125 billion and a derivatives position of over $1 trillion. Unfortunately LTCM had a big position in bonds and, when Russia defaulted, its bond holdings collapsed in value. The risk to the markets of LTCM's collapse was so great that the Fed (the US central bank) had to step in and arrange a $3 billion-plus bail-out to prevent a systemic market failure.

Yet between 1994 (when it started) and 1998, LTCM had generated returns of 40% and it was led by some of the cleverest brains on Wall Street, including John Meriwether (ex-Salomons) and two Nobel Prize winners, Myron Scholes and Robert Merton, who had worked with Fischer Black on the Black-Scholes options pricing model that everyone in the IFMs used.

LTCM's strategy was to find securities which were similar ('fungible') but priced differently, to buy the less liquid one and sell the more liquid one (being more liquid it was easier to sell) and keep the difference. This strategy worked well until markets fell – sparked by Russia defaulting on its sovereign bonds. But as markets started to move together (as they do when they fall) LTCM's positions – picked because they didn't appear to correlate and so appeared to provide risk diversification – all fell together. And the ones LTCM had been keeping were the less liquid ones, so were harder to sell.

In addition LTCM was reliant, like all hedge funds, on high leverage (which had flattered previous results). To keep its strategy secret it tended to spread its matching trades amongst a number of brokers all of which required collateral, again sapping cash. Finally, it didn't realise how much its own ⇨

> trades – which had to be big to make them worth doing at all – were themselves moving the market or the extent to which, as a result, banks had sussed what it was doing and had started to bet against it by taking opposite positions.
>
> LTCM's underlying strategy was in fact correct: bond values did eventually move in line with its predictions but by then LTCM was history. As with Nick Leeson and Barings, it was a matter of poor timing and cashflow. LTCM ran out of money.
>
> Amaranth was another high-profile failure which in 2006 lost $6 billion because it made bets that went wrong on the price of natural gas.
>
> It's hard to say which hedge fund is the most successful. But taking longevity and return together, it's probably Renaissance Technologies. Its top fund, Medallion, has averaged a 35% return for 20 years and has been soft-closed for the last 15. Renaissance is run by James Simons, a respected mathematician. His annual earnings are said to be $2.5 billion. Not bad for a 70-year old former academic.

Performance fees

Hedge funds charge performance fees. Merely charging a percentage of a.u.m. (assets under management) is too staid. They do this too, of course – and it tends to be high: as much as 2% of a.u.m. (the norm is about 25 basis points or 0.25% of a.u.m.) But they also charge performance fees: the norm is 20% of any gain (though some stellar names charge more) hence the expression '2 and 20' – an audacious 2% of funds a.u.m. and 20% of any gains.

One change forced on some of them by investors post credit crunch is that losses have to be recouped before performance fees kick in. The point at which performance fees become payable again is called a **high water mark**. Since half of all hedge funds manage less than $100 million – a trifling amount by investment management standards – any pressure on fees could drive many to the wall.

Closed and soft-closed

Hedge funds depend on the cult of the personality. A fund's success or failure is down to the individual (or, occasionally, pair or trio) managing it. The most successful funds are in great demand and tend to be **soft-closed** (they're no longer taking in money unless a new investor is very wealthy or influential or both – hence the 'soft'). This increases their appeal and mystique.

Bernard Madoff, jailed in 2009 for 150 years for a $50 billion fraud on investors in his fund, wasn't a hedge fund manager. But he implied that he used 'black box' investment techniques to generate a smooth return of roughly 10% a year regardless of market conditions, which is unsustainable. He always gave the impression that his fund was soft-closed, that only a few were taken on as investors, and that you were lucky if you were one of them. This meant investors didn't like to ask questions in case they offended him. In fact he was using money from new investors to pay regular returns to old ones, a fraud pioneered by Charles Ponzi in the 1920s (hence **Ponzi scheme**). More on frauds in Chapter 9.

Doing due diligence on a hedge fund (finding out all about it) can take a lot of time (many institutional investors who put money with Madoff failed to do any). And individual hedge funds are inherently risky. So institutional investors often invest in **funds-of-funds**: funds that aren't hedge funds themselves but specialise in researching, investing in, and monitoring the performance of, a variety of hedge funds. The only problem is that you are paying two sets of fees: to the fund-of-funds itself and in respect of the underlying hedge fund investment.

Regulation

Almost all hedge funds are based offshore. They may be run from London, Greenwich, Connecticut and so on but they are legally incorporated and based offshore and that is where their assets are kept (see Chapter 9 for more on offshore). This means that they lie outside any onshore investor protection safety net. Those who invest in them do so at their own risk and can't complain to regulators if they lose their money.

However, the EU has taken an especial interest in hedge funds post credit crunch. It doesn't like what they do (the instability in the IFMs they cause), their degree of leverage or how much they earn. So the EU has tabled the Alternative Investment Fund Managers Directive to regulate hedge funds (and private equity funds – see next section). Yet it wasn't hedge funds that caused the credit crunch, but banks.

So to sum up, hedge funds differ from standard 'long' funds in that they:
- short sell
- use derivatives to speculate
- are highly leveraged through borrowing so they...
- can take highly speculative, big and often illiquid positions which means they have to...
- have lock-ins which enable them to...
- aim for absolute returns, which means they can...

- charge performance fees but...

- are generally based offshore and so are not marketed to the public, which keeps administration costs down and means the barriers to entry are low but the most popular are...

- soft-closed except to the richest investors, and of course they...

- don't hedge!

Prior to the recession, hedge funds were immensely popular with the rich, as well as with institutional investors which would allocate a small percentage (which is still large in cash terms) of their portfolios to hedge funds to generate spectacular returns.

But with so many hedge funds crowding the market it became harder to pursue a differentiating strategy that generated extraordinary returns. In fact some ended up pursuing *long-only*, *equity-only* strategies which made them indistinguishable from the average mutual fund while still charging hedge-fund-style performance fees. Investors were less than pleased. Some hedge funds moved into related activities, such as providing all sorts of financial support to companies – a bridging loan, riskier debt, equity – almost like investment banks. One of these activities – the buying and selling of whole companies – brought hedge funds into direct conflict with another type of fund: private equity.

3. PRIVATE EQUITY

Private equity is exactly what it says it is: it's money to buy equity (shares) that is raised by an investment bank privately from a small number of institutional investors (that is, pension funds and insurance companies) rather than by an issue to the public at large. Allocating shares, bonds or participations in a private equity fund to a small group of institutional investors is called a **placing** or **private placement**.

Apart from investing in shares and bonds, institutional investors have in recent years put money into private equity funds that are run increasingly by investment banks. These funds are used to buy public companies in mergers and acquisitions (M&A). This is called **taking a public company private** or **public-to-private**. It's not to be confused with **privatisation** which is about selling off state-owned industry into the private sector which may involve, confusingly, an IPO on a stock exchange.

Once the company has been taken private, it will be dismembered, its workforce cut back, bits of the business sold off (often for more than the cost of the whole, so generating an immediate premium on the price paid for the company) and the rump refloated on the stock market. If the aim is to do this in three years (a fast turnaround), it's called a **quick flip**.

The US saw the start of this trend in the 1980s with private equity houses like Kohlberg Kravis Roberts (made famous by the book *Barbarians At The Gates* which describes its outrageous takeover and break-up of RJR Nabisco). Soon these boutiques (KKR was owned by the people who started it) were all the rage. In due course venture capitalists saw that their traditional business was the poor cousin so they joined in too.

As in an M&A deal, the **bidder** (here, the private equity fund) will offer to buy all of the shares in the **target**. If the bidder succeeds, it will end up owning all of the shares in the target.

In a traditional M&A deal, where one public company bids for another, the bidder will offer its own shares in payment for those in the target. This means that shareholders in the target, if they accept the bid, will end up being shareholders in a much bigger company that combines the target (their original investment) with that of the bidder.

M&A deals are either recommended or hostile. In a **recommended bid**, the directors of the target recommend the bid to their shareholders, i.e. they advise their shareholders to accept the bidder's offer. But if they don't, if they reject the bid, then the bid becomes **hostile** (or **contested**).

Institutional investors are key in all M&A deals since they own the bulk of the shares in both the target and the bidder. Effectively they decide the outcome of the bid, which is why the directors of both the bidder and the target need to persuade them of the merits of each board's respective case.

In a private equity deal, the private equity fund obviously won't offer shares in itself (those have already been allocated to the small number of institutional investors that have put money into it). Instead, it will simply borrow a lot of money to buy the target outright. This is called **acquisition finance** (see Chapter 8). If the deal involves a very high proportion of debt in relation to the target's equity, the deal is said to be **highly leveraged**, which is why these deals are sometimes called **leveraged buyouts** or **LBOs**.

Whereas leading hedge funds work in the darker and deeper recesses of the IFMs and so are not very well known, private equity houses tend to be on the front pages of the financial papers when they take over and dismember big public companies. The most well known include: Apollo, Blackstone (listed, and in which China has a significant stake), Carlyle Group, CCMP Capital Advisors, Cerberus, Fortress, Kohlberg Kravis

Roberts (aka KKR), TPG and Loan Star. Because they restructure the target business and cut costs and the workforce, they can be unpopular with politicians who get criticised by the electorate for failing to protect companies and jobs from them. This is why a senior German government figure has described private equity funds as 'locusts' (he was actually referring to a hedge fund that was being something of an activist investor in the German market, but let's not split hairs).

Venture capital: private equity's poor relation?

Venture capital (VC) is about making equity investments in small, fast-growing businesses in order to provide them with (1) the cash they need to expand and (2) the cashflow without which they can go bust.

VC used to be a separate activity in its own right but VC providers – a mix of independent boutiques and subsidiaries of banks and insurance companies – have increasingly switched to private equity where the returns can be greater. It's VC money that kick-starts businesses that eventually go on to list (Chapter 2).

The traditional source of equity finance for small businesses is what VC professionals call dismissively the 3 Fs ('fools, family and friends'). But once a business has exhausted those sources it needs to turn to professional equity providers: VC houses.

VC is called 'venture' capital because it is risky. Roughly two out of three start-ups go bust in the first five years (the way a plane is most vulnerable at the point of lift off). Banks are hesitant to lend because there is no upside when you are providing debt and there are few assets to use as security. So the bulk of start-up funding is equity.

Once a business has grown enough, the VC provider will seek an **exit route**. These include a **trade sale** (selling the company to another business), **recycling** (selling to another VC provider), an **MBO** (management buyout – selling the company to the people who run it) right up to a full **IPO** (initial public offering – see Chapter 2). In the case of an MBO where do the managers get the funding?

Venture capitalists don't just fund start ups. They also fund management buyouts. An MBO can occur when a big business decides that part of its operations are no longer core: instead it decides to sell it off. This often follows a takeover or merger where the combined business decides that part of what it has acquired or merged with is not core to its business going forward, so it sells it to the management.

The managers of the business being sold are often the people prepared to pay the best price, because they know the business and the value of what they are buying. And because they own it (with the help of VC backing) they will have the incentive to make it successful.

For tax, legal and regulatory reasons (including restrictions on what pension funds can invest in) private equity funds are often not mutual funds as I described earlier but are structured as **limited liability partnerships** (LLPs) with **feeder funds**. Limited liability partnerships are more flexible than companies (fewer reporting and disclosure requirements) but membership is usually restricted to 20 partners. If more than 20 institutional investors are going to participate, then their money will go into feeder funds and these in turn will fund the LLP. An LLP is used rather than a 'normal' partnership because in a normal partnership each partner is equally liable for all of the partnership's debts. In a limited partnership only the 'general partner' (usually a specially formed company) is liable for the partnership, which means institutional investors are protected.

The activity of structuring these funds and then marketing them to institutional investors to raise money is called **upstream private equity**. Once institutional investor participations have been obtained, spending the money on deals is called **downstream private equity**.

For many private equity funds the credit crunch has been a disaster. They've been unable to sell off their investments and in a depressed market those underlying businesses have often performed poorly. Often it's been impossible to refinance expensive short-term debt, taken out in a rush to get a takeover done, or even to roll it over. (Sound familiar? That's what happened, in a different context, to banks like Northern Rock.)

So now debt is scarce and money isn't available to take large companies private, they are either having to risk more of their own equity or to concentrate on improving the companies they've bought. Where those companies have been in danger of breaking covenants in loan agreements, the private equity owners have been tempted to pump in temporary money – known as an **equity cure**. In these straitened times, some have been looking to an unlikely source of replacement funds: hedge funds.

But the clever private equity houses that raised cash before the crunch (equity from pension funds; cheap credit from banks) have been keeping this **dry powder** as it's called in order to buy distressed debt at rock-bottom discounted prices (much like vulture funds and hedge funds) and generating profits from any recovery.

Two interesting circularities:
■ Private equity sees opportunities in fund management – private equity house Hellman & Friedman owned fund manager Gartmore (prior to its IPO at the end of 2009); and TA Associates backed the management buyout of fund manager Jupiter from Commerzbank.

- Private equity houses do deals with fund managers: KKR has a deal with Fidelity that gives Fidelity's funds access to the retail allocation of IPOs of KKR buyouts. Since KKR owns over 50 companies from hospitals to utilities this gives (a) Fidelity investors access to investment opportunities that might otherwise pass them by and (b) KKR guaranteed retail distribution.

4. HUGE INVESTORS: PENSION FUNDS AND INSURERS

The biggest institutional investors are pension funds and insurance companies.

Pension schemes

The idea of a pension is straightforward. While you work you save money in a pension scheme and often your employer will put money in too. Most big companies have pension plans in respect of which they are the **plan sponsor**. The money is invested by the pension plan, scheme or fund (the terms are synonymous) to get **compound** growth – that is, the income from the investments is itself reinvested. Compound growth has a massive impact on the size of the pot you end up with when you retire. That pot of money is then used to buy an **annuity** which is a contract that pays out a given amount of money a year (hence the name) for as long as you live.

Annuities are provided by insurance companies on the same mutualising principle as insurance in general. Insurance works on the basis that the claims of the few are offset by the premiums of the many who don't make a claim. In the case of annuities, some people die soon after they retire so will not get the full benefit of their annuity while others will live for a long time and cost more than they saved. The money saved on those who die early offsets the cost of supporting those who live for a long time.

Funded v unfunded

The pension fund industry isn't evenly developed around the world. The US and UK are amongst the leaders in having **funded** pension systems (whereas countries that pay their pensioners out of current income are said to have **unfunded** pension provision) but European countries are catching on.

Even in those countries that are funded, it may only occur in the private sector and the pensions of public sector employees may be unfunded (paid out of current tax receipts).

And even in the private sector it may not always be plain sailing: poor investment returns, companies taking **pension holidays** (not paying into their plans), companies going bust and pension frauds – all have taken their

Alternative risk transfer

Insurance meets the debt markets in something called **alternative risk transfer** or ART. When you think about it, insurance is an annual contract to provide a lump sum to tide you over if you suffer a financial loss. The problem is that if you don't suffer a loss you lose the whole premium. Some insureds enter into multi-year contracts of insurance with a premium rebate if in any year there isn't a loss. The effect of the insurance is a bit like a standby facility: just when your credit standing is lowest (because you've suffered a financial loss) you can drawdown on this credit facility to make good that loss.

Alternative risk transfer works just like this. The most colourful instruments are **catastrophe bonds** (cat bonds). These have been used to provide municipalities with earthquake cover. Why would a pension fund bet on whether an earthquake might happen? Answer: it wouldn't. But these bonds are structured in tranches (again) so that the most risk-averse investors can buy the top-most tranche which is unlikely to be breached unless the earthquake is huge – and which therefore carries a much lower coupon. Even for those investors in more-at-risk tranches, they don't forgo their investment: they just forgo interest on that investment for a period – say three years. In the meantime if there is no catastrophe, investors can expect a coupon of as much as 12%.

What this means is that a municipality gets the use of the capital without having to pay interest for the period of greatest need – a kind of interest-free loan for that period. The investors get their capital back but not all of the interest they would have received if an earthquake hadn't occurred. Of course, a cat bond can be structured so that investors lose some of their capital too – but for that they'd expect a much higher coupon.

Don't forget also that, at most, institutional investors would only commit a tiny proportion of their overall portfolio to ART, in the hope of generating some above-average performance on the portfolio's periphery.

This also has the advantage of bringing funding from the capital markets (which are enormous – say $20 trillion) into the insurance and reinsurance markets (which are much smaller – say $500 billion – and tend to contract if there has been a pattern of recent natural disasters).

So far issuance has been small. Swiss insurer Winterthur pioneered the market by issuing a cat bond to protect it against claims from extreme weather conditions (hailstones the size of tennis balls which cause enormous damage to the bodywork of expensive cars in Switzerland). In 2005 cat bond issues were under $2 billion; in 2006 they more than doubled to almost $5 billion.

More sophisticated versions may make the trigger not so much the catastrophe itself but the level of the insurance company's own loss, or the level of industry losses. Here they begin to resemble credit default derivatives (see Chapter 6).

Less extreme applications of ART are for milder storm damage and

⇨ unexpected weather. Using weather derivatives, farmers can insure against the risks of poor weather, tourist resorts against loss of earnings. Energy companies for their part can protect against low demand because of warm weather by using **heating degree days** contracts which work like options. Catex, an electronic exchange for the trading of catastrophe risks and weather derivatives, was launched in 1994. Unsurprisingly, the biggest buyers of cat bonds are hedge funds.

As for earthquake cat bonds, the most famous (and pioneering example) was due to be issued by the California Earthquake Authority in the 1990s. It never in fact happened. Instead the whole risk was bought by an investor well known for his investments in insurance companies. His name? Warren Buffett.

toll. Where companies might have offered a pension based on, say, a percentage of your final salary (**defined benefits**) they have switched to telling you how much to invest (**defined contributions**) but without any guarantee of what that might provide in terms of an annuity.

Demographic timebomb

Those actuaries who specialise in determining pension fund liabilities through statistical analysis of incidence of death are concerned about the demographic time bomb: infant mortality is declining; people are living longer; and retiring earlier. This means that the world's population is tilting in favour of the elderly: within a matter of decades those in work will be outnumbered by the elderly who will be riding on their backs.

This hasn't put off insurance companies taking on pension fund liabilities from companies with pension plans through **pension buy-outs**. In the UK alone £50 billion has been transferred in this way – although this is just a drop in the ocean of defined benefit liabilities which are thought to top £1 trillion. What's in it for insurance companies? Mutualisation, again: they calculate that on some deals they will make a loss but on others a profit.

One idea taking hold is that of **mortality bonds** (aka **longevity bonds**). In 2003 Swiss Re – a major reinsurer – issued a three-year $400 million bond to protect it from catastrophic mortality (for instance from an epidemic). The issue paid 135 basis points over the interbank rate but investors' principal was at risk depending on mortality statistics across five countries (US, UK, France, Italy and Switzerland). If an index of these statistics exceeded the base level by 1.5 times, all principal was lost. For every 0.01 increase investors lost 5% of their principal.

Swiss Re did it because, as the world's largest provider of life and health reinsurance, it couldn't find enough counterparties on which it could offload the risk of extreme mortality. The bond proved popular, especially with pension funds that could see that a catastrophic loss of life (meaning their investment was lost) would be offset by a much-reduced demand on their pension assets (since so many pensioners would have died). So Swiss Re issued a further $362 million bond in 2005.

This is an example of **alternative risk transfer** (see box on previous page). The incidence of mortality can itself be tranched into bonds where liabilities are triggered by the numbers of a specified cohort living at ages 65, 75 and so on (survivor bonds continue to pay until the final member of the cohort dies). Tranching. Sound familiar?

So you can see that this is an area where pensions, insurance and the capital markets are converging.

Insurance and reinsurance

Insurance and reinsurance aren't, strictly speaking, regarded as part of the IFMs. This is perverse because (1) insurance companies are institutional investors, (2) offshore financial centres such as the Bahamas are heavily dependent on the insurance and reinsurance market (Chapter 9), and (3) major insurer AIG for one was wrecked by becoming a significant player in the credit default derivatives market.

Insurance companies take in **premiums** from the public, invest them in the markets and use the investment returns to meet claims and generate profit for themselves. How they invest that premium income is crucial to their financial success. So insurance companies aren't just good at pricing risk. They are investment management machines too.

Traditionally there are two types of insurance and the companies offering these have tended to be distinct. But, as with banking, there has been consolidation in the insurance industry worldwide and now the largest insurance companies offer both types of insurance product:

■ casualty insurance

■ life assurance

Casualty insurance is insurance against the possibility of an event happening. This can be anything from theft of your possessions to your car being damaged in an accident, your house burning down, paint on the carpet, or missing your holiday through illness or the plane being delayed or cancelled. In other words it provides us with financial recompense against unwanted events occurring in our lives. You also get insurance in other contexts: against the possibility of redundancy (in which case you get some income for a limited period); or an extended warranty to protect your TV after the supplier's guarantee runs out; or to meet your mortgage payments.

Life assurance (called 'assurance' because death is assured, that is, guaranteed) is, by contrast, really a savings product, often with generous tax incentives to encourage people to buy it. This allows you to save money on a regular basis so that, when you die, a lump sum is available to support your family. It can also be used to provide critical illness cover (which is where casualty insurance and life assurance converge) in case you are unable to continue working through ill health.

From this **life business** as it's called, insurance companies have moved into providing pensions so that, when someone retires, the pot of money they have saved can be used to buy an annuity which will pay out an income for the rest of their lives (as mentioned above, the insurance company loses money on those who live long but makes money on those who die soon; in the same way it makes money from those who don't have a claim and loses money on those who do).

Reinsurance

Reinsurance is how insurers insure themselves. Insurers don't sit on the risks they insure. Instead they **cede** risk to reinsurers. The risks ceded are called **cessions**. Reinsurers of reinsurers are called **retrocessionaires**. Some reinsurers obtain their business by dealing directly with primary insurers (these reinsurers are called **direct writers**) while others receive business via reinsurance intermediaries (called brokers or **broker companies**). Some do both. About half of all reinsurance is bought through brokers and the other half is arranged directly.

Insurers will routinely lay off risk to more than one reinsurer – often several reinsurers will provide reinsurance cover to the same primary insurer sometimes on the same policy if it is particularly large or risky. The reinsurer who sets the terms is called the **lead reinsurer**, and the others who subscribe are called **following reinsurers.**

Examples of reinsurance contracts include:
Facultative certificate – where a reinsurer covers a single risk and cover takes the form of either a proportion of the claim ('proportional') or a share of the claim above a fixed level ('excess') usually to a specified maximum.

Facultative automatic agreement – which covers many primary policies of the same type on a proportional or excess basis, providing stability over a certain area of primary insurance, usually on a fixed cost basis. Often made at the same time as the primary policy, with the insurer and reinsurer working closely together to decide terms and pricing for both sets of cover.

Treaty – reinsures a particular set of insurance policies (within agreed limits) over a set period. Coverage can include claims made during the period and/or claims made on policies issued in the period, and a premium will be paid depending on the claims made. A treaty means significant sharing of exposure, and can lead to the insurer and reinsurer working closely together.

Insurers also use reinsurance strategically to:
- take on a bigger risk than usual (reinsuring the bit that would otherwise make the risk too big to take)
- spread too great an exposure from a single customer (like the previous example but here it's the customer not the risk that is too concentrated)
- take on more customers without increasing their capital base and without having to turn those customers away
- gain a reinsurer's specific expertise by passing to the reinsurer a risk outside their usual scope of business
- make a turn on the difference between the premium they receive from the insured (high) and the premium they pay to the reinsurer (lower)
- smooth their own financial performance by cutting out big lumpy losses (for instance from natural disasters)

The following are ways of smoothing their financial performance:

Quota-share treaty – a treaty which reinsures a fixed percentage of each policy, useful in part for effectively increasing capital, but mostly for financial management. The reinsurer receives shares of premiums and claims in equal proportions and pays out of that a ceding commission to the primary insurer which is what enables the smoothing of results for the insurer.

Surplus-share treaty – similar to a quota-share treaty, except that the reinsurer covers a variable percentage of each policy based on the limit of the policy and the treaty's agreed net line retention. In the reverse of the quota-share treaty, this mainly provides the insurer with greater capacity and only provides a little financial management.

Excess treaty – reinsures a portion of each claim in excess of an agreed figure and up to an agreed limit. There are many varieties: per-risk, per-occurrence, working cover, higher exposed layer, catastrophe cover, aggregate or stop loss and clash, differentiated by the different kinds of loss they cover, to what limit and over what period. This provides the insurer with stability and also allows it to take on more and larger business.

Finite or non-traditional – these treaties are becoming increasingly popular and are primarily, if not entirely, designed with financial management in mind. Low risk policies are taken up by reinsurers who make very little direct margin, but offshore reinsurers can discount claims on the basis that they will be covered in part by future investment income on the premium, with tax-benefits for the primary insurer.

Lloyd's of London

Although described as an insurance market, Lloyd's of London is actually the ultimate reinsurance market of all. Named after Edward Lloyd who ran a coffee shop in the 1680s, the market became a place where ship owners, merchants with cargoes and insurers met and did business. Although Lloyd's has since diversified so that its expertise lies in pricing large, specialist and novel risks never insured before, its roots lie in maritime insurance (which makes up half its business still). When a large loss is reported it is a ship's bell (taken from the *Lutine*, a ship insured at Lloyd's which sank) that is rung to warn the market.

The turning point for Lloyd's was the 1906 San Francisco earthquake which established its name in the US and worldwide. It prides itself on the fact it has never failed to meet a claim in its entire history.

Until the 1990s its underwriting muscle was provided by individuals called Names who were essentially investors in the market and carried unlimited liability for losses. A long-term Name might make losses one year and profits another, depending on the track record of the syndicates he or she was on. But, like any good long-term investment, the rewards over time could be great.

However, in the 1980s Lloyd's became gridlocked by litigation through a number of factors that coincided: (1) the large number of natural disasters which occurred at the same time; (2) US asbestosis liability from employer liability cover provided in US employment contracts decades before – as elderly workers retired and died from asbestosis, their families sued; (3) fraud – Lloyd's was very much a members' club with managing agents pocketing premiums for themselves and some even absconding with Names' money; (4) the LMX spiral – Lloyd's syndicates passing risks around the market and pocketing a slice of premium as they did so, creating inflated revenues and concentrating risks.

All of this led to litigation and paralysis in the early 1990s. Many Names went bankrupt; some committed suicide. But Lloyd's reorganised. It stuck all its old risks in something called Equitas and started again with corporate capital, phasing Names out. However, at one point it looked as if Equitas would run out of money. But an investor partial to insurance came to the rescue: Warren Buffett.

Credit crunch turmoil in the insurance markets: the story of AIG

Traditionally, insurance and the capital markets don't mix. Although both industries use the term 'underwriting', each operation is very different from the other. In investment banking it means taking on the residue of a securities issue. In insurance it means agreeing to compensate for a loss.

But the two have started to converge: a decade ago, Citigroup merged with Travelers, the huge US insurer (although they've subsequently demerged); major European banks offer bancassurance (selling life assurance and pensions products); pension funds use insurance companies and fund managers to manage parts of their portfolios; insurance companies provide the annuities that pensioners are paid; monoline insurers – which specialise in one line of business – have backstopped bond issues (such as mortgage securitisations, municipal bonds and project financings) for years.

But AIG (American International Group) took this to extremes. A respected US insurance institution and one of the top five largest companies in the world, it went spectacularly bust in 2008. What caused this was a unit called AIG Financial Products which behaved like a hedge fund atop a large and stable insurance company (funnily enough, it was based not in the US but in Mayfair, London's hedge fund district).

Through this unit, AIG wrote credit-default swaps (CDSs) like they were going out of fashion. CDSs pay out on a borrower's default, so they are used by banks keen to insure themselves against risky loans going bad (see Chapter 6). It's a massive market of over $50 trillion. AIG sold approaching $500 billion of them but, as the economy sank and loans defaulted, found itself paying out $50 billion to CDS counterparties (mainly banks) and went bust. But it was too big to be allowed to fail without jeopardising the markets further. So the US government stepped in (at a cost of $175 billion and rising).

This is why reliance on monoline insurers to give guaranteed value to bond issues backfired in the credit crunch: when an insurer looked to be in financial difficulty, and had their credit rating downgraded, this had a knock-on effect on all the municipal bonds that they were insuring. For example, in

January 2008, the rating of Ambac, a leading monoline, was cut from AAA to AA by Fitch, so triggering a simultaneous downgrade of $500 billion of bonds issued by over 100,000 municipalities and institutions.

The monolines for their part have come unstuck too. Aside from Ambac, MBIA (the largest bond insurer in the world), FGIC, MGIC, PMI and others provide bond default insurance which helps weaker issuers obtain a higher credit rating for their issues. This is because these monolines use their own credit-standing to 'wrap' (guarantee) muni bonds by issuers (such as an individual hospital) to command as high a credit rating as the monolines themselves – see Chapter 5 for the resulting problems. They wrap and backstop over $2.5 trillion of outstanding muni debt. But they are by nature thinly capitalised (since they're not lending institutions) and have only $50 billion of claims-paying ability.

As their own ratings declined, so the issues that they wrapped and backstopped went down too, as did the CDSs they wrote (sold). Banks that bought their CDSs suffered over $100 billion in writedowns (several billion of that just down to monoline ACA). This rippled outwards: Swiss Re reported billions of dollars of write-downs on CDSs and US mortgage-related investments. Insurers ING and AEGON had to receive capital injections from the Dutch government. Ironically (given what AIG got up to) it was the widening spreads (the difference between buy and sell quotes) on CDSs available on insurance companies themselves that reflected market concerns. Spreads on the biggest conglomerate insurers like Prudential (US), MetLife and Prudential (UK) went to 600 basis points (six whole per cent).

On top of all of this, insurers braced themselves for the usual crop of insurance claims that occur in a recession, mainly around D&O cover (d = directors; o = officers). This protects directors and officers of companies against claims for negligence and misfeasance brought by shareholders angry that their company's share price has collapsed. And what hits the insurance market today hits the reinsurance market tomorrow as claims are passed up the line.

Further irony: so concerned was the New York insurance regulator (responsible for some of the big monolines) in 2008 that he sought standby funding for MBIA and Ambac to preserve their own ratings – by approaching banks.

One interesting idea put forward is that monolines could set up an excess-of-loss pool, in other words reinsure their own worst tranche of risks. This is (putting it simplistically) monoline insurers using reinsurance to self-insure their own insurance. Good, eh?

New kids on the block: sovereign wealth funds

Some of the biggest institutional investors are sovereign wealth funds (SWFs) which are government-owned investment funds that channel a country's surplus income – from natural resources such as oil and gas or overseas trade and exports – into investments overseas for the benefit of future generations.

The idea of SWFs has been around for 50 years although only recently have they begun to attract much attention. One of the first was started by the Pacific island nation of Kiribati which built a $400 million fund out of its guano exports. The fund is over 50 years old. Another is the Kuwait Investment Authority (and its overseas sibling, the Kuwait Investment Office) which also started in the 1950s. The biggest is the Abu Dhabi Investment Authority ($900 billion). China's is variously reported to be the biggest or to have just $200 billion in assets. Total assets of SWFs are estimated at about $3 trillion.

What's surprising is just how many countries have them, from the State Oil Fund of the Republic of Azerbaijan to Venezuela's Investment Fund for Macroeconomic Stabilisation. An interesting contrast in fortunes is that between Norway, which put the revenues from North Sea oil into an SWF and the UK which didn't. Norway's SWF is now worth about $400 billion. It's a fine line between a country's SWF and its national pension fund. South Korea's $200 billion National Pension Service invests all over the world.

Most striking is how many of these funds are from emerging markets. Apart from Norway, Australia's Future Fund and Canada's Alberta Heritage Savings Trust Fund are amongst the few SWFs from developed economies. And therein lies the political issue. Developed economies, advocates for years of free and open IFMs, don't like it when these SWFs sweep in and buy up swathes of their own economies – especially in the case of China and Russia whose political intentions remain hidden.

In particular, SWFs like financial assets. They have stakes in big banks, private equity houses (China Investment Corporation bought a $3 billion stake in Blackstone; Mudabala, an Abu Dhabi fund, has a stake in Carlyle) and even stock exchanges such as OMX and the London Stock Exchange, over a third of which is owned by Qatar and Dubai.

But developed economies overlook the fact that recently SWFs have been crucial in bailing out banks, such as Citigroup, Merrill Lynch, Morgan Stanley and Barclays, all of which turned to SWFs from China, Singapore, Kuwait and Abu Dhabi for equity injections. Between them these SWFs have pumped in over $40 billion by way of fresh equity. In Citi's case it received over $14 billion, half of that from the Abu Dhabi Investment Authority alone. And SWFs don't always necessarily make a killing: CIC's investment in Blackstone has cost it $1 billion already.

By and large SWFs seem to be long-term, buy-and-hold investors. In response to criticism over opaqueness and lack of transparency, 21 of ➡

⇨ them formed the International Working Group of Sovereign Wealth Funds in April 2008 and published a set of rules called the Santiago Principles in October 2008.

Considering that SWFs are generally answerable to very few people in the world, this strikes me as pretty big of them.

Despite all of this, some insurers and reinsurers believe that investment bankers could learn from their approach to risk management. Since their industry is geared for losses – often unpredictable, infrequent but of high magnitude – they have a healthy scepticism of computer-driven risk management modelling. They use scenario-planning (brainstorming possibilities and their consequences) as well as encouraging insureds to retain part of the risk, so avoiding moral hazard (by contrast the originate-to-distribute model in sub-prime securitisations encouraged moral hazard: originators didn't care who they lent to). Now that's an interesting thought.

Final word: who in these troubled times for monolines set up his own bond insurer and offered to consider bailing out others? Warren Buffett.

5. THE ROLE OF BANKS IN INVESTMENT MANAGEMENT

Investment banks are intimately involved with the Buy Side in all sorts of different ways.

As we saw in Chapters 2 and 3, banks originate, underwrite and distribute **bond and equity issues** which they sell to institutional investors. Bank **research analysts** provide institutional investors with economic and market data that help them decide whether to buy or sell securities, although this can give rise to conflicts if analysts are ramping (talking up) equity and debt issues led by their own bank.

Prime brokerage

Hedge funds in their heyday represented the single most important type of business to a number of investment banks through something called **prime brokerage**. This comprises multifarious services provided by investment banks to hedge funds. Examples include all types of broking (the buying and selling of securities) as well as stock- and bond-lending, short-term liquidity (i.e. loans), the tailoring of exotic OTC derivatives, plus back-office support such as clearing and settlement.

By way of example of how important this business can be to banks, over a period of less than three years, the hedge fund TCI (named The Children's Investment Fund as it pledges a percentage of its profits to a charitable

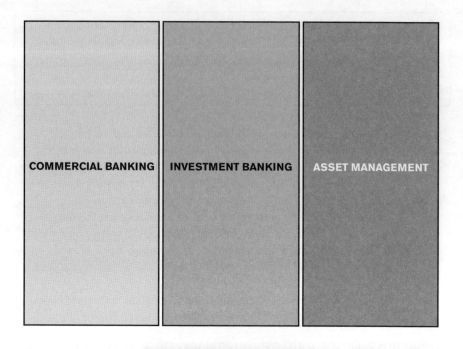

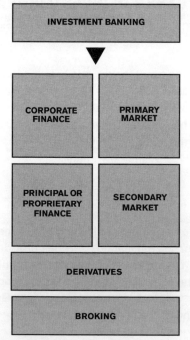

A breakdown of investment banking operations

endowment for children) paid almost $100 million in commissions to its prime brokers.

When the credit crunch hit, a lot of banks took a double whammy: their portfolios were stuffed full of securitisations that were bust; and their biggest business outside that was prime brokerage – accounting for as much as a third of their profits – at a time when hedge funds were also going down the pan.

One strange side-effect of the credit crunch was that hedge funds did better than the banks that lent to them. When Bear Stearns, which with Morgan Stanley and Goldman Sachs had almost two-thirds of the prime brokerage market, went bust hedge funds were hugely concerned. In particular, they were worried about something called **rehypothecation** (hypothecate is the French-based term for mortgage) which means prime brokers using assets (as collateral for their own borrowing) put up by hedge funds as collateral for their borrowing. If your prime broker goes bust your collateral has gone.

Other involvement with institutional investors

- Banks were behind the SIVs (**structured investment vehicles**) which bought so much of the sub-prime securitisations and in which they sold participations to institutional investors.

- Investment banks have been heavily involved in launching and marketing **private equity funds** to institutional investors to raise the money for private equity houses to do M&A deals. Banks have also become involved in these deals as parties in their own right, using their own capital as equity to take businesses over, merge them and sell them off. This is called **principal finance** and can cause conflicts of interest if a bank is advising a private equity fund on a takeover in which it may have a competing proprietary interest. In fact in the run-up to the credit crunch some commentators were suggesting that investment banks like Goldman Sachs, with their extensive proprietary trading in derivatives and equity investment in principal finance deals, were themselves 'private equity hedge funds'.

- Banks have their own **asset management** arms through which they manage money on behalf of clients. Examples include UBS Global Asset Management, Goldman Sachs Asset Management, Bank New York Mellon Asset Management, JPMorgan Asset Management and HSBC Global Asset Management, but many sold their asset management businesses after the credit crunch in order to rebuild their capital base and because the apparent synergy (an asset management arm that can buy issues led by the bank) actually causes conflicts of interest. A recent notable deal was the sale of Barclays Global Investors (by Barclays to rebuild its balance sheet) which BlackRock bought for $13 billion, making it the biggest fund manager in the world. Divesting themselves of asset management arms leaves banks free to find the best investment products for their clients across the industry – this is called **open architecture**.

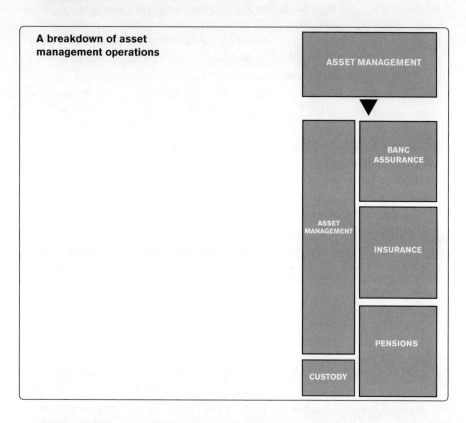

A breakdown of asset management operations

- Investment banks (Morgan Stanley in particular) have been key in developing **alternative risk transfer** which, as we've seen, is a way of encouraging institutional investors to widen their range of asset classes.

- Institutional investors use banks to look after their securities, receiving interest and dividends from their investments around the world, reclaiming tax and doing the currency conversions. This is called **global custody**. It isn't regarded as especially glamorous but, if done on the right scale with computerisation, can generate steady fees which at times of volatility can be attractively predictable. The biggest bank names in this business include: Bank of New York Mellon, State Street Bank, Chase Global Custodians (part of JPMorgan Chase) and Northern Trust.

- Banks, especially European ones, have moved into the business of insurance and pension provision, which is called **bancassurance**.

- Banks and insurance companies have owned each other (Citibank/Travelers, Allianz/Dresdner, Credit Suisse/Winterthur) though not always successfully.

- The final irony is that the collapse of banks – especially regional banks in the US (25 in 2008, almost 40 in the first half of 2009) – soon had investors circling seeking rich pickings. And who were they? Not big banks seeking consolidation – they had no cash to spare and their own problems to sort out. Answer: private equity funds.

So it all connects.

Talk of banks takes us on to what commercial banks did originally which, compared to all this capital markets activity, may seem rather dull: lending money. But first, let's visit Frankfurt: equally dull, I'm afraid.

HOW IT ALL CONNECTS

- Institutional investors are the biggest buyers of shares (Chapter 2), bonds (Chapter 3), money market instruments (Chapter 4), securitisations (Chapter 5) and derivatives (Chapter 6)

- Banks also have asset management arms

- Insurers have helped to bail out the banking sector – Ping An, China's largest insurer, bought a 4% stake in Fortis

- Insurers have become exposed to bank credit markets through writing credit default derivatives (Chapter 6)

- Hedge funds have been big buyers of distressed banks' debt and distressed banks themselves – hedge fund SRM at one point held over 6% of Northern Rock

- Venture capital finances start-ups which may in due course become public companies (Chapter 2)

- M&A deals are done by public companies using their own shares instead of cash (Chapter 2)

DAY TRIP TO
FRANKFURT

It's hard not to feel sorry for Frankfurt. It's a small, neat, tidy place, a European version of Singapore. But it's not Singapore (which we'll come to later). And even though in surveys of IFCs Frankfurt is always trotted out as Europe's leading IFC after London, that's like comparing a toy train set (Frankfurt) with a real railway (London).

If the bankers and burghers of Frankfurt have any regrets, it must be ones of size and location. Frankfurt feels small, too small. This lack of size points to a lack of infrastructure – from a paucity of professional support services (accountants, actuaries, consultants, lawyers, and the like) to a mere carapace of cultural and sporting life outside work. There isn't enough here to sustain the 'work hard, play hard' culture of the IFMs. Frankfurt is too small to make it big as a financial centre.

As for location, Frankfurt must wish it were somewhere else. Germany has some great cities, all of which in their own quirky ways would have been better bets: Hamburg, the fabulous port city and media capital, with its Hanseatic and Baltic trading history, and notorious night life; Munich, a centre of industrial and technical innovation, Germany's motor trade, European intellectual property and the October beer fest; and, of course, Berlin, the centre of government and history, with empty windswept blocks set against the amazing futuristic hotels on Potsdammer Platz, with Checkpoint Charlie, the Reichstag and the Brandenburg Gate reminding you just how close below the surface history is, and a cultural heritage stretching from *Cabaret* to Rammstein, both engagingly bonkers in their own ways.

But no, we're not there or anywhere. We're in Frankfurt. And it could have been so, so different.

The 1990s were Frankfurt's decade. In 1993, Deutsche Börse (DB) took over the operation of the Frankfurt Stock Exchange (FSE) from the Frankfurt Chamber of Commerce and Industry. In 1994 Frankfurt fought off stiff competition to become home to the European Central Bank, and therefore the euro, positioning it to become the gateway to east European economies. In 1996 it launched its *Finanzplatz Deutschland* initiative to propel it into the top tier of global IFCs. The vision was to create an integrated market around bonds (its core strength), stocks and futures.

In 1997, DB launched the Neuer Markt (New Market), a junior market for start-ups and fast-growing smaller companies which quickly established itself as the German market for technology and high-growth stocks, a serious rival to NASDAQ. That same year DB also launched Xetra, an electronic trading platform, that made the FSE far more of an international market with almost half of the 300 market participants outside Germany.

1998 also saw the creation of Eurex, a merging of the Swiss and German futures exchanges which overtook CBOT in volume. Eurex promptly set about negotiating a strategic global alliance with CBOT which resulted in the launch of a new joint trading platform in 2000. So far so good.

But it's been downhill from there ever since. The FSE may be ranked eighth by domestic market capitalisation and eighth for bond trading (continental investors are more into bonds than equities) but Frankfurt is a financial centre in decline. Even the banks have been deserting it: Deutsche and Dresdner do their euro-trading in London in preference.

The Neuer Markt was ravaged by the dotcom boom and bust in 2000 and between then and 2002 lost 96% of its value. Its closure soon after was a huge reputational blow for Frankfurt. The FSE was further humbled by several failed takeover attempts of the London Stock Exchange (LSE) and Euronext, the French-based pan-European exchange, which marked a retreat in equities. By 2005 the FSE was hosting just 20 (mostly small) IPOs a year, with just five in 2008.

The FSE's first effort in May 2001 to form a joint pan-European exchange almost yielded results, had it not been for the OMX's bid for the LSE in August 2001. DB's bid for LIFFE (London's futures market) to consolidate DB's presence in German bond futures, also in 2001, came to nothing too.

That same year, insurer Allianz bought Dresdner, one of Germany's three principal banks based in Frankfurt (the other two are Deutsche and Commerzbank). Allianz is based in Munich, to where control shifted. There were rumours too that Deutsche – with two-thirds of its earnings coming from its London and New York investment banking operations – would move its HQ to London.

Undaunted, in 2002, DB took full control of Clearstream, the securities clearing and settlement house in Luxembourg – the idea being that it would offer an integrated service in international bonds and equities. But major clients UBS and JPMorgan Chase promptly defected to rival Euroclear.

DB's next assault on LSE came in December 2004. LSE rejected the bid, saying it was too low at 530p per share, while being open to further talks. But later that same month, Euronext announced its interest in bidding for LSE. DB revised its offer in January 2005 but withdrew it two months later in the face of continued hostility from LSE and from DB's own shareholders.

In 2006, DB tried to form an alliance with Euronext. But Euronext chose a bid by the New York Stock Exchange (NYSE) instead. In November 2006, DB finally dropped its ambitions to win LSE.

DB is currently the only major continental exchange that has not consolidated with another exchange. Euronext's merger with the NYSE put France ahead in the race for financial consolidation on the continent. Having managed to wrest trading in German bond futures from London, DB still believes that it has a strong enough presence in the fixed income and derivatives markets (through Eurex) to ensure its future.

Two reforms have helped. In 2003, the FSE restructured its listing of German stocks. It introduced its Prime and General categories. Prime listings have more stringent transparency and reporting requirements and are for top companies seeking interest from international investors. A third tier, Entry standard, was created in 2005 via the Open Market (the regulated unofficial market) as the new segment for small and medium-sized companies.

This last was part of an 11-point plan drawn up in 2005 to enhance Frankfurt as an IFC. Other proposals included: cutting taxes on foreign nationals; improving business education and research (this has led to the 'House of Finance' – a centre for financial studies in conjunction with the Goethe Business School); and the introduction of real estate investment trusts (REITs) in 2007.

REITs are funds that invest in commercial property. They turn an illiquid investment (commercial property) into a liquid one (transferable securities) because investors trade in and out of the REIT rather than the underlying property investments. This has particular appeal to international investors and over the next decade the market could be worth a staggering €140 billion.

For Frankfurt's sake, let's hope so.

Chapter 8

Commercial Banking

SPEED-READ SUMMARY

- Commercial banking is the taking in of deposits and the making of loans

- Retail banking (commercial banking for individuals) is a local rather than international activity

- Bi-lateral lending is a loan between a bank and a borrower

- Syndicated lending occurs where a group of banks lend a large amount to a borrower using the same loan agreement

- Financial covenants are designed to ensure the borrower manages its business prudently

- In the credit crunch, banks accelerated the repayment of on-demand loans which undermined perfectly sound businesses

- Acquisition finance enables a bidder to take over a target company

- Asset finance (aka finance leasing) is a tax-efficient way of funding large items such as planes, ships and oil rigs

- Trade finance uses letters of credit which are traded in the *à forfait* (secondary) market

- Project finance is used to fund large infrastructure projects and is limited or non-recourse

- Islamic banking is compliant with Sharia law which forbids interest and speculation – and is a fast-growing industry

- Microfinance – another fast-growing part of banking – is the provision of financial services to the world's poorest people and is based on microcredit (lending tiny amounts to many)

- Private banking is essentially asset management for the rich

The most basic financial activity in the world, lending (so old it's mentioned in the Bible), is also the least international. The act of taking in deposits is retail and local, a far cry from the wholesale IFMs we've visited so far. Only when the amounts being lent become huge do banks club together in international syndicates to provide the loan. These are done most obviously for sovereign borrowers (i.e. countries), which we'll come back to.

So commercial banking (as lending is called) comes almost last on our list. It's also the least typical of the trading frenzy that has gripped the IFMs. True, it's the securitisation of basic lending that led to the sub-prime credit crunch (Chapter 5). And loans are these days designed to be tradable in the secondary markets, so they are no longer the static, fixed assets on banks' balance sheets that they once were.

It's also true that the way in which loans are syndicated is much closer to the bond markets as syndication techniques in equity IPOs and debt (bond issues and loans) have converged – not least because the biggest banks these days are both investment and commercial banks.

LOCAL, NOT INTERNATIONAL

But, by and large, retail banking is a local, national activity: major US bank Continental Illinois went spectacularly bust in 1984 because its deposit base was too narrow, restricted by state law to Chicago and its environs; just over 20 years later, UK bank Northern Rock went spectacularly bust because it tried to augment its local depositor base by the short-term funding of long-term mortgages in the interbank market.

In the intervening 20 years the IFMs have gone trading crazy. Everybody's been in on it, from investment banks and brokers to institutional investors, hedge funds and private equity houses. The proliferation of derivatives has made it that much easier. Even in retail finance people have started using credit cards like never before.

So it comes as a slight shock to realise that lending became a bit of a sideshow, unless of course you were lending for private equity purposes, to fund a takeover (acquisition finance), or to hedge funds (prime brokerage), or were simply using depositors' money to buy US securitised mortgage-backed bonds (before the market crashed). Surprisingly (or not) those banks that emerged relatively unscathed from the credit crunch (for instance Santander and BBVA in Spain) were the ones that had simply stuck to what they did best: prudent lending to local customers.

GOLDSMITHS AND ROTTEN BENCHES

Lending is probably the oldest form of financial transaction. Bank notes began when people left their gold with goldsmiths for safekeeping in return for receipts. They then used the receipts to pay for goods and services, instead of going back to get their gold out. These receipts changed hands while the gold itself was left with the goldsmiths who were able to start lending it out. This was the start of lending.

In fact the term 'bankrupt' dates from the middle ages when the bankers of Lombardy in northern Italy used to sit on benches which would be broken up if they went bust (*banca rotta*). It so happens those bankers turned up in the City of London, hence Lombard Street by the Bank of England – which just goes to show that the financial markets were international long before the modern era.

Loans themselves were not inherently tradable, but they are now. Originally, the legal means of selling a loan meant you had to tell the borrower, who might justifiably feel annoyed that his relationship bank had passed his loan to a stranger. But securitisation (Chapter 5) changed that; as has the use of derivatives (Chapter 6), such as credit-default swaps which cover banks against losses from borrower defaults.

In fact, bank documentation now routinely contains the right of the lender to on-sell the loan, and the secondary market in loans is well established – all of which are why, these days, banks syndicate loans and bond issues in much the same way, and the two forms of raising debt finance have converged.

1. BI-LATERAL LENDING

The two principal types of bank debt funding are **bi-lateral** loans (bi = two parties: lender and borrower) and **syndicated lending** (syndicate = several banks lending to one borrower on identical terms contained in one loan agreement). Syndicated lending tends to occur where a single borrower wants more money than one bank is prepared to advance because of the credit risk.

Matched funding

Banks don't just lend out their deposits. They also borrow money on the interbank market. In practice, when a bank knows it is going to lend an amount of money, it gets those funds in the interbank market and it does so by borrowing those funds for a set period – three or six months (the interbank market is a short-term market; banks don't want to be lending to each other for long periods – it ties up their money).

Common bank lending terms

Overdraft – just like a personal overdraft and repayable on demand – i.e. whenever the bank asks for it back.

Revolving credit facility (called a **revolver**) – a more sophisticated form of overdraft, it 'revolves' in the sense that the company can reborrow whatever it has repaid, i.e. it can utilise repaid amounts – this is called a 'rollover'.

Term loan – a loan of a fixed amount for a fixed period.

Letter of credit facility – used in less sophisticated markets where the bank issues a letter of credit (a bit like a cheque drawn on the bank) that the company can borrow against.

Drawdown – the procedure for, and moment of, actually borrowing money under the loan.

Event of default – a breach by the borrower of any term that allows the lender to accelerate the loan (demand early repayment).

Repayment of principal is usually by way of:

- **Amortisation** – principal repaid by equal instalments; or

- **Balloon** – if the amount of the repayment increases with each repayment; or

- **Bullet** – all in one go on maturity. If the borrower is in breach of its obligations the bank can accelerate the loan (demand immediate repayment).

On demand repayment – the bank can demand repayment of the entire loan for no reason: this is what happened in the credit crunch as banks tried to shore up their balance sheets; which is what drove perfectly good businesses to the wall, as they were starved of credit and cashflow.

So the bank borrows short and lends long and funds itself for each loan period by a matching interbank deposit. This is called **matched funding**. It means that if anything goes wrong with the loan – for instance the bank gets repaid too early or gets repaid too late by the borrower, this gives the bank a problem. If the bank is repaid too early, it is sitting on funds on which it is paying interest in the interbank market; if it is repaid too late, it isn't able to repay its own loan on the interbank market. Both scenarios are painful to bankers. Both of them are examples of **broken funding**.

Yield protection

So the loan is made on a **cost-plus basis**: the borrower pays the bank's cost-of-funds plus its margin. In other words, a bank will work out the cost to it of making the funds available to the borrower and add a margin. Much of the loan documentation is about yield protection ('yield' here meaning 'return'): ensuring the bank covers its costs and gets its expected profit.

Security

Commercial banks will always seek security – i.e. other sources of funds that they can tap if the borrower defaults (by contrast, bond issues are almost invariably unsecured). Security often takes the form of a charge over the borrower's assets. If the borrower is a subsidiary of a group, there may be a guarantor that guarantees payment of the interest and repayment of the principal. The guarantor is usually a parent company hence the guarantee being known as a parent company guarantee or, if it's not as strong as a guarantee, a comfort letter. (Note: this use of the word 'security' is not to be confused with 'securities', meaning bonds and shares.)

Financial covenants

In every loan agreement, the borrower makes certain promises (called 'covenants'). Some of the key ones affect the way the borrower can run its business and are called financial covenants. They include:

- **Negative pledge** which prevents a borrower from pledging (i.e. mortgaging) its assets to any other creditor in preference to the lending bank, and so ensures the bank retains its priority over later lenders.

- **Pari passu** which is crucial in a syndicated loan since it ensures that all lenders are treated the same, and the borrower can't favour one lender over another by repaying or prepaying one before another.

- **Restrictions** on disposals so the borrower cannot asset strip, change its business, or favour some creditors over others (by handing them assets).

These, and covenants defining **financial ratios** (e.g. minimum net worth, minimum working capital, interest cover, debt-to-equity ratio, etc.), set the parameters within which the borrower may operate its business. They enable the bank to monitor the borrower's position and **accelerate the loan** (require it to be repaid early) if there is any breach by the borrower (called an **event of default**) or – even more importantly – any **prospective breach**. This is because the bank needs to be able to get in first and accelerate its loan before any other lender does so with theirs, so it has more chance of getting its money back first and getting out whole.

Prior to the credit crunch, when credit was cheap and banks were falling over themselves to lend, they would attract borrowers by offering cov-lite (**covenant-lite**) loans where some of these financial covenants were relaxed or omitted altogether.

Other events of default

Other key events of default include **payment default** (non-payment of interest or principal when due), **material adverse change** (fundamental change in the borrower's financial position) and **cross default** (if the borrower defaults under any other loan agreement because that indicates it is probably close to insolvency anyway).

When the borrower goes bust

Three aspects of the most recent credit crunch have been:

- **Leaderless creditor groups** – securitisation has meant that once loans were turned into bonds it was much harder for those owed money by a borrower (called **creditors**) to identify each other and work together because they lacked that direct contact with the borrower you get through a loan.

- **Pre-packs** – when a borrower does go bust, an **administrator** (usually an accountant) is appointed by the creditors to gather in the assets, realise them (turn them into money) and distribute that money according to the local insolvency rules, usually to the most senior creditor first and ending with the shareholders (who usually get nothing). Those with

---

Sovereign lending

By definition, the most international loans are **jumbo** (big) loans for large amounts requiring syndicates of 50-plus banks where the borrower is a prestigious sovereign. All banks want to get in on that. Every so often a generation of commercial bankers has the same bright idea: let's lend to countries because they will always be there unlike corporate borrowers which can go bust, get wound up and disappear.

This rush of blood to the head happened most spectacularly in the 1970s after the 1973 oil shock created the need to recycle the earnings of oil-producing countries which meant that big loans were made to Latin American and African countries.

In August 1982 Mexico suspended payments under its sovereign loans (in other words it defaulted). This was followed by more than 70 other sovereign defaults (roughly half in Africa and half in Latin America). The **sovereign debt rescheduling** crisis took a decade to work through and was only resolved when defaulted bank loans were relaunched as **Brady bonds** (named after the US Treasury Secretary Nicholas Brady who was their main architect – the bulk of lending banks affected had been US commercial banks).

Between 1990 and 2005 there were a further 40-odd defaults, mainly on African syndicated loans and Latin American bond issues (by now Latin American countries were used to issuing bonds, African countries less so).

However, it was Russia, which defaulted on its bonds in 1998, which caused the most mayhem. Hedge fund LTCM collapsed as a result (see Chapter 7).

security (a charge over the borrower's assets) are able to exercise that charge and recover what they are owed from selling the underlying asset. If possible, an administrator wants to sell off the business as a **going concern** because that will raise more money for the creditors. A **pre-pack** is where all of this has been planned in advance (a 'pre-packaged' insolvency and administration) which is how some businesses are sold off almost on the day they are declared insolvent (bust).

- **Debtor-in-possession financings** – where insolvent companies can file under US insolvency law (known colloquially as 'Chapter 11' which is the relevant part of the US bankruptcy code) and carry on trading under court protection against their creditors. Debtor-in-possession financings are ones where Chapter 11 allows 'new' lenders preference over 'old' lenders because companies in Chapter 11 need access to fresh funds and won't get it unless the banks prepared to provide it are given seniority over previous lenders.

2. SYNDICATED LENDING

Everything mentioned above applies equally to syndicated loans. When a borrower wants to borrow more than its bank is prepared to lend, the bank will pull together other banks to form a syndicate.

Syndicated lending is the backbone of international commercial banking. It is usually a bit more expensive than a bond issue (cheaper to arrange but carrying a higher interest rate) because it is difficult for a bank to get out of a loan or sell it on once the loan has been made, so the syndicate members can be stuck with the borrower for the term of the loan and want to be rewarded for that risk (whereas a bondholder can just sell the bond in the market to get rid of that particular exposure).

But there are times – depending on the yield curve, the state of the banking industry and so on – when syndicated loans are cheaper for borrowers than bonds. In any event they offer borrowers a different source of funds.

The syndicate will lend to the borrower on the same terms using the same loan agreement but there are additional roles made necessary by the fact that the lender is not one but several banks:

- **Arranger** is the bank awarded the mandate (instruction to put together the loan) by the borrower. It retains a portion of the proposed loan and undertakes to syndicate the rest among other banks with the help of a book runner/syndicate coordinator.

- **Book runner/syndicate coordinator** (in large syndications these will be different banks) actually undertakes the syndication: the arranger tells it how much exposure to the borrower the arranger wishes to retain and, therefore, what the target fundraising is.

- **Agent** which collects interest and repayments from the borrower and distributes them to the syndicate, monitors the borrower's financial covenants and administers waivers and amendments to the loan documentation.

Sharing clause

A key clause in a syndicated loan agreement is the sharing clause which says that if any bank receives a payment from the borrower, it will share that payment with the other syndicate members. This is to prevent the borrower from preferring one lender over another, for instance if the borrower has a separate bilateral loan with one of the banks.

Loans v bonds

Nowadays, many loans are as tradable as bonds and are constructed from the outset so that participations can be sold on. This and the way they are syndicated is much closer to the way bonds are: in both cases you can have **bought deals** where the lead bank agrees to provide all the funding then syndicates to other lenders subsequently. This can be done on an absolute basis, best efforts or reasonable basis (the first means the bank has to; the last two mean that if it can't the proposed loan is cancelled).

Two traditional differences still apply:
- **Bond documentation is simpler** and the covenants less demanding. This is because bondholders can always sell in the market if the borrower's credit-standing deteriorates, whereas traditionally lenders were stuck with the loan come what may so they required much more comprehensive, fuller loan agreements.
- **Loans are more flexible** – for instance as to staggered repayment and renegotiation of terms: it is easier for a borrower to negotiate with lenders than an issuer to do so with bondholders (since the issuer won't know who they are) unless, which is unusual, the issuer has structured the bond so that there is a **trustee** which can negotiate with it in bondholders' best interests.

3. ACQUISITION FINANCE

Acquisition finance means lending to fund **M&As** (mergers and acquisitions between companies). Acquisition finance was one of the first victims of the credit crunch. But at the height of the boom as more and more M&A deals became **highly leveraged** (a lot of debt supported by little equity), acquisition finance was all the rage.

It included **whole business securitisation** (Chapter 5) which is a way of turning a business's revenue stream into a capital amount which can then be used to buy that business. It also funded **LBOs (leveraged buyouts)**. In banking circles, acquisition finance is said to be **event-driven lending** rather than general corporate lending.

M&As are generally funded by the bidder's equity ('paper') such as a share-for-share acquisition or rights issue. But debt finance is often more attractive to the:

- **Target's shareholders**, since they get money not the buyer's shares.

- **Buyer**, since the costs are tax-deductible (whereas dividends are paid out of after-tax income).

- **Buyer's shareholders**, since any additional issue of equity may depress the buyer's earnings-per-share (since there are more shares in issue) which is a key profitability figure.

In a private equity bid it's essential since the private equity fund won't be offering its own paper (which is owned by its investors).

Acquisition finance can take one of two forms: a loan or a bond issue. A loan can provide some advantages over a bond issue:

- **Renegotiation** – it's easier for the borrower to negotiate a waiver or amendment with a syndicate of bankers than to try to alter the terms of a bond (since it won't necessarily know who the bondholders are).

- **Flexibility** – a loan tends to be more flexible for the bid stage of an acquisition, before the buyer's longer-term financing needs are ascertained (e.g. the buyer may in fact intend to sell off bits of the target).

Most syndicated loans are done on a best efforts basis, and the arranger makes this clear in its offer letter to the borrower. But in acquisition finance, the borrower will want **committed funds**. It's no good to the buyer for the bank to come back empty-handed and say 'No one wanted to join the syndicate so you can't have the money'. The buyer has an acquisition to finance. So the bank advising on the acquisition may underwrite the syndicated loan process – i.e. it will commit to lend the full amount if necessary but can syndicate the debt to other banks either before or after signing. In short the arranger generally makes an underwritten offer.

Market flex

The syndicated loan and bond markets are converging, using similar techniques to achieve syndication. The loan market has borrowed something called the 'market flex technique' from the bond market – that is, the final pricing and structure are only determined after market soundings have been taken (rather than being fixed prior to syndication). This is often built into the term sheet (the memo the lender and borrower sign which highlights the terms to be put in the full loan agreement). This means the bank reserves the right to change the pricing and other key terms if necessary to syndicate the transaction successfully.

High-yield bond

If the bidder does decide to issue a bond it will usually be at a high rate of interest to attract investors and will be for a short term – six months or a year – with a view to refinancing on more preferable terms. By then the acquisition will have been made and integrated and the bidder's credit standing is likely to have risen, making any refinancing cheaper. This is an example of a bond being high-yield without necessarily being junk.

Covenant-lite loans

Cov-lite loans (mentioned above) were especially prevalent in acquisition finance. The covenants that were relaxed included the more subtle ones designed to ensure the borrower doesn't borrow too much from elsewhere (leverage covenant), maintains sufficient funds to cover interest payments (coverage covenant), doesn't give other lenders security over its assets (negative pledge covenant) and maintains certain margins (financial ratios).

Banks were especially happy to offer these if the loans were subsequently going to be securitised or the borrower's credit risk offset by a credit default derivative. Sounds familiar? Of course, the downside to lenders was that cov-lite loans were more difficult to declare in default when credit markets tightened.

A lot of acquisition finance loans ended up as CDOs or CLOs (**collateralised debt** or **loan obligations**), that is securitised issues backed by leveraged loans (Chapter 5). These enabled investment banks to package up issues that combined senior debt (which is the top slice, most likely to be repaid) with high-yield debt in such a way that the senior debt might not be paid off (amortised) during the life of the security at all, but only later.

This was especially popular in LBOs where businesses were being bought and the debt could be paid off by PIK certificates (**payment in kind** where fresh bonds or even shares are issued to refinance those about to expire) or even – shades of ninja loans here – '**pay if you can**' loans. All of this is fine of course just so long as it's done in a rising market where the debt is more than covered by an increase in value of the underlying business or collateral (the home in the case of sub-prime). Which it wasn't.

In fact PIKs, apart from receiving no cash interest, tended to be well removed from any assets in the underlying business. As cheap credit dried up in the credit crunch, loans that were meant to provide temporary acquisition finance couldn't be refinanced so banks were left holding the temporary loans – known as **hung bridges**.

4. ASSET FINANCE (FINANCE LEASING)

Asset finance is a banking industry in its own right. It's a way of funding the acquisition of big bits of kit like aircraft, ships and oil rigs by getting the bank to buy the asset and **lease** it to the company (called the **lessee**) that would otherwise have borrowed the money to buy it. The lease will be for the asset's **useful economic life** (say 15 years in the case of an airplane) over the course of which the company makes quarterly **rental** payments until the bank has recovered the cost of the asset and the implicit interest charge over the 15 years (a bit like a repayment mortgage to buy a house).

Asset finance (also called **equipment leasing** or **finance leasing**) is attractive because it can be cheaper for the company than simply borrowing the money and buying the asset itself. This is for two reasons:

- **Credit risk** – the bank actually owns the asset so it feels safer than if it had merely a security charge over the asset. This means that the deal has a lower credit risk which is reflected in a lower implicit interest rate.

- **Tax allowances** – most developed economies provide tax advantages to encourage industry to invest in plant and machinery and so remain competitive, so the bank gets these tax advantages and passes on part of the benefit to the lessee by way of reduced rentals.

The lease contains promises (**covenants**) by the lessee, such as:

- **Payment of rental** – to pay the amounts due under the lease when they fall due.

- **Maintain and repair the asset** – the bank may never see the asset and it certainly has no technical knowledge about it, so the lessee must bear the burden of maintaining it, not least to maintain the value of the bank's property.

- **Insure** – again, this is the lessee's duty, with the bank's interest noted on the policy so that if there is a payout the money goes to the bank as owner, not the lessee.

- **Not to sell or charge the asset** – so the lessee doesn't try to sell the asset or use it as security for another loan (in certain countries the bank will put a notice on the asset, for instance in the aircraft's cockpit, which serves as legal warning to third parties).

- **Not to jeopardise the availability of the tax breaks** – otherwise the lease is collapsed into a loan at a higher rate of interest to compensate the bank for its loss.

Breach of any of these covenants is an event of default which allows the bank to take back the asset and sell it to make good any loss.

What happens at the end of the lease

At the end of the **primary lease term** (that 15-year period in the case of a plane), the bank has been paid out (both interest and principal) and really has no further financial interest in the asset. One of two things can happen. Either the lessee can continue to lease the asset for a **secondary** term for a nominal amount (called a **peppercorn**); or the asset can be sold by the lessee acting as the bank's agent.

If the asset is sold, the bank will share the proceeds with the lessee, often allowing the lessee to keep as much as 90% of the proceeds. This is because whatever the asset is worth in the second-hand market will be a reflection of how well the lessee has maintained it, and the bank will have been paid out anyway. However, in certain countries the lessee can't keep all of the proceeds of sale otherwise it will be treated as the asset's owner and the tax breaks may be jeopardised.

Double dips

Finance leasing is a huge industry that spans the globe. Clever lawyers and bankers can structure deals so that the bank is treated as owner in one country and the lessee in another, so that two sets of tax allowances become available. This is called a **double dip** and is a battleground between tax authorities and bankers. As soon as one double dip opportunity is closed, the bankers and their lawyers discover another.

Finance lease v operating lease

Finance leases should not be confused with operating leases. If you rent a car when you go on holiday, that is an operating lease: it's not for the car's useful economic life and you certainly don't expect to maintain it or insure it. The hire company does that. In fact if the car goes wrong you just call them up for a replacement. And once you've returned it, the hire company leases it to another holiday-maker, and so on. Funnily enough, the hire company may itself be funding its fleet of hire cars by leasing them from a bank under a finance lease.

5. TRADE FINANCE

Asset finance is an international banking activity. So too is trade finance, one of the oldest. Trade finance is a way for manufacturers to export their goods knowing they will be paid by the importer who may be on the other side of the world, and someone they've never met but only corresponded with. It's linked to shipping (see Chapter 10).

A **bill of exchange** is a promise-to-pay under which a company (the buyer or **drawer**) agrees to pay the seller (**drawee**) a given sum of money at some point in the future – usually three months ahead. It's a sort of post-dated cheque. To make it more acceptable, bills of exchange were **endorsed** (guaranteed) by prominent merchants (which is how 'merchant banks' started).

Bills of exchange are similar to **bankers' acceptances**, which are also promises-to-pay issued by companies to banks in return for short-term loans. The banks resell these promises-to-pay in the market at a discount, but guarantee payment. **Discount houses** started by buying bills of exchange at a discount to face value. They funded their holdings of bills by borrowing from banks, one of the precursors of the money (short-term debt) markets (Chapter 4). These bills were either held to maturity or sold in the **discount market** and brokers began in order to match buyers and sellers in return for a commission.

This was how international trade developed – at a time before the telephone when exporters (sellers) and importers (buyers) on different sides of the world might not know each other and business was conducted by letter. The exporter wouldn't ship the goods without being sure of payment; the importer wouldn't pay for the goods in advance without sight of them or, at least, assurance as to their quality and proof of shipping and insurance. This is where trade finance houses and banks stepped in. The exporter would have the goods inspected by an independent third-party agency, would ship the goods, and insure them while in transit. It would deposit the bill of lading (shipping confirmation) and certificates of inspection and insurance with its bank.

À forfait market

The importer would deposit the purchase price with its bank which would issue a **letter of credit** (like a bill of exchange) payable in three months' time. This letter of credit could be sold in the market for immediate value at a discount (to allow for the three months before it could be presented for payment). This international market for letters of credit is called the *à forfait* **market** and is a form of factoring.

Factoring is where a bank buys a company's receivables for immediate cash. The receivables (invoices issued to customers) may take some time to be paid so the bank pays the company a percentage (say 90%) of their face value and the company gets immediate cashflow. A lot of businesses use factoring – it's a specialist area of banking in its own right – and is similar to a banking activity called **invoice discounting**.

6. PROJECT FINANCE

Project financings can be immensely complex deals that take years to come to fruition. They also tend to be highly international, bringing together lenders from developed economies to help construct infrastructure projects in emerging economies. What makes them different from standard commercial lending is that they are often **limited recourse** or **non-recourse** meaning that the lenders will not look to the borrower for repayment.

At first sight this looks crazy – banks not expecting repayment from the borrower – but in fact it means simply that they look to the proceeds of the project itself to repay the loan, not the borrowing vehicle set up to initiate the project. In a limited recourse financing the banks reserve the right to seek repayment from the borrower if they aren't repaid as originally intended out of the project's proceeds.

A typical project might be a dam that creates hydro-electric power in an emerging market, a typical natural resource project; or infrastructure improvements (e.g. ports, airports, roads, bridges and tunnels); or new industrial plant projects (such as paper mills and aluminium smelters). In fact the techniques to do this, which were exported from developed economies in the 1970s and 1980s, have in recent years been re-imported by those developed economies in order to build public sector projects such as hospitals, schools and roads, but with private sector financing. This keeps them off government balance sheets (like securitisation, another example of OBS – off balance sheet – financing) so reducing the apparent level of government borrowing.

Many of the countries in which project financings have traditionally taken place are poor credits. They may have borrowed extensively in the IFMs and even rescheduled (see sovereign lending box earlier). So project financing is a way of continuing to lend to such countries but without lending directly to the indebted government. In this sense project financings are often ring-fenced: the money must be used for the project and the project only.

Step-in rights

A major source of complexity in a project financing is the time it takes to come

Who is involved in a project financing

The parties include:

Project company, a special purpose vehicle which is the borrower, owns the project and will run it once it's built.

Project sponsors – these are the multinational companies keen to get the project off the ground, often the contractors that build the project or supply heavy plant (such as turbines) to it.

Banks funding the project.

The Government in whose country the project is being built, which will either buy the project's output, or guarantee the purchase of it.

Export credit agencies – every developed country has an ECA which helps to finance the sale of its exports to other markets. They include US Ex-Im (the US Export-Import Bank), JBIC (the Japanese equivalent) and Coface (France). ECAs will help companies from their country participate in major projects by providing soft loans to the project, that is, loans on preferential terms (called co-financings where funding comes from commercial banks as well as ECAs) and by providing insurance against political risk (the risk that the project may be nationalised or affected by political unrest). ECAs – from both the public and private sectors – are also heavily involved in trade finance (mentioned earlier) for which they also provide political risk insurance.

Multilateral lending agencies such as the World Bank, Asian Development Bank (ADB), and the European Bank for Reconstruction and Development (EBRD) which are like ECAs but have a supranational remit so will become involved in projects that offer major infrastructural benefits in emerging markets. Their involvement (by providing finance or guarantees) often encourages commercial banks to participate.

on stream. Funds will go into the project during its construction phase and will only be recouped during its operation. This means there is always a risk – compounded by the complexity of vast construction projects in markets not used to them – that the project will run out of money before it is completed.

So, during the project's construction, the banks have **step-in rights** to take over the project to ensure it is finished. Having lent money once they won't want to do it again so the funds necessary to take the project forward to completion will be provided under a **completion bond** (a form of insurance) provided by a **monoline insurer** (them again, this time specialising in construction projects). Completion bonds are also used in the movie business to ensure a film can be finished and distributed (movies can also be funded through finance leasing – see earlier).

Most projects are built on a **turn-key basis** – after the builder has finished, the project is ready to go (e.g. like starting a car). There will be a **long-**

stop date by which the project should be completed, and a **drop-dead date** by when the project must come on stream to meet the debt service and repayment projections.

Offtake or take-or-pay agreement

What makes a project economically viable is the cash it will generate once it comes on stream. This alone will service and repay the debt incurred to build it. The banks are therefore concerned with the risks of the cashflow being disrupted – they are lending on the cashflow of a future business that consists of a single income stream.

So the key to the financing is how the borrowing will be repaid. This is done through an **offtake** contract where the government agrees to buy the project's output (such as electricity) to distribute to its citizens. Not all projects have an offtake agreement – for instance a motorway operating on a toll basis simply earns money from the users, while an oil project will usually have its product sold in the open market.

But where the only customer will be the state or a state agency, the offtake arrangement will be critical since it will be the sole source of the project's income and, therefore, viability – which is why the agreement is also called a **take-or-pay** (meaning that the project output has to be paid for whether or not it is wanted or used).

The lending banks will be keen throughout to ensure that the funds are not diverted for other purposes and that the money earned by the project once it has come on stream is not diverted away from the lenders. This last is often achieved by having offshore **escrow accounts** (escrow is where a bank or trust company holds funds for the benefit of the parties to that agreement) into which the income generated by the project is paid and over which the banks have a charge, to ensure they are paid out first.

Project financing took root in developing economies to provide much-needed infrastructure. But, as mentioned, these techniques have been exported back to the developed economies from which they came and are now routinely used to build hospitals, schools, roads, bridges and so on but off the government's balance sheet. Macquarie Bank has been a pioneer in investing in infrastructure projects worldwide on an equity basis.

Some of the biggest project financings are taking place in the Gulf (especially Saudi Arabia) using Islamic banking principles, which takes us to...

7. SHARIA OR ISLAMIC BANKING

Sharia is the system of Islamic law which, when applied to banking, bans the payment and acceptance of interest (**riba**). Since 20% of the world's population is Muslim and less than 1% of securities are Sharia-compliant, the scope for growth should be huge.

Total assets held in Sharia-compliant products is still under $1 trillion although (1) Islamic banks have been around for over 30 years (Dubai Islamic Bank which began in 1975 is thought to have been the first), (2) they are present in over 75 countries and (3) the annual rate of growth has been 10–15% for a number of years. However, that figure has trebled in the last ten years. Some estimates put the expected figure at close to $2 trillion within the next five years.

One brake on growth is that all Sharia transactions have to be approved by a board of scholars. There are many such boards around the world but they do not all adopt the same approach. This is because Sharia law is, like any system of law based on religious principles, a matter of doctrinal interpretation.

Malaysia, for instance, which is a leading centre of Islamic banking, is regarded as liberal (which may explain in part its market position) – possibly too liberal according to scholars in, say, Saudi Arabia. (There is nothing new under the sun in finance. Jesus may have thrown the moneylenders out of the temple. But it was in sixteenth-century Venice that modern moneylenders are said to have charged interest for the first time, using a loophole in the Bible, specifically Deuteronomy Chapter 23, to do so.)

This lack of uniformity has hindered the development of global products as Muslims in different regions cannot always use products blessed under a different interpretation of Sharia. However, this is changing, partly because the most prominent scholars belong to several boards spanning the globe, partly because of the work of the Malaysia-based Islamic Financial Services Board, which seeks to set standards for the industry, and partly due to the work of the International Sharia Research Academy for Islamic Finance. As a result, more Islamic instruments are uniformly accepted than not.

The ban on riba – imposing an interest charge that doesn't vary despite fluctuations in the value of the underlying asset – works in tandem with a ban on speculation (**gharar**). This rules out highly leveraged debt, derivatives, insurance and gambling.

It follows that Islamic banks don't get involved in the money markets and wouldn't have touched sub-prime although, interestingly, asset-backed securitisations (because they are based on real, tangible assets – an important principle in Islamic banking) are acceptable.

So it's hard to see how the credit crunch could happen to Islamic banking. In fact there's an argument that Sharia-based principles will appeal to ethical investors who aren't Muslim since investments in alcohol, munitions, tobacco and casinos, among others, are not permitted.

Sharia financial centres

Dubai is the hub of the Islamic banking world, followed by Bahrain. Beyond the Gulf, Malaysia and Singapore are the largest centres for Sharia finance. Malaysia dominates the sukuk (bond) market, accounting for an estimated two-thirds of the worldwide market.

The Malaysia International Islamic Finance Centre (MIIFC) acts as a cluster: it attracts Islamic banks, offers a comprehensive regulatory and Sharia framework, operates Sharia-compliant markets, serves as a regional hub, and provides a pool of trained Islamic finance professionals. It operates alongside Malaysia's conventional financial markets and the governor of Malaysia's central bank is also the chair of the MIIFC.

In Europe, London is seen as the market leader, with the UK government announcing in 2006 that it wished to be seen as a gateway for Islamic trade and finance. By contrast, New York is a small and insignificant player, with, so far, little appetite from its investors for Sharia products. London claims to offer a substantial cluster of expertise in the City, with over 25 banks, ten fund managers and several international law firms with specialist Islamic banking divisions. The UK is the only Western country that features in the top ten list (9th) of countries with the largest amount of Sharia-compliant assets ($10 billion).

It's clear that Islamic banking isn't just for devout Muslims. It has moved firmly into the mainstream with international banks such as HSBC, Deutsche Bank and JPMorgan Chase entering what is seen as a new, huge and lucrative market. Sharia-compliant investment funds launched in the west totalled over 500 by 2007 (with over 150 new funds launched in that year alone) and this figure is predicted to double.

The 1997 Asia credit crisis spurred Malaysia to focus on Islamic banking (see box above). This credit crisis has had the same effect on Bahrain which wants to be the centre for the **sukuk** (bond) market. In 2007 sukuk issues reached almost $50 billion but collapsed in 2008. Gulf states, hardly in need of cash, issued billions of dollars of eurobonds in 2009. The thought is that they may do the same again, but this time with sukuk, to provide a deep enough market to encourage secondary market trading which in turn will encourage further primary market issues by sovereigns and corporates.

How Islamic banking works

Islamic finance is more akin to asset finance. Islamic banks don't make loans but fund assets for customers by buying the asset then selling (simultaneously or at a later date) to the customer for payment at a later date with a mark-up, which is the bank's return. This is called **murabaha** or a **mark-up transaction**.

There is in fact a finance leasing equivalent called **ijara** where the asset is funded by selling a rental participation to the investor who effectively buys a share in the underlying asset, with the rental return pegged to a benchmark.

Project financing is achieved through **istisna-ijara** financing (**istisna** is a form of deferred vendor financing – the seller provides the loan).

The underlying concept is one of the sharing of risk with the attendant sharing of profit. It follows that there isn't the equivalent of the general purpose loan where a company borrows the money without specifying what it will use it for; instead this is special-purpose funding where the amount in question is applied to a specific purpose.

Bonds

Bonds are banned because they pay interest so **sukuk** securities effectively act as securitisations, backed by an underlying asset in respect of which a return or cashflow is generated. The sukuk holder has a share in the underlying asset, receives an income from the asset and shares in the responsibility for its maintenance. Special purpose vehicles can be set up as intermediaries and structures vary according to the underlying financing, the most common being **ijara**, **mudaraba** and **musharaka**. Mudaraba and **musharaka sukuk** are partnership arrangements (see below under 'Equity investments').

Just like conventional bonds, sukuk can be issued by sovereigns, corporates and public bodies in any country – they are not confined to Islamic states. Japan and China have issued sukuk and Western governments – especially those with indigenous Islamic populations – have indicated an interest in doing so too.

Sukuk can be traded in the secondary market, although to date liquidity has suffered because most sukuk investors tend to buy-and-hold. The main ratings agencies all rate both corporate and sovereign sukuk.

One notable sukuk deal was signed in 2004 by Hanco, a Saudi Arabian car leasing and rental company. The deal entailed Hanco selling its entire fleet of vehicles to the intermediary bank, which then offered a stake in the fleet to investors. Hanco continued to act as manager of the fleet on investors' behalf, receiving management fees for operating and maintaining the fleet, collecting income and disposing of vehicles. The biggest sukuk issue (in 2006) was by Nakheel, the developer creating the artificial islands off Dubai's coast.

Derivatives and hedge funds

There are Sharia-compliant derivatives and hedge funds. This is despite the Sharia ban on excessive risk-taking or uncertainty (*gharar*) which would appear to prevent short selling and derivatives trading. But some of the more liberal interpretations of Sharia (see 'Sharia boards' below) argue that there may be circumstances where risk management tools are allowable: for genuine hedging (reducing risk) and where there is a clear link to an underlying asset.

This has given rise to a fledgling OTC Islamic derivatives market with the most common transactions being swaps and index-linked derivatives. The first Sharia-compliant hedge fund was launched in June 2008 by Barclays Capital and the Dubai government.

Equity investments

Equity investment is permitted – indeed it falls clearly within Sharia principles of risk- and reward-sharing, and venture capital and private equity lend themselves to Sharia financing. Understandably, Sharia proscribes investment in businesses that are contrary to Islamic principles which ban gambling, pornography, pork and alcohol. This has parallels in ethical or socially responsible investment elsewhere.

The two most common structures (both partnership arrangements) are mudaraba and musharaka sukuk. Mudaraba (trust financing) is similar to venture capital in that it is a partnership between an investor and an entrepreneur (**mudarib**). The profits resulting from the venture are distributed in agreed proportions. Musharaka has parallels with joint-venture investments. The bank and its client share the capital investment, and profits are divided according to a pre-arranged formula, while losses are borne in proportion to the original investment.

Because of the demand for Sharia-compliant equity investments, a number of Islamic market indices have been launched as benchmarks. The best known are the Dow Jones Islamic Market Index, launched in 1999, the FTSE Global Islamic Index series and the S&P Sharia Indices launched in 2006.

Sharia boards

Every transaction must be submitted to a board of religious scholars for approval. They will issue a **fatwa** (a religious edict) declaring the deal to be **halal** (lawful). Sharia regulations are open to interpretation and Sharia boards in Southeast Asian countries such as Malaysia are regarded as being less stringent than those in Middle Eastern countries such as Kuwait. So, for example, while it's clear that no Sharia board would approve an investment in a whiskey distillery, what about a hotel which has a bar? Some would say no; but others would approve. Equally, highly-leveraged deals would not find favour because of the excessive risk involved, but some Sharia boards allow investments in companies with a debt level of up to 30%.

Possibly the biggest challenge facing Islamic banking is a philosophical and ethical one. Under the Qur'an, is it enough to pursue profit without pursing ethical and societal ends too, such as the alleviation of poverty? In other words, must Islamic banking further philanthropic aims as well? Some argue that it must build a profitable global business first before being saddled with, and possibly shackled in its growth by, a social burden too. Which brings us neatly on to microfinance.

8. MICROFINANCE

Microfinance is the business of providing financial services to vast numbers of poor people in developing economies. **Microcredit** is the provision of tiny loans (**microloans**) to poor individuals to spur entrepreneurship. These individuals lack collateral, steady employment and a verifiable credit history and cannot meet even the most minimal qualifications to gain access to traditional financial services.

Microfinance has been a success story since starting in the 1970s, spearheaded by Grameen Bank in Bangladesh which over the last 25 years has lent almost $7 billion and whose founder, Muhammad Yunus, was awarded the Nobel Peace Prize in 2006. Microfinance was seen as the private sector successor to state-owned agricultural development banks. They had been present in developing countries from the 1950s, providing subsidised agricultural credit to small and marginal farmers in the hope of raising productivity and incomes. But they were branded a failure, often inadvertently undermining the development goals they were intended to serve.

During the 1980s, **microenterprise credit** concentrated on providing loans to poor women (considered a safer and more conscientious customer base than men) to invest in tiny businesses, enabling them to accumulate assets and raise household income and welfare.

There are over 4,000 **microfinance institutions** (MFIs) serving over 150 million poor people in 100 developing countries, with about $30 billion out on loan and $15 billion in deposits. Seven out of ten are in Asia and two out of ten in Latin America. The bulk of MFIs are found in India and Bangladesh (home to a third of the world's poorest people) but the top fifty MFIs are found in countries as diverse as Morocco, Ecuador, Ethiopia, Serbia, Bosnia and Herzegovina as well as Russia. The UN declared 2005 to be the International Year of Microcredit.

Challenges

The MFI industry faces challenges. The first is **outreach** – the ability of an MFI to reach poorer and more remote people. Grameen Bank was able to build its success by serving a tightly-knit population and initially required groups of borrowers to guarantee loans to their individual members. But while microfinance has achieved a great deal, especially in urban and near-urban areas and with entrepreneurial families, its progress in delivering financial services in less densely populated rural areas has been slow. There are still three to four billion people globally who are **unbanked**. Brazil is the success story, with 95,000 access points, through post offices, branch networks of big banks and kiosks at petrol stations and shops (the kiosks are part of an MFI called Lemon Bank).

Second is **sustainability** – the ability of MFIs to cover their costs, in particular the transaction costs of lending very small amounts to very many people. It's an issue faced by all retail commercial banks – the operating costs of maintaining customer accounts: there is a break-even point in providing loans or deposits below which banks lose money on each transaction they make. Poor people usually fall below it and this is compounded amongst thinly-spread rural populations where the costs of a rural branch network are prohibitive.

MFIs offset these by charging high rates of interest which can appear abusive, especially when the borrowers are poor. When Compartamos, a Mexican MFI, made its founders multimillionaires in its $467 million IPO in 2007 it was heavily criticised for its high rates of interest of 85% annualised. But microloans tend to be very short term. And lending small amounts of money is expensive. A $10 loan for three months that costs $1 in interest has an effective annual rate of 40%. The median interest rate for sustainable (that is, profitable) microfinance is about 25%. It may be high but it's better than moneylenders extorting many times that.

So high rates are necessary to enable MFIs to survive. It's why interest rate ceilings intended to reduce exploitative practices can actually hurt poor people by preventing MFIs from covering their costs, which in turn chokes

Social responsibilities

There has been criticism that microfinance institutions (MFIs) turn borrowers almost into indentured workers, selling crafts or agricultural produce through an organisation controlled by the lending MFI.

The desire of MFIs to help their borrowers diversify and increase their incomes has sparked this type of relationship in several countries, most notably Bangladesh, where hundreds of thousands of borrowers effectively work as wage labourers for the marketing subsidiaries of local MFIs. Critics maintain that there are few if any rules or standards governing working hours, holidays, working conditions, safety or child labour, and few inspection regimes to correct abuses.

The MFIs for their part argue that they are providing the very basics of economic existence, such as demand for goods, and the conditions – though no match for their Western counterparts – raise their workers' standards of living far above that of their non-working neighbours. BRAC (Bangladesh Rural Advancement Committee) provides education and health services in addition to being an MFI, and is often tagged the world's largest NGO (non-governmental organisation).

Indeed, microfinance programmes may even be doing social good. By providing access to financial services principally through women – making women responsible for loans, ensuring repayment through women, maintaining savings accounts for women, providing insurance cover through women – microfinance programmes have improved the status of women within the family and the community. In regions where their mobility is restricted, women have become more visible. They own assets, including land and housing, play a more prominent role in decision-making and there are even reports of declining levels of violence against women.

The real concern is that Western banks, spotting an opportunity, will rush in, flood MFIs with credit, seek to skim off a hefty return, and cause a credit crunch of a different order.

off the supply of credit. Annual interest rates that reach 25% or more allow for local inflation and the MFI's bad debt profile. Muhammad Yunus has recently made much of this point, arguing that MFIs that charge more than 15% above their long-term operating costs should be penalised.

Funnily enough, those most affected, the **microborrowers** themselves, are least concerned. They often prefer to stick with the moneylenders they are familiar with and are prepared to pay very high interest rates for services like quick loan disbursement, confidentiality and flexible repayment schedules. They don't always see lower interest rates as adequate compensation for the costs of attending meetings, attending training courses to qualify for disbursements, or making monthly collateral contributions. They also don't like being forced to pretend they are borrowing to start a business, when they often borrow for other reasons (such as paying for school fees, dealing with health costs or securing the family food supply).

Microfinance is attracting a flow of private sector money: private equity fund Sequoia and hedge fund Sandstone have stakes in SKS Microfinance, India's largest MFI; mutual funds – such as AXA World Fund, Dexia Micro-Credit Fund, BlueOrchard Debt Sub-Fund, MicroVest and Gray Ghost Microfinance – have attracted over $2 billion. Some provide a 3% return which currently is pretty good. Others, such as Truestone's Luxembourg-based fund, are more like hedge funds. It requires a minimum investment of $50,000, imposes a one-year lock-in, and aims for annual returns of up to 10% on a five- to seven-year horizon.

Securitisation has a role even here. Morgan Stanley has led two securitisations for BlueOrchard, BOLD 1 (in 2006) and BOLD 2 (2007) – BOLD stands for BlueOrchard Loans for Development – totalling $200 million. BOLD 2, the larger of the two, involved securitising a portfolio of unsecured loans to 20 different MFIs in 12 different countries. In 2006 BRAC (see 'Social responsibilities' box on previous page) securitised receivables worth $180 million.

But over half the $10 billion committed to MFIs in 2008 came at sub-market rates from donors such as aid and multilateral agencies (especially the International Finance Corp, part of the World Bank, the Dutch Development Finance Corp, and KfW Bankengruppe).

Financial systems

Of course, the costs of providing microfinance could be met, at least in part, from the provision of savings services to customers (remember, we're talking here about microfinance, not just microloans) – not least since the informal methods of saving open to microsavers (such as savings collectors) are very unsafe and lose them on average a quarter of what they save. But MFIs that take in deposits do need some degree of regulation.

Critics complain that the microcredit era which began in the 1970s has lost its momentum and is being replaced by a **financial systems** approach, with a move over the last 40 years from informal financial service providers (such as moneylenders and savings collectors) to member-owned organisations (such as credit unions) to the emergence of non-governmental organisations (NGOs) such as BRAC that provide financial services for the poor. In the 1990s, so the argument goes, many of these NGOs transformed themselves into formal financial institutions in order to access and on-lend client savings, so enhancing their outreach.

This helps explain the immense diversity of MFIs serving poor people in the developing world today and an increasing awareness of the diversity of financial services they need and the diverse settings in which they live and work.

Peer-to-peer platforms

But the slow progress in developing quality savings services for poor people has led to **peer-to-peer platforms** which expand microlending by sourcing funds from individual lenders in the developed world. The last five years have seen the launch of Kiva, MicroPlace and United Prosperity in the US, MYC4 (Denmark), Rang De and dhanaX (India), Veecus and Babyloan.org (France) and United Youth Development Organisation (UK) with just over $50 million channelled through them so far. For example, MicroPlace.com, owned by eBay, allows retail investors in the US to buy securities that are effectively securitised microloans. MicroPlace is tapping into the increasing desire among Western society for socially responsible investment. This can channel greater capital to microcredit.

However, the rate of capital flow into microfinance is a risk unless well managed. There are obstacles to building a sound commercial microfinance industry, such as inappropriate donor subsidies, poor regulation and supervision of deposit-taking MFIs (governments get twitchy when depositors' money is at issue, but the costs of regulation and compliance could derail MFIs); the fact that few MFIs meet the needs for savings, remittances or insurance; institutional inefficiencies and the need for more dissemination and adoption of rural, agricultural microfinance methodologies. However, the most pressing is probably limited management capacity in MFIs.

Those who feel that microfinance has deserted its origins are pioneering **social finance** and **impact investing** which seek to fund healthcare and basic needs such as clean water that are of direct help to the world's poorest people.

Pre-bankable

Owing to the widespread success of the microfinance movement, the traditional banking industry has begun to realise that microcredit borrowers should be more correctly categorised as **pre-bankable**. Seasoned observers have made the point that what small businesses in emerging markets need is microfinance rather than a local stock market (Chapter 2), something we'll come back to in Chapter 10. Microcredit is gaining credibility in mainstream finance: banks and other financial organisations are considering microcredit projects as a source of future growth.

After all, microfinance has been exported to the biggest financial market in the world. In the US, 37 million people (an eighth of the population) live below the poverty line. Grameen Bank opened in New York in April 2008. Yet, in the home of capitalism, some economists think that microloans may have less appeal in the US than elsewhere because those most in need think – just get this, coming from the country of capitalism – that it's too difficult to escape poverty through private enterprise.

This leads us on to the final section in this chapter – financial services for those at the opposite end of the social and economic spectrum: the very rich. If microfinance is new and for the masses, private banking is old and for the elite.

9. PRIVATE BANKING

You may be wondering why there's been nothing so far on **retail finance**. That's because retail finance – the provision of financial products from debit and credit cards and checking accounts to unsecured overdrafts, loans, mortgages and insurance – is almost by definition a local activity: people go to banks within their country. Occasionally a cross-border product – a mortgage denominated in another country's currency to enable people to buy holiday homes there – appears. But for the most part this sector of banking, though perhaps the biggest globally, is the most local and least international.

The most international part of retail finance is in fact private banking, a service provided to the rich (called **high-net-worth individuals** or **HNWIs**). It's actually an asset management service (see Chapter 7): managing HNWIs' portfolios for lucrative fees and in return providing upmarket loans, credit cards and banking facilities. The term 'private banking' conjures up small, select financial institutions furnished like gentlemen's clubs where obsequious bankers dressed like butlers speak in hushed, reverential tones to their clients and give them discreet access to safe deposit boxes held below in vaults.

This is still true – in part. Private banking is at one level ordinary retail finance but for the very rich or HNWIs. But because the rich have money, these HNWIs are really deposit-makers: in return for entrusting their wealth to a private bank (and often private banks are private in that they are privately owned or are the wholly-owned subsidiaries of publicly quoted banking groups) they expect a high degree of personalised service that extends beyond gold-plated checking accounts, debit and credit cards – retail finance with knobs on. They expect to be made to feel welcome and important. But, apart from that, the bulk of what they need by way of financial services is actually wealth management. So everything you learnt about investment management in Chapter 7 is relevant here. In fact, as much as one-third of the money invested in hedge funds comes from HNWIs.

Swiss discretion

Gold-plated retail finance, wealth management and tax minimisation, all carried out under a cloak of discretion in an environment that smacks of centuries of quiet and understated tradition: no wonder the heart of private banking is and remains Switzerland.

UBS is the leader in the field but wealth management – on the face of it a stable and consistent fee generator – is not always plain sailing. UBS decided in 2008 to withdraw its private banking business from the US following allegations from US regulators and tax authorities that it had colluded in shielding US citizens' income from US tax. This was a major blow for UBS: over a third of its profit comes from wealth management and a quarter of its staff are based in the US.

What was seen as a good banking fit – investment banking for its spectacular boom and busts and private banking for its steady fee-income – led big banks to move into the HNWI field. The thinking was that investment banking produced financial products that HNWIs could invest in. The first creates financial products and the second provides the buyers.

But this raises huge potential conflicts of interest – the investment banking side wins a mandate from an issuer and then stuffs its securities into the portfolios of the HNWI clients of the private banking arm. This is why some big banks have been selling off their private banking business to private banks like Lombard Odier, Pictet and Julius Baer (all Swiss). They in turn have been effectively recreating themselves as onshore private banks as Switzerland has moved away from majoring in bank secrecy (see Chapter 9).

For the future, Asia – as in many areas of the global economy and IFMs – is the place with the greatest potential for private banking, especially Islamic banking for Muslim HNWIs. There are over 350 million Muslims in the rapidly expanding and entrepreneurial economies of India, Indonesia and Malaysia. The small proportion that are or will become HNWIs represents a big slug of private banking business, and they are all keen to buy Sharia-compliant financial products. Malaysian banks, in particular, have been at the forefront of developing Sharia-compliant financial products for HNWIs.

Much private banking is carried on in offshore and low-tax IFCs – which are covered in the next chapter.

We can now see how commercial banking fits into the picture of the universal or conglomerate bank (see diagram below) which we'll also explore in Chapter 9.

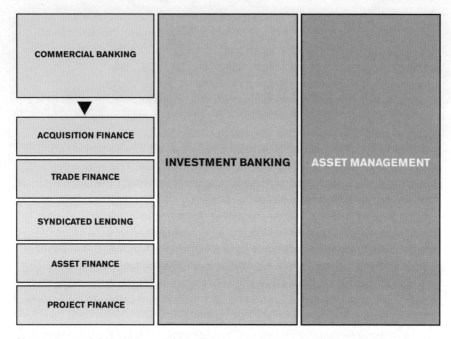

How commercial banking activities fit into the picture of a universal bank

HOW IT ALL CONNECTS

- Commercial banking was the poor cousin of investment banking (Chapters 3 and 4) but after the credit crunch looks much more attractive

- Securitisation (Chapter 5) is what made commercial bank loans tradable

- Private banking is really a form of asset management (Chapter 7)

- Securitisation (Chapter 5) is increasingly used to fund microfinance institutions

- Sovereign borrowers (Chapter 9) borrow from international syndicates of commercial banks

DAY TRIP TO
SINGAPORE

Singapore is the model for any new IFC bootstrapping itself into existence. It is a city-state – comparable to Monaco or Luxembourg – perched on the southern tip of the Malay Peninsula. It has a population of just under five million but its GDP of $240 billion translates into a respectable $50,000 per head, ranking it fourth in the world by purchasing power parity. A tightly-run republic since 1965, Singapore has built its position as an IFC carefully, piece by piece. Its GDP is ten times the level it was 30 years ago – earning it the label 'economic miracle'.

It is rated the easiest country in the world in which to do business and is regularly rated the third best IFC, after London and New York, beating Hong Kong into fourth spot. Singapore is cosmopolitan in every sense, with four official languages (Mandarin Chinese, Malay and Tamil, with English the most widely spoken) and a variety of religious faiths: Christians, Muslims, Taoists and Hindus, with Buddhists forming the bulk.

Singapore has next to no natural resources and – like London – owes its success to history and geographical location. The Port of Singapore is the busiest container terminal in the world (although Shanghai is catching up fast) and handles half the world's supply of crude oil. Originally a British colony, Singapore was a key *entrepôt* when Britain's trading empire was at its height, set at the cross-roads of the world's trading routes. Singapore is totally reliant on trade. Its exports are worth over 150% of its GDP. Like Hong Kong, but more visibly independent, Singapore is a conduit between established markets in Europe and North America and emerging markets in east Asia. It's in the same time zone as Beijing.

Compared with other east Asian cities – sprawling, noisy, dirty, gridlocked, choked by smog and blaring traffic – Singapore is clinical and antiseptic, small and compact, leafy, clean and efficient, which makes it feel European.

It feels like Asia's answer to Switzerland. The comparison is apt. It's the strategy Singapore has been pursuing with stealth over the last few years.

Singapore has always been a vibrant IFC – the Singapore stock exchange (SGX) has over 200 foreign listings on it, over half from China, and market capitalisation of $350 billion – not bad for a market that's comparatively recent. It's the world's fourth largest centre for currency trading and its futures market, Simex, was where trader Nick Leeson famously blew up Barings Bank in 1995. Singapore's professionals are clever and industrious and its accountants and lawyers among the best in Asia.

But the real story is that over the past few years Singapore has been turning itself into Asia's number one offshore financial centre (OFC – see Chapter 9) for wealth management, which is at the heart of private banking (see Chapter 8).

At a time when Switzerland has been dismantling bank secrecy laws (that allow bank account holders to remain completely anonymous and shield their financial details from tax authorities) Singapore has been doing the opposite. In 2000 it strengthened its bank secrecy laws so that they now offer depositors greater protection than Switzerland's. In 2004 it revised its trust laws – often at the heart of legal structures designed to protect assets from tax – and it has declined to sign up to the European Union's withholding tax and exchange of information directive.

Singapore now allows foreigners to buy land and become permanent residents if they satisfy certain wealth thresholds. Its tax regime exempts foreign investors from tax on gains, income or overseas income (Singapore only taxes income at source). Its top rate of income tax is around 20%, making it an attractive destination for those with high levels of income from elsewhere.

Above all, Singapore has made itself a beacon for fund management – the equivalent of Geneva or Boston – and has even set up a Wealth Management Institute to plug the gap in local professional money management talent. Although Switzerland is a long away ahead, Singapore is now number two in the world for private banking and holds about $300 billion or 5% of the world's private banking assets (Switzerland holds about $2 trillion, about a third).

In under ten years, private banking assets have multiplied six times and the number of private banks operating in Singapore (most of them subsidiaries of the world's biggest banks and the leading Swiss private banks) has more than doubled to over 50. Singapore is no longer seen as a safe Asian haven just for European HNWIs (high-net-worth individuals): the current inflows of HNWI assets are from India, China and Indonesia.

There is significant foreign investment (around US$300 billion) in Singapore, principally from the UK, followed by the Netherlands, the US, Japan, Switzerland and India.

The only risk is that financial services could outgrow the rest of the economy – as happened disastrously in Iceland (see Chapter 10) and which could to a lesser extent happen in London. A third of Singapore's working population is in professional or technical jobs, with about a quarter (the next largest) in clerical, service and sales-related jobs. Only one in five works in manufacturing, although Singapore has done well to attract multinationals in pharmaceuticals: GlaxoSmithKline, Pfizer and Merck all have production facilities in Singapore. Almost 70% of Singapore's GDP is made up of services, with manufacturing and construction making up the remainder.

Perhaps most significantly, Singapore is one of those countries with sovereign wealth funds, one of which (Temasek Holdings) is worth around $150 billion. One of its best investments has been an 18% stake in Standard Chartered, a UK bank prominent in east Asia that managed to avoid the worst excesses of the sub-prime credit crunch. Like Singapore itself.

Chapter 9

Offshore Financial Centres and Regulation

SPEED-READ SUMMARY

- Offshore financial centres (OFCs) are mainly former colonies (the majority of them British) that have found a living by offering low-tax havens for asset location

- Under prolonged international pressure, OFCs are shedding bank secrecy to prevent tax evasion

- Now, leading OFCs are specialising, for instance as centres of insurance or asset management

- Regulation focuses on banks, securities and insurance

- Regulation tends to be either rule based or principle based – the latter is becoming more prevalent

- Central banks are responsible for monetary policy which includes money supply, interest rates and volume of credit

- Central banks also generally supervise their national banking system and individual banks

- The biggest banks are involved in commercial banking, investment banking, asset management and bancassurance

---

I've already introduced you to one geography of IFCs that isn't just about London, New York, Tokyo and so on, and that was in the field of fund management (Chapter 7). Now we're going to visit another one: that of offshore financial centres (OFCs).

OFFSHORE FINANCIAL CENTRES (OFCs)

They're called OFCs because originally many really were offshore: Bermuda, Bahamas, Cayman Islands and so on – in fact these days any palm-fringed, sun-baked atoll that hasn't turned itself into an OFC has really missed a trick. But some aren't islands at all: Switzerland and Liechtenstein are landlocked.

Leading Offshore Financial Centres (islands and landlocked)	
Bahamas	Isle of Man
Bermuda	Liechtenstein
British Virgin Islands	Monaco
Cayman Islands	Switzerland
Channel Islands (Guernsey & Jersey)	Mauritius

Originally many of these were places where you could incorporate a company, vest the shares (bearer anyway) in a trust so no one knew who owned them, appoint a shadow board of directors made up of local lawyers and accountants (or even other companies) and open a local bank account with no questions asked and no tax payable, all evidenced by a thin file in a lawyer's office.

Local trust companies, law firms and accountants prospered mightily on the back of this prosaic business. Some islands – populated by more palm trees than people – were able to boast tens of thousands of companies with little more than brass plates to evidence them.

Life has moved on a little since then. What all OFCs share in common is: a financial and professional services infrastructure far greater than the needs of the local economy; plus a company registry for businesses that have no real physical presence there, but can claim legal establishment while actually operating elsewhere.

OFCs are able to do this because they have (1) the ability to make their own laws, which is what enables them to offer a no-tax or low-tax regime for those businesses registered there, (2) light regulation, (3) bank secrecy laws that allow local financial institutions to conceal the financial details and identities of customers from tax and other authorities in those countries where those customers are actually based and would normally be accountable and (4) legal structures based on trust law that enable the beneficial (that is, actual) ownership of financial assets to be hidden. They don't as a rule offer investor compensation schemes to protect against loss through local fraud or corruption. The cost of doing so would negate their low tax advantage.

In other words, if you're an individual or business with assets you want to shield from potential creditors, tax authorities or law enforcement agencies, stick them in an OFC.

No wonder the popular misconception of an OFC is of a place where despots of banana republics stash billions of dollars looted from their countries or criminals launder their fortunes. However, before becoming too hypocritical, it's worth making two points.

First, almost all OFCs of any note are former colonial possessions. In return for the colonial power's continued military protection, a system of law and tax breaks, these islands were able to forge their own futures without troubling the colonial overseer for continued financial support. As one senior figure from an OFC has said: 'How else were we supposed to earn a living?'

Second, many of the low- or no-tax breaks originally offered only by OFCs have been copied or utilised by at least some leading IFCs – the most obvious being London to attract, amongst others, the economic cluster of Greek shipowning dynasties (subsequently put at risk by personal tax hikes).

And I say 'popular misconception' because this has all begun to change over the last few years in response to a changing morality in the financial markets.

International pressure

In 1998 the OECD (the Organisation for Economic Cooperation and Development, a club of 30 developed economies) published a seminal paper called 'Harmful Tax Competition: An Emerging Global Issue'. At a time when estimates put assets vested in OFCs at over $6 trillion, the OECD criticised OFCs for their bank secrecy laws (allowing local banks to protect the secrecy of depositors' financial affairs even where criminal activity or tax evasion was alleged elsewhere).

Since then the intergovernmental Financial Action Task Force (FATF) on money laundering and terrorism has taken up the cause. And, most recently, the G20 (the group of leading global economies) declared at a summit in 2009 that 'the era of bank secrecy is over' and said it was committed to helping developing countries benefit from 'a new cooperative tax environment'.

Tax is a central issue. Tax bodies and professionals have argued for years that tax revenues diverted to OFCs from poor countries would, if retained by those countries, do far more for their development and their people's well-being than all of the developed world's aid programmes put together.

The World Bank estimates that cross-border flows from criminal activity, corruption, capital flight and tax evasion come to over $1 trillion a year, half of which comes from developing economies or transitional economies (moving from planned to market). Yet aid programmes amount to just $100 billion – a tenth of that – a year.

Both the OECD and FATF have maintained blacklists of OFCs that refuse to share information with other countries. The OECD has been happy to transfer OFCs to its white list if they enter into TIEAs (tax information exchange agreements) with a dozen countries. TIEAs with the Nordic block have been popular – you get seven of the 12 required TIEAs in one go. But these TIEAs only entitle the counterpart country to ask questions in relation to a named account at a named bank. In other words, the tax authorities have to be able to name their man and his bank to get the relevant financial details. Big deal.

The Cayman Islands, for one, has opted for automatic exchange – for example, it routinely reports income from savings accounts to the relevant EU country where the account owner is a citizen. Critics say the OECD and FATF have been too soft. The OECD has removed all but three OFCs – Liechtenstein, Andorra and Monaco – from its blacklist of uncooperative tax havens, while FATF has removed them all.

As attitudes harden, it becomes a no-win situation for OFCs. If they don't clean up, they will lose business. But if some reform too quickly, they will lose business to other OFCs that move more slowly, such as Liechtenstein and Switzerland. The US is closing loopholes that allow US companies to use OFCs to avoid tax. Bermuda has seen companies quit, including management consultancy Accenture, for reputational reasons. Some newly nationalised banks may sell off private banking operations because of political pressure on bank secrecy. AIG sold its Zurich-based private bank in February 2009.

The more sophisticated, self-respecting OFCs have moved with the times. They've renounced bank secrecy laws. They've set up regulatory bodies to vet the quality of the business they attract. They've bowed to pressure from the OECD and others to share information and be more transparent. And these measures are beginning to work.

Indeed, a number of OFCs resent being called offshore financial centres at all and prefer being known as international financial centres (IFCs), like London, New York and so on. In fact they argue that London is as much an OFC as they are since by some standards it is a low-tax haven, deliberately made so by the UK government to attract and retain wealthy foreigners as residents on the basis that they bring their business and employment with them. The Netherlands, for example, has for many years encouraged multinationals to put a Dutch holding company at the heart of their European operations because of the favourable tax treatment they obtain.

Specialisation by OFCs

Although all OFCs continue to cater for rich individuals (see private banking in Chapter 8), the leading OFCs have made a name for themselves in particular financial niches, for example:

- Attracting multinational companies wishing to locate their corporate place of registration in a low-tax environment to increase the fiscal efficiency of their worldwide operations.

- The establishment of special purpose vehicles (SPVs) as off-the-shelf companies with no assets (shell companies) for securitisations and repackagings – the reason for locating SPVs in no-tax jurisdictions is to avoid any tax take ('fiscal drag') on wafer thin cashflows circulating around complex legal structures which would otherwise make these structures unprofitable.

- Investment management – Jersey has an extensive regime of different corporate and limited partnership vehicles and different types of fund depending on who they are being sold to, such as 'very private', 'expert', 'listed', 'unregulated' – vetted by the Jersey Financial Services Commission, a mini-SEC. Jersey is the first UK dependency to introduce foundations, a concept familiar in Asia and the Middle East, as an alternative to trusts.

- Hedge funds – the Cayman Islands are the offshore capital of the hedge fund industry: there are 8,000 registered there (like the Bahamas and

Trust us

OFCs and those who work in them have often been (unfairly) pilloried: OFCs for being attractive locations able to offer low or no tax environments, often sheltering under the protection of a former colonial power but free to make their own laws; and those who work in them for claiming to be professionals of specialist expertise when all they do is incorporate companies, hold 'board meetings' and establish trusts – all pretty routine stuff. And be paid royally for it. Maybe this is just the economics of envy, but onshore IFCs resent the unfair competition OFCs provide. The following will give you an idea of what they resent.

In the 1980s OFCs developed the international business corporation (IBC): basically a company registered in an OFC but which, provided it did business elsewhere, was subject to no local taxes, filing requirements or reporting (no need to keep a register of shareholders) and which needed just one director and shareholder (which in each case could be another IBC). In other words IBCs were invisible but for their name. The OECD has led moves to persuade some OFCs to drop IBCs.

Another aspect of OFCs that onshore IFCs resent is the manipulation of trust law. A trust is a vehicle to which an individual (a settlor) transfers property for the benefit of others (beneficiaries).

It's often used in families to transfer assets to the next generation pending their coming of age. The point of a trust is that the settlor loses control over the assets – because they are no longer his or hers – and so, among other things, is not subject to tax on them. But what if you could use a trust to lose ownership for tax purposes but retain control for your purposes?

This is what a number of OFCs have done. Because at law there has always been uncertainty over the degree of control a settlor can assert before the trust is regarded as a sham, settlors have been careful not to interfere in the running of trusts they've created. But some OFCs have gone so far as to pass legislation that specifies what a settlor can and can't do, and barring beneficiaries from enforcing a trust in their favour. The result is a negation of what trusts are meant to be.

It's not all bad. A more recent development is that of segregated account companies known as cells. Each cell is like a separate company with its own accounts, assets and liabilities but the whole is run as a single company, reducing the need for separate sets of directors and cutting back on administration and filing costs. Investment managers can use cells to keep separate client accounts under one umbrella. Insurance companies that want to pool their reinsurance in what is called a reinsurance captive can club together using a cell company – one cell per participating insurer.

Bermuda, the Cayman Islands benefit from being a quick plane flight away from New York). The funds are, of course, managed from New York and London.

- Reinsurance captives, that is, offshore reinsurers set up by groups of insurers or reinsurers to enable group members to self-insure by keeping the risk (and the premium) within the group, but in a separate offshore entity – especially useful at times when market rates are high. Bermuda has the world's biggest cluster of reinsurance companies and the second biggest of captives – 1500 insurance and reinsurance companies (Cayman comes second with 900).

- Shipping – some OFCs (BVI, Liberia and Panama) offer flags of convenience, that is, ship registries where the costs of registering a ship are low and the costs of compliance (such as safety standards for crew) are less demanding than in onshore registries.

A number of OFCs, such as Bermuda and the Cayman Islands, have set up stock exchanges to attract the listing of funds, debt and derivatives issues, as well as multinationals wishing to add a further listing. Bermuda's, which trades electronically, has over 500 listed companies with a market

---

Central banks, monetary policy and Basel 2

Central banks (CBs) are part of government. They regulate banks in their country, act as lender of last resort (that is, bail out any banks that are bust to ensure the integrity of the financial system), often borrow on behalf of the government and set interest rate policy (see Chapter 4).

Every country has a central bank whose role can include any or all of the following:
- Issuing its country's **money supply** (notes and coins)
- Supervising the national financial system (**macroprudential supervision**)
- Supervising individual banks (**microprudential supervision**) to ensure they maintain sufficient **regulatory capital** (in keeping with

local requirements as well as international requirements such as 'Basel 2' – see below)
- Managing the country's gold and currency **reserves** (which can be used to influence the country's **exchange rate**)
- Acting as **banker to the government, managing the national debt** and **arranging government bond issues**
- Acting as banker to individual banks as the **lender of last resort**: if a bank hasn't enough cash to meet customers' withdrawals of deposits, the central bank will supply cash to the banking system to relieve the liquidity shortage.

In particular, CBs are often put in charge of their country's **monetary policy** which is the control of money variables such as interest rates, ⇨

⇨ money supply and the volume of credit in the economy. Typically, a CB will have control of the country's **interest rates** as a means of **controlling inflation** (see Chapter 4) which it will do through **money market operations**.

It will buy in government bills and bonds to increase liquidity and reduce interest rates. It will sell them to soak up liquidity and increase rates. In normal times this is sufficient to influence interest rates on much longer term instruments, from 12-month corporate loans to 30-year mortgages. In the recent credit crunch this didn't happen as money markets froze up so CBs moved into longer-term markets – lending to banks for longer periods and extending guarantees of longer than a week. CBs don't like doing this because it could saddle the government with long-term liabilities – as indeed it did when ultimately governments had to take banks over (see Chapter 5).

CBs have their own central bank – the Bank for International Settlements in Basel – through which they agree on capital adequacy requirements (how much cash banks have to retain as their capital cushion against depositor redemptions) which were revised in 'Basel 2' to include risk weightings for the different assets banks hold (part of the macro- and microprudential supervision mentioned above).

Note that **insurance** tends to be regulated separately. In the US there are state insurance commissioners. The same is true of **securities regulation**, the main purpose of which is the protection of the investing public. And **deposit insurance** (part of bank regulation but to protect others from banks) can be provided by the central bank (as lender of last resort) or can be offered by a separately constituted government body, as in the US (the Federal Deposit Insurance Corporation or FDIC).

capitalisation of $200 billion: 20% are hedge funds; 60% are offshore funds and alternative investment structures such as SPVs and SIVs.

Leading OFCs are now able to claim genuine specialist expertise. Of course, there will always be shady OFCs out there: the more shady, the less salubrious the customers they attract. As one expert in OFCs told me: 'There are some OFCs where you can hide your money so well that even you won't be able to find it again.'

Discussion of OFCs and their increasing regulation brings us to the topic of regulation of the IFMs in general.

THE ROLE OF REGULATORS

The pressure put on OFCs by leading economies is one example of intergovernmental cooperation. This is true of regulation in general as the

IFMs and those who operate in them straddle national boundaries. Regulation can appear complex – multiple agencies with different acronyms and overlapping jurisdictions – and it doesn't always work. But in essence it's simple. It has two purposes:

(1) Protecting financial institutions from themselves and each other – this is about making sure that a bank or insurance company doesn't take on so much risk that it endangers itself or its counterparties in the IFMs otherwise there's a risk that the financial system will collapse like a row of dominoes. This is what bank and insurance regulation is about. The credit crunch showed that this aspect of IFM regulation was flawed. Banks and insurers went bust unexpectedly.

(2) Protecting others from financial institutions – this is about making sure that investors and buyers of retail financial products are not misled or defrauded. This is what the bulk of securities regulation is about. Insurance regulation can overlap with this where it extends to the products and policies that insurers sell. Banking regulation extends to this where it provides for deposit protection and compensation. The purpose of this is to encourage people to save, to put their cash in banks, and to safeguard themselves through insurance.

The overall objective is to preserve the integrity of the financial system. Governments need an efficient financial services system in which people have confidence and which:

■ Provides citizens with useful retail financial products encouraging:

- ■ Upwards social mobility
- ■ Acquisition of their principal domestic residence
- ■ Self-help financially (savings)
- ■ A sense of safety and security (insurance)

■ Enables capital to be channelled to the most deserving businesses

■ Costs governments as little as possible while encouraging a buoyant economy in which tax receipts are maximised

■ Enables governments to borrow cheaply

■ Enables inflation to be kept in check

Every IFM will have one (possibly more – which can create confusion) regulatory body operating in each of the three fields of **banking**, **insurance** and **securities**. As the financial institutions they regulate straddle sectors and geographies, so the matrix of supervision at a **sectoral**, **national** and **international** level becomes more complex, the need for coordination, communication and common standards increases, as does the risk that something will fall through the cracks.

Global regulation and supervision

The national supervisors come together in supranational bodies to share information and pool experiences:

- IOSCO (International Organisation of Securities Commissions) for securities

- Bank for International Settlements, based in Basel and known as the central banks' central bank, for banking (the latest Basel Accord, known as 'Basel 2', sets out what a bank's regulatory capital should be and is tied to how risky its loans and assets are)

- The International Association of Insurance Supervisors (and in particular its Insurance Core Principles) for insurance.

Research by Martin Cihák and Alexander Tieman, published in an August 2008 IMF working paper on global financial regulation, led them to conclude that ongoing financial globalisation makes individual country systems much more closely linked, and increases the need for effective cooperation between regulators within and across national boundaries. Building on previous research published in IMF working papers, they identified four key areas of focus and a further four key areas in which regulators could do better (below).

The four areas of regulatory focus

Regulatory governance	Objectives of regulation Independence and adequate resources Enforcement powers and capabilities Clarity and transparency of regulatory process External participation
Prudential framework	Risk management Risk concentration Capital requirements Corporate governance Internal controls
Regulatory practices	Group-wide supervision Monitoring and on-site inspection Reporting to supervisors Enforcement Cooperation and information sharing Confidentiality Licensing, ownership, corporate control Qualifications
Financial integrity and safety nets	Markets (integrity, financial crime) Customer protection and compensation Information, disclosure, transparency

Key areas where regulators could do better

Banking	Supervision of all risks Connected lending Money laundering Supervisory objectives, powers, resources Remedial measures Consolidated supervision
Insurance	Market conduct issues Internal controls Derivatives and off-balance-sheet items Organisation of supervisor Corporate governance Asset management Licensing Cross-border business operations
Securities	Enforcement powers, compliance programmes Capital and other prudential requirements Powers, resources and capacity Operational independence, accountability

The key failing of the pre-credit crunch regulatory environment was its focus on individual institutions (known as **microprudential supervision**): if each individual institution was OK, then regulators believed that the sanctity of the overall financial system followed. But this completely ignored **systemic risk**. Post credit crunch the talk is of macroprudential supervision which takes into account the wellbeing of the overall financial system in the context of where the world is in its economic cycle: the credit crunch brought to an end an unprecedented bull market in which the price of assets such as houses and securities had risen inexorably and had become grossly inflated (known as an **asset bubble**).

Regulators can be fiercely national and protectionist, partly because they look after their own, but mainly because if anything goes wrong in their country, then their government will have to meet the cost of any fraud, default or bailout.

Regulatory arbitrage

This can lead to turf wars which players in the IFMs can exploit by using the less-regulated of two markets (this is called **regulatory arbitrage** – locating your operations to minimise the level of regulation to which they are subject). Basel 1 came about because Japan went from having one bank in the global top ten in 1980 to nine by the end of the decade, made possible because of its more generous view of bank regulatory capital which gave its banks an unfair advantage (according to US and European competitors). Basel 1 was an agreed approach to bank regulatory capital that redressed this imbalance.

More recently, the US found itself disadvantaged because of the legislation (Sarbanes-Oxley, known as 'SOX') which it introduced post-Enron. This put New York at a competitive disadvantage and drove prospective listings by foreign companies from the NYSE to the LSE in London.

Now London for its part is being criticised because the UK switched banking supervision from being the sole responsibility of the UK's central bank, the Bank of England, and shared the job out so that the Financial Services Authority (the UK's SEC) and the government itself were also involved. Result: Northern Rock went bust with queues of depositors lined up around the block, a scene not seen in the UK since 1866 and the spectacular failure of the UK's then biggest bank Overend Gurney. Observers suspect this may have given the initiative to the EU to regulate for all European banks. Certainly, the EU is keen to regulate hedge funds and private equity players through its Alternative Investment Fund Managers Directive.

Rule-based v principle-based regulation

The way in which regulation can be undertaken falls broadly into one of two categories: **rule-based** or **principle-based**.

Rule-based is simply an extensive set of detailed rules with which an institution either complies or doesn't. This approach provides certainty and avoids the application of discretion on the part of the regulator. But it can be over-prescriptive and formulaic and lead to an inflexible tick-box approach which achieves nothing. Rule-based regulation can also be expensive to implement and supervise in terms of low-level administrative cost. Innovation is stifled because it cannot be accommodated within the existing rule framework.

Principle-based regulation (PBR) involves less detailed prescription of what is right and wrong, less codification and less rigidity of rule book interpretation, as well as less volume of actual regulation. It is said to encourage innovation and competition. PBR sets out the broad principles on which markets should function and is 'based on getting the regulated to adhere to the spirit of the regulation while a rule-based approach is intent on the regulated obeying the letter of the regulation' (according to the National Stock Exchange of India which is moving from a rule-based approach towards PBR as pioneered by the UK in 1997).

Of crooks and conmen

IFMs attract crooks because – as bank robbers are fondly quoted as saying – that's where the money is. Every year there are stories about individual rogue traders ripping off their bank. These tend to be contained.

More worrying are the frauds that wreck the lives of many people. Charges levelled by the US against Sir Charles Stanford over an alleged $8 billion fraud, if proved, will wreck the island of Antigua and the livelihood of its people since he controls most of Antigua's economy, including its largest bank.

Bernard Madoff was jailed in 2009 for 150 years for defrauding his clients of $50 billion – even by today's standards a staggering amount of money. But then he had been doing it for decades, and was only caught out when the credit crunch increased the number of investors wanting out. Madoff's fraud, like most, was a **Ponzi scheme** (taking in money from new investors and using it to pay out above-market returns to old investors) named after Charles Ponzi who did this in the 1920s. Perhaps most shocking of all, Madoff was a former chairman of NASDAQ.

Madoff was offering consistent returns of 10%. Typical scams involve the promise of, on the one hand, investment in safe instruments such as government securities with, on the other, a level of return which such safe investments simply can't generate. It takes a sucker to be suckered. The only extraordinary thing is how often governments have been forced to bail out victims of their own greed.

A variation on the Ponzi is the **pyramid scheme** where current investors are incentivised to find new ones whose money effectively pays them out (like a chain letter). These were popular in the 1990s in former east European countries where free markets were introduced without sufficient protection for the public. Romanian savers lost about $1 billion between 1991 and 1994 in the Caritas scheme. Two-thirds of the Albanian population invested in pyramid savings plans that collapsed in 1997, prompting the overthrow of the government and intervention by the IMF.

Then there are professional frauds endemic to IFMs. These include **insider dealing** or **insider trading** – buying or selling of securities on the basis of information that isn't in the public domain. By definition this is a crime carried out by market professionals, either directly or by tipping off others who act on the information. It occurs most often prior to the announcement of an M&A deal: since the bidder is going to want the target's shares, these will go up in price as soon the bid is announced; a price spike just prior to the announcement in expectation of this is the tell-tale smoking gun.

Stock exchanges are as diligent in pursuing insiders as the authorities for reputational reasons – investors won't want to use a market where share prices are adversely affected by insider trading. Galleon, the hedge fund accused of insider dealing, was caught out by the NYSE's systems. However, convictions are hard to achieve since the passing on of tips doesn't leave much of an evidential trail. And in ⇨

⇨ some IFCs it's only recently been made a crime (Hong Kong, for instance, since 2003).

Of course, there are plenty of other professional scams but these attract less interest because they are more technical and less brazen. They include **front running** (where a broker trades for its own account before filling a client's order, knowing that the client's order will move the market in its favour), **market timing** and **late-trading**. The last two occur where a mutual fund allows favoured investors (usually market traders) to buy units at prices below their actual value, based on valuations of the underlying assets that are no longer current. These hit the headlines in New York in 2003 involving over 20 funds managing over a fifth of US mutual fund assets. Shockingly, the scams unearthed included webs of collusion where investors (often hedge funds) left 'sticky assets' in one fund in return for beneficial trading in another, related fund.

More prosaic are **pump and dump** strategies (also known as **stock ramping**) where positive, but false, rumours are spread about a stock which can then be sold at a profit once the price has risen in response to the rumours.

THE ANATOMY OF A BIG BANK

What the credit crunch pointed up is the failure of regulators at both a national and international level to have a sufficient grip on what big banks do. We saw in Chapter 3 how the division between investment and commercial banks through Glass-Steagall in the biggest market of all (the US) was eroded and then swept away. We also saw in Chapter 3 what investment banking is. We saw in Chapter 7 how banks have moved into asset management and bancassurance and in Chapter 8 what commercial banking comprises.

Put these together and you have massive financial institutions which as commercial banks take in deposits from the public and as investment banks take enormous own-account risks with their capital. In many respects big banks these days are accidents waiting to happen.

They also benefit from the notion that they are too big to be allowed to fail without jeopardising the sanctity of the world's entire financial system. This leads to moral hazard: enormous risks being taken in the certain knowledge that if they go wrong, the government will step in. This is what led to the international condemnation of the bank bonus culture: profits are privatised (pocketed by the bankers) and losses socialised (parked with the taxpayer). There is talk now not just of limiting bank bonuses, but of breaking up big banks – a return to Glass-Steagall perhaps.

But when you look inside a big bank you can see how challenging it is for regulators to get an accurate picture of what is going on. You'll recall the division of a big bank's operations into three:

COMMERCIAL BANKING	INVESTMENT BANKING	ASSET MANAGEMENT

COMMERCIAL BANKING

Under commercial banking we have acquisition finance, trade finance, syndicated lending, asset finance and project finance.

ACQUISITION FINANCE

TRADE FINANCE

SYNDICATED LENDING

ASSET FINANCE

PROJECT FINANCE

Then under investment banking we have corporate finance (advising companies on IPOs and M&A, the way the old UK merchant banks did), we have equity and bond origination which is primary market activity, then we have secondary market trading and market making in those securities.

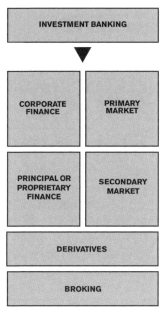

We also have banks using their own capital to buy and sell (including private equity activity) under principal or proprietary finance. Then we have anything to do with OTC derivatives. Any of these trading activities that are done for clients comes under broking.

Finally, on the right we have asset management, which is made up of asset management itself, custody services for institutional investors, and bancassurance, including insurance and pension products.

Which, when you put it all together (and make the connection between lending and acquisition finance and derivatives and the prime brokerage the bank provides to hedge funds), leads to this:

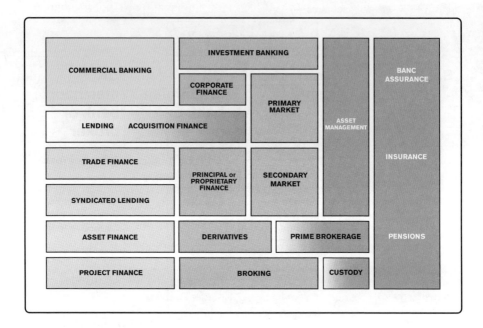

No wonder banks are hard to supervise – and this schematic is a simple, one-dimensional picture which fails to capture the extent of their risks, exposures and liabilities which are dynamic, changing from moment to moment all the time, depending on the time zone, the IFC, and where trading has propelled each IFM at that particular moment.

What the biggest banks do: everything

The world's major banks combine commercial and investment banking, such as:

- taking in deposits, borrowing on the interbank market and lending

- originating and trading securities, both bonds (debt) and shares (equity)

- market-making (keeping and trading an inventory of securities)

- broking (dealing in securities with and on behalf of investors)

- using their own equity to invest in and buy and sell businesses and assets (proprietary trading and principal finance)

Of these activities, the first is commercial banking and the other four are investment banking activities, involving trading of one sort or another. It is trading that has come to typify banking activities over the last two decades.

The following shows how some of the world's biggest banks got to where they are:

Bank	Commercial bank	US investment bank or broker	UK merchant bank or broker
Citigroup	Citibank	Salomon Brothers Smith Barney	Schroders (part)
JPMorgan Chase	JPMorgan Chase Manhattan (inc Manufacturers Hanover and Chemical Bank)	Bear Stearns	Robert Fleming Schroders (part) Cazenove (part)
UBS (Union Bank of Switzerland)	Swiss Bank Corp	PaineWebber Kidder Peabody	SG Warburg
Deutsche Bank	Deutsche Bankers Trust	Alex Brown	Morgan Grenfell Phillips & Drew
HSBC (originally Hongkong and Shanghai Banking Corporation)	Midland (UK)		Samuel Montagu James Capel

We saw how banks – not hedge funds or private equity funds, surprisingly – caused the credit crunch (in Chapter 5). Now in Chapter 10 we'll see how concerted action on the part of governments bailed them out and averted global financial destruction.

But before that we'll just pop over to Dubai, a dramatic example of how a financial centre can turn itself from an OFC mirage into an IFC oasis (and back again, depending on the outcome of its 2009 default).

HOW IT ALL CONNECTS

- Much private banking (Chapter 8) is provided offshore

- Hedge funds (Chapter 7) are often registered in OFCs for tax and regulatory reasons

- Regulation of the securities ties in with the in-house regulation stock exchanges undertake to reassure their investors that they are level playing fields (Chapter 2)

- A lot of the SPVs used in securitisations and CDOs (Chapter 5) are incorporated in OFCs

- Credit default derivatives (Chapter 6) that caused so much havoc in the financial meltdown may be commoditised and moved on-exchange to reduce their attraction in the OTC market by reducing the margins CDS sellers can generate

- Glass-Steagall was introduced in the 1930s to prevent commercial banks from speculating in securities (Chapter 3) – might this division be reintroduced?

- This time round it's been commercial banks (Chapter 8) backed by government-guaranteed deposit insurance that have emerged the stronger

- Much of the world's shipping (Chapter 10) is registered offshore under what are called 'flags of convenience'

- Securitisation (Chapter 5) is being used to securitise insurance liabilities

- Links between China (Chapter 10) and the Bahamas: Chinese conglomerate Hutchison Whampoa has invested over $1 billion in the Bahamas, including the development of deepwater and container ports

DAY TRIP TO
DUBAI

It is incredible, extraordinary: a city built on, well, sand. If you start from nothing you can build whatever you like.

Dubai is the way you'd create a city from scratch. Everything about Dubai is larger than life, from the world's tallest building, the world's largest airport (Al Maktoum International), the world's largest man-made port (Jebel Ali) and one of the world's largest free zones. Dubai is home to Palm Deira island – visible from space as a palm frond built in the sea – and World, a man-made archipelago of islands in the shape of, well, the world. Yet it has a population of less than two million, almost a fifth of whom are transient workers required to leave within a month of being out of work, as many have had to do recently.

Dubai's economy (like that of the United Arab Emirates more generally – Dubai is one of the UAE's seven emirates) was traditionally dependent on oil, which is now in Dubai's case all but exhausted. But it diversified. Funds from the oil industry were, under the guidance of Dubai's first Emir, ploughed into creating the huge man-made port (owned by Dubai World, one of three government-controlled holding corporations) and then more widely into transforming Dubai into a centre for global business.

Dubai's main economic activity takes place in several zones including the Dubai International Financial Centre (DIFC), Jafza and Dubai Internet City (a centre for internet-based and telecommunications businesses) among others.

The DIFC is a state within a state. It is run by the DIFC Authority, has its own legal system (based on common law countries like the UK, US, Australia and Hong Kong), is administered by the DIFC Judicial Authority which is headed by a former UK judge, and has its own regulatory body, DIFC Financial Services Authority. Foreign banks are welcome but can only operate in the DIFC: doing business outside the DIFC is banned. If you trespass outside, local law applies. It is completely different.

Separate licences are available for specific IFM activities which will be familiar to you now: banking services (investment banking, corporate banking and private banking); capital markets (equity, debt instruments, derivatives and commodity trading); asset management and fund registration; insurance and reinsurance; Islamic finance (expected to be a major source of growth since the UAE is predominantly Muslim); and professional service providers (law, accounting, etc).

Locating in the DIFC attracts a number of benefits: 100% foreign ownership is allowed (outside the DIFC, only 49% ownership is permitted); there is no tax of any kind levied; it's a US dollar denominated environment (the local currency, the UAE dirham, is pegged to the dollar); there are no currency or capital transfer restrictions; and the artificially created legal system will be instantly recognisable to any international financier and is written in plain English. Over 50 banks are present in the DIFC, over half foreign-owned. DIFC's aim is to quadruple the financial services sector's contribution to Dubai's GDP by 2015.

You can also list on NASDAQ Dubai, the local stock exchange, which was launched in 2004 and has almost 800 companies already listed on it. NASDAQ Dubai (formerly the Dubai International Financial Exchange) began trading in 2005. It was one of the first international stock exchanges to bridge between western Europe and east Asia and is situated in the DIFC. In 2006 the Dubai Ports, Customs and Free Zone Corporation (PCFC) listed a $3.5 billion sukuk (Islamic bond – see Chapter 8), the largest Islamic bond ever listed. In 2008 the exchange underwent significant change and a rebranding, following NASDAQ OMX's purchase of a one third stake, including the launch of a derivatives market. By 2009, NASDAQ Dubai had 29 member brokers, including international and regional banks, and volume of almost $2 billion.

Dubai itself is home to several exchanges. The Dubai Financial Market (DFM) began trading in March 2000 and is located in the Dubai World Trade Centre. It currently has 65 companies listed, capitalised at over $80 billion. The Dubai Gold and Commodities Exchange (DGCX) started in 2005 and was the first international commodities derivatives market in the Middle East, with an annual volume of almost $60 billion.

Jafza itself is a geographic zone built around the Jebel Ali terminal. It contains over 6,000 companies – many of which benefit from close proximity to the port – and over 150,000 people work there. Its purpose is to attract FDI (foreign direct investment) by making it easy to set up and run an international business there (this is called a 'free zone' because it's free from tax and regulation). As with the DIFC, businesses in Jafza are treated as if legally outside the UAE (Jafza's legal system being similarly closer to English than local law). Again, they can be 100% foreign-owned. They and those who work in them are exempt from all import and re-export duties, all personal income taxes and corporate taxes. There are no currency restrictions.

In the wake of the global credit crunch Dubai's growth ground to a halt – particularly in real estate. Palm Deira and World had been thrown open to foreign ownership and deposits of just 10% meant speculators had bought tens of properties, much as they might futures. Many construction projects have either been scaled back, as in the case of the Palm Deira, or halted altogether. Dubai's total liabilities were thought to be about $80 billion. In February 2009 Abu Dhabi (which has the lion's share of the UAE's remaining oil reserves) bought $10 billion of Dubai five-year bonds. This prompted speculation in the west that Abu Dhabi might seek to rein in Dubai's exuberant expansionism.

Then in November 2009 Dubai World sought to renogiate $60bn in debt, causing panic across IFCs and leaving Dubai's shiny, long-term future in doubt.

Maybe a castle built on sand after all.

Chapter 10

The
Bigger Picture

SPEED-READ SUMMARY

■ The credit crunch was caused by a failure in macroprudential regulation

■ Governments responded by easing fiscal policy (cutting taxes and increasing public spending) and monetary policy (reducing interest rates and increasing money supply)

■ By bailing out individual banks and flooding the IFMs with liquidity they pulled the global economy out of a steep dive

■ This will have an inflationary impact down the road, leading to higher interest rates and taxes and reduced public services

■ Iceland was hit badly because its financial services sector dwarfed its domestic economy

■ The US has relied on China to use its trade surplus to support massive US borrowing – this won't continue indefinitely

■ It may be that the US is hoping that this debt will be inflated away

■ In time the US dollar may lose its supremacy as the world's reserve currency

■ We are at a point where the old developed world is ceding economic supremacy to emerging markets and, in particular, China and India which together with Brazil and Russia form the BRICs

■ Emerging markets can be destabilised by tidal flows in and out of foreign capital

■ Emerging markets don't necessarily need their own stock markets but benefit from stable bank funding and developing local bond markets

■ Countries may erect protectionist barriers against world trade, but these lead to uncompetitive industry and stunt longer-term growth

■ Shipping is crucial to world trade and faces a recession of its own

In this final chapter we step back from the IFMs and set them in context. We look at how governments clubbed together to save the world from almost certain financial death and at what cost. We look at how governments interact with the IFMs and big-picture global economics (known as **macroeconomics**).

We start by looking at the role and purpose of governments in economic terms. Take a company. At its most basic, a company's job is to make profits for its shareholders. But nowadays that's not enough. It has to serve the interests of its stakeholders (not only shareholders but also employees, customers and the local community) and generate a profit in a sustainable way that is socially and environmentally responsible and respects applicable codes of corporate governance.

What about a country?

The economic purpose of government

A government has four economic goals: to achieve **full employment** with little or **no inflation** in an economy **with a high rate of growth** and a **balance of payments** (imports and exports cancelling each other out meaning a balanced external current account). This all sounds a bit philanthropic. Why should a government trouble to do any of this? Because (at least in a Western liberal democracy) that's how you ensure you get re-elected. 'It's the economy, stupid': make the electorate feel well off and they'll keep you in office for ever. Punish them in their pocket and you'll be thrown out at the next election. We're talking about politicians and the desire for power.

A government has two ways of influencing the economy: **fiscal policy** and (through its central bank) **monetary policy** (see central banks box in Chapter 9). Fiscal policy is about (a) government income through taxes and borrowing and (b) government spending (aka **public spending**) on defence, housing, health, education, transport and so on.

But if the global financial system – which funds growth, mediates the balance of payments, and either causes or controls inflation – collapses, then all of this is put at risk. The global economy goes into reverse. That pushes countries into recession and puts people out of work. This costs governments elections. Which is why they care about this stuff. But the global credit crunch did more than that: it put the world as we know it at risk. So how did governments react – and at what cost?

HOW GLOBAL FINANCIAL DOOMSDAY WAS AVOIDED

We know from Chapter 5 that a **liquidity crisis**, caused by the short-term money markets grinding to a halt, spread out into a **credit crisis** as banks, unable to fund their short-term assets (or value them), called in as many loans as they could in a bid to shore up their balance sheets. In this way a purely financial crisis spread like a stain into the wider global economy.

Deleveraging of financial assets

The fashionable term for what banks did is 'deleveraging of financial assets' (**deleveraging** has been described as 'the flight from debt and the dash for cash'). Short of capital (money), they reduced their loans so that whatever capital they had was sufficient to support the loan book that remained.

The original idea behind securitisation was to free up banks' balance sheets so they could continue lending without having to increase their regulatory capital. Imagine that a bank has regulatory capital of 5%. It then buys structured products of the type we've been discussing – mortgage-backed bonds. At the time these are triple A credits but as soon as the US real estate market starts to collapse they fall in value. Let's say they fall by 20%. If a bank has 10% of its assets in these bonds, it has now lost 2% of the asset side of its balance sheet which is 40% of its regulatory capital. See how quickly misfortune can turn into crisis – a sort of gearing effect in reverse.

Under the Basel rules the bank must now shrink its assets to restore its **capital-to-asset ratio** to the original 5% level. This means it must sell assets, at a time when all the other banks are doing the same. Deleveraging means unwinding, especially of debt – selling it into a falling market, which just accelerates the downwards spiral, turning it into a vortex.

This vortex is called **debt deflation**. It's exacerbated if there isn't a ready market for assets such as mortgage-backed bonds, which means there is no way of ascribing accurate **values** to them (**marking-to-market** – remember from Chapter 6?). As prices collapse, the ability to value assets disappears which leaves banks, their assets and their capital-to-asset ratios, in freefall.

Add to that the closure of the interbank market (which means that banks dependent on short-term money to replenish their regulatory capital can't roll over their positions so that their capital is itself shrinking) and you have a double whammy of shrinking capital and declining asset values. Result: banks are left holding assets they can't value or sell – in other words the bad stuff; they have zero cashflow; and they go bust. Without the oxygen of cash they asphyxiate.

Rescuing banks and buying the bad stuff

Governments can only do two things: rescue banks; or buy the bad stuff. Rescuing the banks means they end up owning them. Buying the bad stuff restores order and value to the markets.

Which is what governments did. They had no choice. It helped that various policy makers around the world were students of the 1930s recession. They knew that failing to shore up banks and failing to flood the market with liquidity would plunge the world into a terrible penumbra of depression lasting a decade or more. It took the collapse of Lehmans and the domino effect on everyone else to convince them of that.

In terms of **monetary policy**, governments (1) **cut interest rates**, (2) **guaranteed the banks' liabilities**, lent them money, injected equity capital and finally took them over in whole or in part, effectively nationalising them and also (3) **printed money** (not necessarily literally – they did it through quantitative easing as we'll see below).

In terms of **fiscal policy** governments **cut taxes** and **increased public spending**.

All of this costs money. We will all feel it as soon as governments sense we are over the worst. Then interest rates will rise (to put the lid back on inflation and restore monetary policy); taxes will rise; and public services will be cut (to restore public finances to some semblance of health and get fiscal policy back on track). Still, it could be worse. You could live in Iceland (see box on p227).

How the US saved the West

Since (1) the sub-prime credit crunch started in the US, (2) the US is the largest global economy, and (3) US financial institutions as a whole dominate the IFMs, what the US government did was key for the rest of us.

A year after the credit crunch first became apparent in 2007, the US Fed and Treasury over a two-week period nationalised Fannie Mae and Freddie Mac (you'll remember them from Chapter 5), took over AIG (Chapter 7), extended government deposit insurance (usually just available to bank deposits) to over $3 trillion in money market funds (which people treated as cash on deposit anyway even though funds aren't banks – hence the nickname the 'shadow banking system').

The US pumped fresh equity into various banks and/or guaranteed their liabilities – in the case of Citibank by ringfencing and guaranteeing $300

Lessons from the credit crunch: where banks could do better

The credit crunch exemplifies the big theme of this book: the move from lending to trading. And not just sub-prime, but an explosion of financial speculation across IFMs.

Investment banks moved from agency business, such as underwriting and providing M&A advice, into principal finance and proprietary trading – making their own private equity investments and betting their own capital in the IFMs to make bigger profits but with bigger risks. Some critics have called for the separation of the 'utility retail commercial banks' from the 'casino investment banks' and for banks to get back to serving customers and undertaking activities that consume less capital.

This crisis has shown up a weakness in short-term wholesale funding which rolls over quickly but lacks the government guarantees of commercial bank deposits. There has been a call for a move away from short-term wholesale funding to 'stickier' deposits. It has also been pointed out that the real contraction in credit came from non-bank providers – money market funds, hedge funds, SIVs and so on, dubbed the **shadow banking system** which melted away from the money markets at the first hint of banks in trouble.

Possibly the biggest outcry following the credit crunch has been about the size of **bankers' bonuses** which can make footballers' pay packets seem reasonable and which appear to reward failure. UK bank RBS's departing chairman caused a scandal by retiring aged 50 with a £16 million pension pot paying £650,000 a year (since scaled back).

Bank bonuses started when banks switched from being private partnerships, owned by the partners who worked in them (as law firms are still). They felt custodians of their partnership for future generations (this was certainly the philosophy at Goldman Sachs). But then they incorporated and went public in order to attract the level of capital that banks operating in IFMs started to need to underwrite, market make, provide clients with financing options such as the bought deal and, ultimately, to trade for their own account and take proprietary positions in the markets.

Those who worked in banks no longer had substantial ownership of them (the exception was Bear Stearns where just under half the bank was owned by employees – which meant that when it went bust many lost not only their jobs but their savings too). So bankers demanded to be rewarded by paying themselves substantial bonuses in the name of attracting and retaining talent. Institutional investors looked on supinely: corporate governance will always be observed in the breach so long as institutional investors can simply sell their position rather than sit down with management and take an ongoing interest in the companies they've invested in, which is much more time-consuming.

What people really object to is what the credit crunch revealed:

➡ that **bank profits are privatised** (pocketed by the bankers) while **losses are socialised** (passed on to the taxpayer); this implicit state guarantee means banks get cheaper funding to bet the ranch all over again. This is why many central banks and bank regulators are starting to doubt the wisdom of having **banks that are too big to fail**. The **moral hazard** (meaning that there is no downside to excessive risk, no incentive to stay safe) is too great. Hence talk of breaking big banks up. There is also talk of 'resolution regimes' specific to banks (ways of winding them up cleanly) for example through 'living wills' that each bank is required to draw up which applies if it ever becomes a 'zombie bank'.

Governments in the 2008 financial meltdown moved from providing guarantees and taking on banks' most toxic assets to taking shareholdings in the banks themselves (nationalisation, however you like to nuance it) on the basis that if there is any upside to be had when times get better they might as well have some of that too, and not just get landed with the liabilities.

It's still unclear whether government shareholders will play an active part in supervising their newfound investments. Early reports suggested crackdowns on high executive pay and bonuses and a requirement that banks get back to doing what they were supposed to be doing all along – funding businesses, especially those in most need: small, fast-growing ones.

It was also said at the time that this was the last gasp of Anglo-Saxon-style banking, exemplified by the rise of investment banking, trading, derivatives, private equity and hedge funds. Instead there'd be a move towards the **social model of financial services** where banks are long-term shareholders in the businesses they fund – a model practised in, for example, Germany and (at least until a few years ago) Japan.

billion of its assets. The US also announced its Troubled Asset Relief Programme (TARP), a $700 billion government rescue package to buy up the worst derivatives, sub-prime mortgages and toxic assets that banks couldn't get rid of. Some observers say the cost of all of this may eventually rise to $2.5 trillion. (The UK's equivalent, its Asset Protection Scheme, has led to it guaranteeing £600 billion of banks' assets.)

One option not pursued by the US is that of sticking the bad stuff into 'bad banks' set up for the purpose (a bit like Equitas – see Lloyd's of London in Chapter 7). In the early 1990s, Sweden responded to its own banking crisis by setting up two bad banks, Securum and Retriva, into which it transferred the worst assets of Nordbanken and Gota Bank, two nationalised banks. This time round, Switzerland backed UBS's plan to do the same with $60 billion of its bad assets. The UK is doing this with Northern Rock.

Overall, governments are thought to have pumped almost $500 billion of capital into banks and guaranteed almost ten times that amount of bank debt.

Credit easing or quantitative easing

The question is: how did the Fed (and other developed economies like the UK which followed suit) do it? Where did this 'money' come from?

Answer: they did it by **increasing the money supply**. The Fed increased its reserves from $11 billion to $900 billion in order to use these newly created funds to buy securities (not just the toxic ones, but government bonds and corporate assets). By buying in these assets in return for this new cash, the Fed increased liquidity.

This is called variously **credit easing** or **quantitative easing**. Some call it printing money. But central banks would argue that buying in these assets increases liquidity in the short term but in the longer term the assets are sold back (so that the money paid back is cancelled) or, in the case of government bonds, they are simply retired so that, either way, the overall money supply is not increased.

Printing money (without intending to collect it back in again) is called a **helicopter drop**. Or a government can announce a tax rebate (fiscal stimulus), issue bonds to fund it, and lodge them with its central bank in return for a deposit – which is the same as a helicopter drop but neater because it bypasses the banks and money markets. This is called **monetising part of the public debt**.

Essentially, if a government then wants to rein in the money supply to drive inflation down, it issues debt (bonds) which soaks up money or liquidity as it is called. But if – as here – it wants to loosen money supply, to encourage economic activity (which can be inflationary but may be necessary to stave off a recession or collapse in the banking system as in 2008), it redeems government debt so releasing cash into the monetary system. In short, governments pursued a twin policy of increasing the fiscal deficit (public debt) with expansion of the money supply.

Expansionary fiscal policy

Governments also needed to use **fiscal stimulus** to encourage economic activity. Fiscal stimulus (or expansionary fiscal policy – EFP) simply means governments reducing taxes (to make people feel richer to get them to spend more) and increasing public spending (so that the government becomes an engine of demand – Japan famously did this in the 1990s,

Land of ice and (no) money

The country to suffer the most in the credit crunch has been Iceland. In a global financial meltdown, those countries with greatest exposure to the IFMs relative to their size will suffer the most.

London is the leading *international* financial centre with a financial sector whose balance sheet, at 450% of GDP, is far greater than a country the size of the UK needs.

But Iceland's was double that. By the end of 2007, Iceland's top three banks (two of which had been in state ownership only five years before) had $180 billion outstanding in loans, 900% or nine times the country's economy of about $20 billion. But with a population of just 300,000, less than a third of those loans were backed by domestic deposits. The rest was funded in the international interbank markets.

The money had been spent on extensive overseas acquisitions – ranging from prominent high street retail chains to football clubs. Household debts were double disposable income (elsewhere it's about 1.5 times).

When the interbank markets dried up, the Icelandic banks had no cash to support their loans. They had to be re-nationalised. Still worse, to the extent the banks had tried to attract deposits – via internet accounts from overseas – they ended up owing foreign investors over $8 billion. Iceland's currency collapsed.

Independent from Denmark for only 65 years, Iceland's continued economic independence is under threat. Iceland went to the IMF (the International Monetary Fund) which, with various European countries, put up $10 billion, equivalent to half the country's GDP. At the IMF's behest Iceland put its interest rates up six percent to 18%. Inflation hit 20%.

Iceland's citizens are expected to face 70 years of high taxes, reduced public services and declining living standards. Iceland may yet be forced to join the EU, abandon its currency in favour of the euro and surrender its fishing rights, about which Icelanders feel extremely strongly.

The IMF has said the collapse of Iceland's banks is the biggest financial failure ever in proportion to the host country.

commissioning 'white elephants', such as motorways that went from nowhere to nowhere, just to keep contractors busy).

The problem is that this can put the government into debt because it is receiving less in tax (which it has cut) yet is spending more. If government expenditure exceeds income it's called a **budget deficit**, whereas if government income exceeds expenditure it creates a **budget surplus**. So EFP means a government has to borrow (unless it has a previous budget surplus it can use). Government borrowing is fine, but can cause problems of its own, as we shall see.

EFP leads to: a higher budget deficit or lower budget surplus; an increase in **aggregate demand** (AD) as well as increased imports and inflation; and a reduced current account.

AD is the total of a country's expenditure on goods at a particular price. Everything in the world leads back to you and me. Businesses manufacture and provide services, and banks offer finance, so that you and I can buy what we need and want. What you and I buy is part of AD, which is consumption. Consumption isn't the only ingredient in a country's GDP (gross domestic product). GDP includes consumption, investment, government spending plus exports minus imports. All of that is AD.

EFP will increase AD since lower taxes mean people can spend more and increased public spending itself adds to AD.

So EFP can bring an economy out of recession by increasing employment. But it tends to be inflationary. It isn't always: if money is not circulating but is stashed in reserves or under mattresses it cannot boost spending or push up inflation. So these moves may not be inflationary: however, if that's the case, as reserves swell, credit growth wilts.

Inflation v deflation

Besides, a little inflation is all right. It has the effect of gradually increasing asset values (e.g. house prices) which increases the feel-good factor. The opposite of inflation – **deflation** – is worse: consumers don't spend because there's no point in buying until tomorrow when things will cost less (but which of course never comes, because tomorrow you postpone buying until the next day, and so on) leading to permanent postponement of purchases. Demand dries up, driving the recession deeper. Industry falters and the economy grinds to a halt. Prices go down which means that debts (such as household mortgages and corporate loans) get bigger in real terms.

Deflation is difficult to get out of. Japan was in a deflationary environment for over a decade and interest rates fell to zero – because no one wanted to borrow. The same deflationary environment has affected Germany in the past. So inflation can be welcome in a deflationary environment – it lifts asset prices and eases the real debt burden on borrowers (by eroding the real value of that debt). But it hurts savers (by eroding the real value of their savings) as do cuts in interest rates (savers get a reduced return on their deposits).

Classical v Keynesian economics

Just in case you're wondering, EFP is not really a long-term solution anyway. Economists bicker over this. Classical economists say EFP cannot in the long term affect output so cannot influence unemployment (though, as we've seen, it can lead to higher prices and increased inflation). Keynesian economists say EFP can lead to higher output and lower unemployment without increasing prices (inflation). But once full employment is achieved EFP can only stoke inflation which is called **overheating** (increase in inflation with no increase in output). So Keynesians say EFP can affect both inflation and unemployment because it can affect both output and prices.

What this means is that in the short term, EFP can increase short-term growth but, in the longer term, growth is a function of the **supply side** – that is, investment, education and technology which drive competitive advantage, nationally and internationally. **Demand side** policies are fiscal policies that affect AD. Growth in the long term is unaffected by AD unless lower interest rates encourage investment which in turn increases supply side output. Economists called the global credit crunch a demand shock: the standard response to a demand shock is through monetary policy – cut interest rates and increase money supply, which is what happened. Keynes showed that supply does not always create its own demand, hence the need for demand management as well as EFP. Keynes also believed that financial crises aren't aberrations in otherwise rational markets. He said they are inherent to the financial system and governments have to prevent them from tipping the world into depression. Keynes would not agree that markets regulate themselves or that all risk can be accurately priced – tenets of the rational expectations theory of boom and bust.

Tightening fiscal policy

EFP on the scale required to address the credit crunch is expected to be highly inflationary.

Developed economies responded to the credit crunch by recapitalising banks (through lending to them, guaranteeing their liabilities, injecting fresh equity, and nationalisation) and guaranteeing troubled assets. They flooded the markets with liquidity by buying bad assets and printing more money, increased their borrowings, lowered their taxes, launched more public projects to stimulate the economy, thus stoking inflation and ensuring (at a time when tax revenues from lower output fell; and unemployment and other social costs rose) that future generations suffer high taxes, low public services and diminished real asset values (at least inflation reduces the real value of debts). Of course, all of this was essential to prevent a complete financial collapse, to counter the slump in private demand and forestall a full-blown depression.

But an increase in inflation will prompt central banks to increase interest rates in due course. Then consumption will go down (it costs more to borrow). Investment will go down (because new investment by industry will

Interest rates: the complete picture

1. When interest rates go up (to control inflation):

- Bank deposits become more attractive in relative terms – so more investors rush to put their money with banks, which means that:

- The stock market goes down because:

  - Bank deposits are now more attractive because they offer a higher return with lower risk, so money is diverted from the stock market and put on deposit instead

  - The cost of borrowing to companies has increased so their profitability goes down so shareholders will get lower dividends so share prices go down

- The currency goes up because in order to deposit money with local banks, overseas investors need to convert their currency into the local currency

- This makes exports more expensive expressed in other countries' currencies so, again, corporate profits (to the extent domestic companies export) will be hit, so contributing to the decline in the stock market

- Bond yields go up, to keep pace with the increase in interest rates, so bond prices go down.

2. The exact reverse happens when interest rates go down (to stimulate demand):

- Bank deposits become less attractive in relative terms so investors put their money into:

- The stock market, which goes up, and

- The bond markets so bond prices go up and bond yields go down as the coupon bonds are paying is relatively more attractive to investors, meanwhile

- The cost of borrowing for companies goes down (note that when interest rates come down, companies tend to retire old debt at the higher interest rate and refinance it at the new, lower rate) so increasing their profitability, which makes their shares more attractive which also drives the stock market up

- The currency goes down as international investors withdraw their deposits and convert them out of the local currency to invest elsewhere

- This makes companies' exports cheaper for overseas customers to buy, so increasing the profitability of exporting companies, making their shares attractive and, again, helping the stock market climb.

Note: markets may not move if they've been expecting these interest rate changes.

be less profitable). There will be fewer exports and fewer imports (the latter will be cheaper because the currency will be stronger – hence reduced exports – but there will be less ability to buy). Consumption will also be down because savings will increase (to get the better interest rate return) but asset prices (houses, etc) will also go down.

Reversing EFP means adopting a **tightening fiscal policy** (**TFP**), that is, increasing taxes, reducing public spending, or a combination of both. TFP reduces inflation and imports, increases the supply side's search for exports and improves the current account, but leads to higher unemployment and lower growth. On top of that there is economic capacity that is never fully replaced and so is lost forever, which is how past economic loss depresses future recovery. So how does this all work at an international level?

BALANCE OF PAYMENTS AND MACROECONOMICS

Imagine you are China, the world's fastest-growing economy. You are importing raw materials and commodities (such as steel) and producing goods for internal consumption and export. Your exports are snapped up around the world because your labour costs are low and your currency weak (which is what you want).

This generates a massive trade surplus which you need to invest somewhere: you're faced with the same consideration as any HNWI (high-net-worth individual) – you have so much money you have to do something about it to preserve its value. But if you're China, you can't just convert those overseas earnings into your local currency (yuan) because that will create demand for your currency which will cause it to strengthen and reduce your low-cost advantage abroad, damaging the very trade that generated the surplus in the first place.

So what do you keep your profits in? The answer is the world's **reserve currency** (that is, the currency that is used for the bulk of international finance and trade). And that is the US dollar. How do you do that? By buying US Treasuries (US government bonds).

Now, imagine you are the US. You are the biggest economy in the world – in fact, but for your lack of oil, you are completely self-sufficient and don't really need to trade with the rest of the world at all. But, as the world's biggest consumer economy, you import more than you export and you are therefore the world's biggest borrower. What you have in your favour is (1) because of the size of your economy and its impact worldwide, your currency is the world's reserve currency and (2) you can borrow as much as you like because the world knows that, if you default, capitalism as we know it is toast, so you won't.

So, although you are the biggest borrower in the world, you are regarded as one of the most creditworthy and therefore can continue to borrow. This explains why, since 2001, foreign investors have acquired about $5 trillion in US securities (more than doubling their holdings of US equities and bonds) as both public and private inflows have financed record US current account deficits.

Now you can begin to see how interconnected the world's economies are. China holds these dollars partly through government reserves (managed by its State Administration of Foreign Exchange), partly through its sovereign wealth fund (China Investment Corporation (CIC)). Apart from its overseas exports, China's current account surplus is buoyed up by foreign direct investment (money invested in China by foreign companies setting up operations in China and investors buying Chinese property). China is estimated to have roughly $1.5 trillion in dollar assets (about two-thirds of its current-account surplus), half of which is in US Treasuries. The rest is in US equities – including CIC's stakes in private equity firm Blackstone and US bank Morgan Stanley – as well as corporate bonds.

The dollar accounts for two-thirds of the world's currency reserves. The euro represents a quarter. Three-quarters of all reserves are in the hands of emerging market economies. China holds one-third of the global total. Government bonds are seen as risk free in the home economy because the government has the power to print money and raise taxes. Since the US is the world's largest economy, has the most liquid markets, and operates the world's reserve currency, Treasuries are seen as risk free, while the dollar's reserve currency status lets the US borrow cheaply causing the country's credit and housing bubbles to persist for longer than they would have done.

China v US: 'don't love you, can't leave you'

So China, as the US's biggest creditor, is effectively subsidising its political nemesis and the world's biggest borrower, which in part is what enables the US to continue buying China's exports in the first place (after the EU, the US is China's biggest export market). Bizarrely, China is peculiarly dependent on the US because the way the US treats its currency affects the value of China's dollar holdings.

A run of big budget deficits increases the risk that a government will default or repay its debts only by getting its central bank to print money, creating inflation. The US won't default (if it does, that's Game Over for the IFMs). But the US has an interest in seeing the value of the dollar decline because that reduces the real value of its debt (how much ultimately it has to repay) and makes its own exports more competitive.

It can do this by pursuing expansionist fiscal (public spending) and monetary (increasing the money supply) policies, which is what the recession requires. Printing money devalues the existing currency because there is more of it available represented by the same level of wealth or assets. In this way, the US's debts might eventually be inflated away, to the cost of foreign investors. An extreme example is pre-war Germany where hyperinflation was chosen over paying the reparations bill leading to scenes of people needing a wheelbarrow full of deutschemarks to buy a loaf of bread.

As the US's self-interest in seeing the dollar devalue against other currencies (to reduce the real value of its debt) increases, those countries holding dollars become increasingly nervous. This is why the People's Bank of China (the central bank) has suggested switching some of its foreign-currency reserves out of US dollars and has been calling (along with the other BRICs – see later) for a new global reserve currency (comprising the yen, the yuan, the euro and gold) in preference to the US dollar. China has also proposed a widening of IMF Special Drawing Rights (see next box on 'World Bank') to replace the dollar as the world's reserve currency.

China would like to diversify away from dollars but any attempt to dump its stock of dollars would risk triggering a plunge in the US currency, so would be self-defeating. But if China wants to reduce its exposure to dollars it must let the yuan rise which would give it a loss on its dollar holdings – so maintaining its current exchange rate policy is helping to keep the dollar dominant and Chinese exports cheap. If China is trying to maintain the value of the yuan by tying it to the dollar, China must continue to buy dollars.

The risk is that as the US falls into greater debt so foreigners may be less willing to lend to it – which could lead to an abrupt halt to the funding of its debt (sound familiar?) and plunge the dollar into decline. It was possibly for this reason that US bond yields shot up almost a whole percentage point at the beginning of 2009, the worst spike in decades.

Perhaps what all this signals is that in future US consumers will no longer be the engine room for China's export-led growth nor will Chinese savers continue to finance US borrowing.

In fact there's no reason why the US dollar will always be the world's reserve currency. It hasn't always been. Two thousand years ago it was the denarius (Rome) then the solidus (Byzantium) and in the seventeenth century – when the Dutch dominated international trade and finance – the guilder, followed by sterling (Britain) until the 1950s. The US dollar accounts for two-thirds of global foreign exchange, down from four-fifths in the 1980s, and the euro is creeping up on it.

World Bank, IMF and SDRs

There is one type of bank we haven't discussed: the supranational.
Supranational banks include the European Investment Bank (actually a commercial bank), the European Bank for Reconstruction and Development, the African Development Bank, the Asian Development Bank, and so on.

They are all part of the big daddy of them all, the **World Bank**, which is owned by developed economies and is charged with the mission to pump investment into less developed economies to turn them into Western-style economies.

The poorest countries are helped by the International Development Association which is part of the World Bank but is often described as a **multilateral agency** with developed economies as direct stakeholders.

The World Bank is headquartered in Washington DC and the US is its single biggest funder. So too is the **International Monetary Fund (IMF)** but its role is helping to maintain global economic stability. Unlike the World Bank, the IMF has spent much of its time recently acting as lender of last resort to developed economies which go to it for funding when they face economic difficulty. Iceland did so (see earlier box). So, more recently, have Mexico, Romania, Ukraine, Hungary and Pakistan among others.

What borrowers don't like is that the IMF imposes conditions when lending in order to help a country sort itself out (Iceland had to jack its interest rates up to 18%). These usually necessitate politically unpopular domestic economic policies which risk alienating the electorate and can lead to the particular government (which went to the IMF) being voted out of office. The IMF also regularly issues reports on countries telling them where their governments need to improve their financial management. Again, a bit embarrassing.

The IMF's unit of account is the **SDR** (**special drawing right**, which is made up of a basket of the leading currencies – the dollar, euro, yen and pound). The G20 summit in London in 2009 authorised the IMF to issue $250 billion in new SDRs and for its overall resources to be increased by $500 billion to $750 billion.

Countries with strong foreign currency reserves such as China can buy SDRs from countries that don't, so providing those countries with much-needed hard (real, usually dollars) currency. SDRs were designed as a reserve currency but never took off (they represent less than 1% of total global reserves).

China wants SDRs expanded to include other currencies, notably the yuan; as well as an SDR fund managed by the IMF into which dollar reserves could be converted.

Like the World Bank, the IMF is dominated by the US. The US, together with Japan, Britain and France, accounts for over 30% of its votes (half of that is the US alone). In due course these will need to be rejigged to give emerging economies a bigger say.

The dollar dominates because hitherto the US has been a large and stable economy with open, deep and liquid markets and low inflation. In other words, people generally have confidence in the dollar as a store of financial value. Confidence is important in the IFMs. In times of trouble the so-called 'flight to quality' sees investors move their financial assets into gold, a singularly useless mineral except as a store of wealth which is worth what it is because people believe it is; after all, the test of any currency is whether people believe it is worth more than the paper it's printed on.

Whether the euro or the yuan or another currency eventually inherits the dollar's mantle will depend on where the global economy is heading over the next several decades.

Tariffs, protectionism and trade

For any country, if its exchange rate goes up, exports will decline and imports increase so the **current balance** will go down. This could lead to lower domestic investment and lower growth longer-term. A fall in exchange rates will improve the current balance (exports up, imports down). If a country has too high an **external trade surplus** (for instance from oil exports), its own currency will appreciate (as those surpluses are translated back into its currency). By keeping its surplus in foreign exchange reserves, it keeps its own currency cheap, as China has done so far.

One way of protecting domestic employment is to put up **protectionist barriers** against imports, by imposing high taxes (**tariffs** or **customs duties**) and **quotas** (limits on imports). But protectionism is likely to lead in the longer term to lower economic growth as a country's shielded supply side loses competitive edge internationally.

Different countries develop different specialisations that will give them an **absolute advantage** (meaning the ability to produce a specific good or service more cheaply than anywhere else – this is based on classical economist Adam Smith). Where two countries have a **comparative advantage** (one over the other in a particular commodity) David Ricardo, another renowned economist, said they would find it mutually beneficial to trade.

The balance of payments current account is split into two components: **visibles** (the trade in goods – from raw materials to semi-manufactured to manufactured goods); and **invisibles** (trade in services, investment income and other receipts). The UK and Iceland are good examples of countries where financial services are a significant invisible export. Turmoil in the IFMs has crippled Iceland and weakened the UK.

If an economy spends more on goods and services than it earns, it has to borrow the money from overseas. A **current account deficit** is undesirable because longer term it is unsustainable: foreign countries at some point refuse to lend any more so the domestic economy has to cut down on imports and export more. Domestic consumption and standards of living fall. This is what happened to Poland, Brazil and Uganda in the 1980s, and Thailand and South Korea in the 1990s.

A current account deficit is OK if it is fuelling growth leading to increased exports.

Deficits aren't always disastrous. Italy and Japan have run debt/GDP ratios of more than 100% for years without complete meltdown. France's is 75% but it is in the eurozone, and the euro is also acting as a reserve currency so central banks have to hold euro-denominated assets. The US's is almost 80% but investors hitherto have held US Treasuries as the dollar is the reserve currency, which is why the US can run up a much higher debt even though the US has spent it on consumption. And as countries borrow more, their cost of borrowing goes up – bond markets push up the cost of government debt.

However – just to bring this back to the IFMs – the main determinant of net debt owed by countries is not the current account deficit: it is stock and bond market prices in the IFMs. In short, it is changes in asset values.

Flying the global economic plane

You can begin to see now that controlling an economy is a bit like flying a plane. You want interest rates to be low enough to encourage economic activity (buying, which encourages production) but high enough to stop inflation (caused by too much demand). You want a balance that means commerce and industry are at their optimum, providing employment for as many as want it (which in turn puts your tax take up and reduces the amount you need to spend on social policies). You want your currency to be strong enough to mean that buying goods and services overseas is not expensive but weak enough to make your own goods and services attractive overseas (because that, again, is good for your own businesses, for employment and the tax take).

So you want to be constantly trimming course, altitude and speed to keep everything at the best balance and your fuel consumption optimal. However, the global economy has been more used to boom and bust than steady flight – with individual countries buffeted by turbulence, falling towards the ground then being wrestled back up into the air until they fly too high and come back down towards earth – a bumpy, uncomfortable flight. Imagine all of these planes in the air together with an air traffic control made up of lots of countries with no single one in overall control and that's what the global economy is like.

More than one market observer has likened the global economy to a plane powered by a single big engine – the US consumer – which was fuelled by debt, meaning that the plane was always going to come down at some point.

So the decision in the face of the credit crunch was relatively easy: open up the pumps and flood the economy with money otherwise we're going to fall to earth with a bang (the 1930s depression was caused by a failure to rescue the banking system and to expand the money supply). In other words, pour petrol into the engines to keep the plane in the sky and worry about the cost later.

However, in future, the global economy will be kept aloft by many small(er) engines – emerging markets (EMs) and in particular the BRICs (Brazil, India, China and, to a lesser extent, Russia).

EMERGING MARKETS

Emerging market (EM) is the term for any country that is underdeveloped economically. These range from countries of vast size but tiny populations, for instance in Africa, to former communist bloc countries in eastern Europe; countries in Latin America and Asia; to the likes of China, Russia and India. Indeed, those three plus Brazil are classified separately and known as the BRICs (see below).

EMs need capital like any fast-growing businesses: they are the equivalent of economic start-ups. The poorest EMs live off foreign aid but larger ones are more dependent on foreign capital. There are three possible sources:

- **Foreign direct investment** (FDI) – this is where overseas companies set up local operations and foreign investors buy local land: these investments are stable in that they can't be withdrawn instantly.

- **Portfolio equity investment** (aka **foreign indirect investment**) – this is where investors buy shares in local companies or foreign companies that are exposed to the local economy (for instance, because the latter are themselves direct investors): this is less stable than FDI in that it can be withdrawn simply by selling equities in local and global stock markets, but the world's largest institutional investors need exposure to emerging economies, so it's more stable than might appear.

- **Foreign credit** (lending) – this is lending by foreign banks and purchases of government bonds: fickle if dependent on the wellbeing of foreign (Western) banks; and especially risky if the borrowing is in dollars rather than the local currency.

Their economies are so immature that capital flowing in and out like the tide can have a profound and unsettling impact. So EMs were initially less badly affected by the credit crunch because their fledgling banking systems were less exposed to sub-prime instruments and their governments had to spend less on stimulating their (fledgling) economies.

But then, because of the credit crunch in the developed world, foreign capital fled, confidence evaporated, EM stock markets plunged and local currencies tumbled. The collapse in the credit markets caused havoc as foreign banks stopped lending and providing even basic services like trade finance. For instance, in 2008, the flow of foreign capital to Latin America dried up, leading to a steep rise in borrowing costs for governments and companies: a record inflow of $180 billion in 2007 was followed by $80 billion in 2008 and a paltry $40 billion in 2009 as foreign banks cut back credit lines, especially in trade finance.

Private inflows of funds into EMs generally fell from $1 trillion to $800 billion in 2008. Developed-to-emerging deals (foreign direct investment, M&A) fell to a six year low in 2008 – with around 230 transactions in the second half

Global payment flows

Cross-border claims (meaning banks' deposits with, and loans from, each other – this is the language of the Bank for International Settlements) are a staggering 30 times larger than they were 30 years ago.

They took off in the 1960s when banks in London were allowed to take non-sterling deposits. These banks attracted US dollars because they faced lower regulatory costs than banks in the US and these dollars became known as eurodollars as the Middle Eastern oil-exporting countries sought Europe as an alternative to the US to store their hard currency.

Over the 30 years from 1977, these 'claims' (mainly loans) increased from $680 billion to $23 trillion, the bulk of them funnelled through: London with strong links between the UK and the rest of Europe; Japan with Hong Kong and Singapore; and the US with OFCs such as the Bahamas, Cayman Islands and Netherlands Antilles, as well as with the UK, Europe and Japan.

In the 1990s, the net flow of funds was from the UK and Japan to the US (around $500 billion) and in the 2000s from Japan to Europe and from the UK and OFCs to the US. These flows, leading largely to the US, accord with the growth in its current account deficit. However, oil-producing nations have tended to channel their funds through Japan and Europe rather than the US.

Trade and shipping

A massive rebalancing is starting to take place in world trade flows between the unsustainable surpluses of China and other big exporters.

The shipping industry is a bellwether for international trade and so for global economic activity. Four-fifths of the world's freight is moved by ship (not air) so if demand worldwide is going up, so will the cost of cargo-carrying capacity (called **charters**).

London is the international centre for the shipping industry although Piraeus is a competitor (since much of the global maritime industry is controlled by Greek shipping dynasties). One reason for London's desire to be seen as a low-tax haven for foreigners is to keep Greek shipping families in the UK.

The Baltic Dry Index (the Baltic Exchange is the historic name for the London shipping market) tracks freight rates for shipping dry bulk cargoes such as iron ore and coal (the most frequently traded cargoes) from producers such as South America, India and Australia, to markets in the US, Europe and China. It hit a high in May 2008 – prompted by China's demand for raw materials such as steel – then fell almost 95% by December, then oscillated wildly during 2009.

This spells disaster for the shipping market which had a vast pipeline (worth $500 billion) of tonnage in the dry bulk and container sectors coming on stream from 2009. Most of this is surplus to requirements as key freight markets have collapsed and many owners are already under pressure without the additional financial burden of expensive new ships. Cancelled or defaulted orders would have a knock-on effect for funding banks (some Nordic and German banks specialise in maritime finance) – with the risk of creating for the shipping industry a credit crunch of its own. The 'box trade' (container ships) has been particularly badly hit.

of 2008. By contrast, emerging-to-developed economy deals have held up well, down just over a quarter on 2006 but now representing almost half of developed-to-emerging, with the highpoint being India's Tata Steel take over of Corus, the Anglo-Dutch steelmaker. Over the past five years, India has led with almost 400 deals, with just over 100 from each of China and Russia. EMs export capital to developed economies because their own financial systems are too immature to provide trustworthy savings vehicles.

This time around, the debt in question has tended to be more corporate (lent to Indian, Chinese and other EM companies) whereas in the past more was sovereign (Latin American in the 1980s). The Latin American debt crisis in the 1980s was triggered by the ending of the oil boom: oil exporting countries had deposited their windfall receipts with banks in developed economies which had lent them on to EMs. The recycling of petrodollars into EM investment continues to be important to EMs but the deposit outflows have been not from Middle Eastern oil exporters but from Russia (the world's second largest oil exporter), Libya, Nigeria and Angola. Inflows from oil exporting EMs are also recycled to other EMs.

Some EMs have imposed exchange controls to stop capital inflows and the capital flight of hot money. In fact it is far from obvious that EMs benefit from opening up to global capital: the freeflow of capital across borders should make more funds more cheaply available to poor countries and increased investment raises GDP and living standards; but economists have not found convincing links between freer capital flows and speedier economic development.

In general, EM equities dramatically outperformed developed stock markets from November 2008. The reasons were many: China's stimulus package of almost $600 billion; EM banks having avoided sub-prime; investors and banks being more prepared to move into riskier EMs because they seemed in better shape than expected; the G20 pledge to fund the IMF to prop up EMs in trouble which led to a strengthening of EM currencies; and China being a major trading partner for other EMs. This outperformance wasn't universal: by 2009 the lack of foreign capital was beginning to have a significant impact on central and eastern European economies – with currencies, shares and bonds falling and the increased risk of a sovereign default. However, it's questionable whether EMs benefit from having local stock markets at all (see next box).

EMs generally are seen as the drivers of global growth over the next decade. Having suffered a series of crises between 1997 and 2001 (such as Russia's bond default in 1998) they have been paying down debt, increasing savings and building reserves. EMs lead the demand for commodities as they build infrastructure. Leading that consumption will be the BRICs which will account for the majority of it.

BRICs: THE NEW ECONOMIC ORDER

Brazil, Russia, India and China are the four biggest EMs. The figures (based on the S&P Global Stock Markets Factbook) are staggering. At the global economic highpoint just prior to the global credit crunch, the BRIC economies' turnover increased by almost 250% from around $3 trillion (2006) to over $10 trillion (2007). China's market capitalisation increased by over 150% from 2006 to 2007. Their proportion of emerging market turnover almost doubled from around 35% to over 65% and their proportion of global economic turnover increased from under 5% to over 10%; they represented almost 60% of emerging market capitalisation, and went from just under 10% to just over 15% of total world market capitalisation.

Just to put this in perspective, in 2007 the US was the most highly capitalised market in the world at $19 trillion (as one would expect) followed by *China* at $6 trillion and Japan at $4 trillion, the UK (3.8), France (2.7), Canada and Germany (2.1), *India* and Spain (1.8), then *Russia* (1.5), *Brazil* (1.3), Australia (1.2), Switzerland (1.2) and Hong Kong (1.1).

The BRICs represent the new order. They are recovering more quickly from the global recession than developed economies.

Brazil has huge natural resources and reserves, is stable politically (it is the fourth largest democracy), has the highest FDI after China and a pension fund sector that supports equity investment. It is dependent on commodity exports (including oil) and the Bovespa index was up by more than 75% over the 12 months from October 2007 because of commodity price increases and recovering demand.

Russia is the sick man of the BRICs, to the extent that some commentators refer to the 'BICs' without Russia. Oil and gas account for almost three-quarters of its stock market, which took a severe dive in 2008 when prices fell by two-thirds, leading to Russia's main markets suspending trading in shares and bonds for several days in September 2008 after the largest one-day stock market fall in over a decade. But since then Russia's markets and currency have surged.

Even if Russia has fallen out of favour with international investors, the other three are attracting interest at a time when developed economies are unattractive.

India is the least dependent on exports, has a more diversified economy and less exposure to commodities, making it a more stable long-term prospect.

China is the fastest-growing economy in the world and has a population greater than that of the US, the EU and Japan combined. Chinese demand drives commodity prices worldwide. When commodity prices rise, money pours into Brazil and Russia which become targets of the 'carry trade' – investors buying their currencies, having borrowed in stronger ones, to ride the rise. China accounts for 10% of global output. China's position as the world's largest exporter, combined with its protectionist socialist market economic system of the past 60 years, means China has accumulated enormous wealth and has the world's largest foreign exchange reserve at $1.7 trillion.

The BRICs are also recovering more quickly than other EMs. By mid-2009, Bovespa was up 75% from its low in October 2008, Russia's RTS index was

Stock markets in emerging markets

This book started with stock markets (Chapter 2) which is where we return. The number of stock exchanges trebled in the 1990s as many emerging markets (EMs) – particularly in former central and eastern Europe – launched them.

Most started in the wake of privatisations of previously state-owned industries in formerly managed economies (for instance, through voucher schemes: providing citizens with vouchers with which to buy the shares). But liquidity has tended to be thin and new issues sparse.

Take the Budapest Stock Exchange (BSE). It has an annual turnover of under $50 billion and capitalisation of about $30 billion with only about 50 listed shares. Since the end of privatisations in the 1990s, there have been very few IPOs. New IPOs average under five a year and are outnumbered by delistings. MOL, Hungary's biggest company, was in a recent M&A tussle with Austrian company OMV. This has led to a significant decrease in MOL's freefloat of shares and, since they account for four-fifths of the BSE, liquidity and volumes have fallen further. Just three foreign investment companies (based in the Netherlands, Luxembourg and Guernsey) are listed on the BSE. The BSE has been seeking alliances with stronger stock markets and the Vienna Stock Exchange has acquired a stake in it. Tellingly, most turnover in Hungarian securities takes place in London.

There's a case for saying that an EM needs strong government and corporate bond markets first. The Hungarian debt market is bigger than the BSE, at about $60 billion and almost four-fifths of that is government, with corporate less than 5%. But mortgage-backed bonds were introduced in 2001 (to fund local property purchases) and they are the most vibrant part of Hungary's debt market.

Or take the Ukrainian Stock Exchange (USE). A third of the trading on the USE is by foreign investors and IPOs by Ukrainian companies raised about $50 billion in 2008 – but overseas. In fact both Ukraine and Russia have the largest corporate bond markets among European EMs (they both feature investor-friendly bonds with embedded put and reset options): in each case, two-thirds of the market is made up of non-government bond issues. Russia has a stock market capitalisation bigger than its GDP (like the UK) with strong primary market activity (unlike Hungary) – over a dozen IPOs a year with strong foreign investor interest. But Poland has the highest number of IPOs – almost 40 in 2006. Most European EM cross-border listings are in London through GDRs, with almost three-quarters of international trading in European EM stocks taking place in London.

The early penetration of EMs by foreign banks following the privatisation and part-sale of state banks has meant that banks rather than stock markets have played a leading role in funding the corporate sector (in the absence of a developed insurance and pension fund base to provide local institutional investors). ⇨

> ⇨ In fact there's a strong argument that EMs don't need to have their own stock markets at all and – ironic in a book on the IFMs – may not even need the IFMs. Certainly, the emergence of pan-European and pan-global stock exchanges means that local markets just fragment liquidity, although EMs might benefit from local junior markets for fledgling public companies before they list on stock markets in the IFCs or OFCs. What EMs and their corporate sectors need are simple lending banks in the way their populations need microfinance (Chapter 8). Local stock markets are unlikely to be a major force in future, nor will they be able to integrate into the IFMs.

80% higher, China was up 52% and India 46%. The BRICs are less dependent on exports than many EMs – for Brazil and India, exports are less than 15% of GDP. And the BRICs have opened up their financial systems less than many EMs so have been less affected than, for example, eastern Europe. They are also trading more with each other. In a landmark deal, Brazil's biggest oil company, Petrobras, raised $10 billion from China in 2009 in return for supplying Sinopec (a Chinese state oil firm) with a guaranteed supply of oil for ten years. In a clear snub to the US, the BRICs have decided to expand the use of their own currencies in bilateral trade with each other rather than the US dollar.

Of the four BRICs, China is at the forefront. Since 1990 China has grown by almost 10% every year – which means that output is doubling roughly every seven years. China benefits from: a well-educated workforce; an inefficient economy with scope to draw rural workers into more productive urban work (wages are low and there is a large reserve of surplus labour which drives internal migration); the relaxation of communist control over the economy allowing individuals to set up their own businesses; and inflows of money and technological know-how from foreign investors keen to take advantage of cheap labour and what will become the world's biggest market. No wonder China had a trade surplus of $400 billion in 2008, 10% of GDP. Savings, investment and FDI are high. Investment has averaged 35% of GDP for the last ten years. The national savings rate is over 50% of GDP (20% household and 30% from businesses reinvesting profit).

The global economic crisis has accelerated China's emergence as a big player. China's currency is becoming the de facto Asian currency unit and may become that of the BRICs too. China's sovereign wealth has been used to make several high profile investments overseas including significant stakes in Blackstone, the US private equity house, and BP, the British oil company. Most significant of all, China Mobile has taken a $500 million stake in a leading Taiwan mobile telecoms company – even though the Chinese government doesn't accept Taiwan's independence.

This is where the IFMs and geopolitics meet. Tellingly, the gathering of world governments in London in 2009 to address the global credit crunch was not of the G7 (the US, Japan, UK, Germany, France, Italy and Canada) nor of the G8 (plus Russia) but of the G20 which includes both China and India. It was at this meeting that China announced that it would not indefinitely support the US's borrowing. Days before, China's central bank governor had made his SDR proposal. As in the IFMs, timing is everything.

So to our final IFC visit: Shanghai; and the last stop on our trip.

HOW IT ALL CONNECTS

- When governments raise interest rates to control inflation, stock markets (Chapter 2) go down and bond yields go up (Chapters 3 and 4)

- When governments reduce interest rates to stimulate the economy, stock markets go up and bond yields go down

- If a country increases its interest rates its currency strengthens and its exports go down – with a knock-on effect on global trade

- Governments don't like inflation (Chapter 4) but the US wouldn't mind if the dollar depreciates – this will make its exports cheaper overseas and reduce the real value of its mountain of debt

- Governments, through their sovereign wealth funds (Chapter 7), are also investors and as sovereign borrowers (Chapter 8) raise debt finance from international syndicates of commercial banks

- Much of the world's shipping is reinsured at Lloyd's of London (Chapter 7)

- Ship finance is a form of asset finance (Chapter 8)

DAY TRIP TO
SHANGHAI

If London is a highly developed IFC with a smallish domestic market – a big head with a small body – Shanghai is an IFC with an infant head and the body of what looks like being a giant.

Shanghai is the financial centre of the world's most populated country (over 1.3 billion) which will be the next global economic superpower. China is already the second largest economy in the world after the US and experienced phenomenal double-digit economic growth between 2002 and 2007. The world's largest airline, insurance group, telecoms and energy companies are all Chinese, as is the world's largest bank – Industrial and Commercial Bank of China (ICBC) which, when it listed on both the Shanghai and Hong Kong stock exchanges, was the world's largest IPO, raising $22 billion. Three hundred of the world's 500 leading companies have invested in China, despite its comparatively closed and underdeveloped financial system.

As the gateway to this vast potential domestic market, Shanghai is seen as the most open, culturally advanced and business-friendly city on the Chinese mainland. This is partly historic: over the centuries its strategic position at the mouth of the Yangtze River made it a centre for international trade; it became industrialised thanks to Japan after the end of the Sino-Japanese war in 1895; and in the 1930s it was the most important financial centre in Asia and third largest in the world after New York and London, a position it lost after the revolution in 1949 caused an exodus to Hong Kong.

Yet Shanghai suffers from the past: the stock market in its modern guise is less than 20 years old, dating from 1990; and also the present – it is part of a controlled economy with the degree of protectionism and over-regulation which all of that implies or 'a market economy with socialist characteristics' as the ruling communist party puts it.

Shanghai itself has suffered from less than cordial relations with that ruling party. In the 1980s, Shanghai became the largest tax contributor to central government, which stunted its infrastructural and financial development as it was denied the experimental economic reforms that took place elsewhere in China.

Then in 1991 the former mayor, Jiang Zemin, became the Party president, increased domestic and foreign investment and reduced the tax burden. This transformed Shanghai into the main financial and commercial centre in China with above-average economic growth. Now Shanghai is the home to branches or regional HQs of 700 Chinese and foreign financial and industrial institutions, including Bank of America, General Motors and IBM. The Lujiazui finance and trade zone has become China's Wall Street, employing 1% of Shanghai's population. That's a lot of people. The transport and telecoms infrastructures are being continuously improved.

The Shanghai Stock Exchange (SSE) is now the sixth-largest in the world (market capitalisation: $3.7 trillion) and the largest in Asia after Tokyo, having overtaken Hong Kong in 2007. Before 2006, two-thirds of the shares on the SSE were government-owned and non-tradable, leaving a much-reduced freefloat and relatively low volumes.

But, just prior to the global recession, its market value surged by 130% (2006) and 97% (2007) with unprecedented volumes making it temporarily the second biggest stock exchange in the world in terms of turnover. The SSE is expected to become the third largest stock market in the world in less than ten years. It has over 150 members and a trading floor of 3600 square metres, the largest in the Asia-Pacific region.

That all sounds rosy, but comes just after a four-year market slump between 2001 and 2005 that saw the SSE's market value halve from its 2001 peak. In response to the continued deterioration in the value of the stocks listed, the government banned new IPO listings on the exchange between April 2005 and May 2006. This favoured Hong Kong. It also looked as if the authorities had taken against the SSE in favour of the Shenzhen Stock Exchange (SZSE) (the SSE and SZSE were set up in 1990 and 1991 respectively and both remain government-owned). The SZSE is the equivalent of China's junior market, the equivalent of NASDAQ in the US, where smaller companies list.

However, in March 2009 the Chinese government approved a plan to turn Shanghai into a global financial and shipping centre by 2020. The Hong Kong Monetary Authority is committed to helping the SSE improve its trading, clearing and settlement systems and there are plans for Chinese depository receipts to enable the shares of Chinese companies listed overseas to be traded in Shanghai. There are also plans for a derivatives exchange.

There is ongoing rivalry between Shanghai and Beijing to become the pre-eminent IFC in Asia. The majority of domestic financial institutions, regulators and policymakers are headquartered in Beijing's financial zone which extends over 35 blocks and holds 90% of China's banking and 65% of its insurance assets. Many major foreign banks have chosen Beijing as the preferred base for their Chinese operations. Officials have engaged in high-profile European roadshows to market Beijing to incoming companies.

The risk in all of this is the equivalent of split liquidity in equity markets: each of Shanghai, Shenzhen and Beijing could become Asia's top IFC in the absence of the other two. If all three compete then none of them may.

China, the big body with the small head, is trying to keep pace. In this it has been partly successful. The markets' regulatory structure has changed beyond recognition. Previously the People's Bank of China acted as a central bank, commercial bank, deposit taker and regulator. Today, there are several different regulatory bodies, each with a defined area of responsibility and China is experimenting with the concepts of shareholding in banks and occidental systems of capital requirement and corporate governance.

The markets themselves have been a rollercoaster ride as the authorities have struggled to control an overheating economy fuelled by overseas exports. In 2006 and 2007 the SSE experienced a stock market bubble as those profits were repatriated. The country's strict capital controls meant the surplus could only be invested in property or shares so both assets spiked. The government stepped in, made a larger freefloat of shares available on the domestic market and eased restrictions on investment overseas.

Then, in May 2007, stamp tax on stock trades tripled. Volumes on both the SSE and the SZSE fell 60% over the next six months and during early 2008 the Shanghai Composite Index fell by 34%, prompting the government to try to boost the market by restricting the supply of new shares. However, it's not all bad. Foreigners listing or planning to list on Shanghai include the New York Stock Exchange and the Asian life insurance businesses of AIG.

Although foreigners are permitted to participate in a widening range of financial activities (such as insurance), Shanghai – and China – remain relatively closed markets. Foreign investors face a lack of currency convertibility, extensive capital controls, and detrimentally low standards of regulation, with new listings encouraged at the expense of financial transparency. Innovation is stifled as both national and foreign banks have severe limitations on their permitted range of activities which in any case are geographically circumscribed.

However, the commercial banking sector has been transformed from comprising a few, wholly state-controlled and inefficient institutions to a more diverse set of competitive financial enterprises that participate in a wide range of activities. China's financial system is still relatively underdeveloped and highly regulated but it has had just 30 years since the first major reform movement in 1979. Besides, Western models of finance can hardly be held up as shining examples of prudent risk-taking. Commercial banking is a good place to start.

The Chinese can afford to sit back and observe. ICBC is worth close to $200 billion which means it can buy up HSBC twice over as well as several of the largest US banks. The Chinese government owns almost three-quarters of it.

Which is a fitting place to end, since these banks are at the heart of the IFMs and the IFCs and could be where latter-day communism meets present-day capitalism, were China to flex its financial muscle.

Goodbye to the old world, welcome to the new. The future starts here.

JARGON BUSTER

If you can't find what you want here, try:

- www.wikipedia.com
- www.investopedia.com
- *A–Z of International Finance: The Essential Guide to Tools, Terms & Techniques* by Stephen Mahony

A forfait	The *trade finance* market where *letters of credit* are traded
ABS	Asset-backed securities (includes *MBSs*)
Absolute return	A positive return that a *hedge fund* manager aims to generate regardless of market movements
Accelerate	What a lender does to have a loan repaid early, usually because of an event of *default*
Acquisition finance	Short-term loans or bonds used by a bidder to fund the takeover of a target company, usually at an above-average rate of interest with a view to refinancing once the takeover is complete
Agent or agent bank	The bank that gets the *mandate* from a borrower to arrange a *syndicated loan* for it and collects the repayments from the borrower during the life of the loan to distribute to the other *syndicate* members
Aggregate demand (AD)	Economics term meaning the totality of a country's expenditure on goods at a particular price
AIM	Alternative Investment Market – the junior market to the London Stock Exchange, designed for younger companies with short trading histories (usually because they are in hi-tech and bio-tech fields that require substantial initial investment)
Alternative risk transfer (ART)	Ways of funding insurance risk through capital markets instruments (such as a *catastrophe bond*)
Amortisation	Paying a loan back in a series of instalments
Annuity	A contract bought with pension plan proceeds that provides an annual income until the pensioner's death
Arbitrage	The act of simultaneously buying and selling in two separate markets to gain from pricing differences between them
Arbitrageur	Someone who practises *arbitrage*
Arranger	In a syndicated loan, the bank awarded the mandate by the borrower to arrange the loan

Asset finance	Tax-favoured way of funding an asset where a bank (lessor) buys the asset and leases it to the borrower (lessee) for the asset's useful economic life in return for regular payments (rental) paid by the lessee over the life of the lease to reimburse the lessor for the capital cost of the asset plus interest. Also known as *finance leasing*
Auction	Market makers quoting prices at which they will buy and sell (compare *order driven*)
Balloon repayment	Used in loans and *finance leases* where the final instalment to be paid by the borrower under the financing is much larger than earlier instalments
Bancassurance	Banks offering insurance and related financial products such as pensions
Bank	An institution that is licensed to conduct banking business – see *Commercial bank* and *Investment bank*
Basis points	Hundredths of a per cent (0.01%) – so bankers talk about a bond being priced at 25 basis points over Treasuries, meaning 0.25% over the rate US government bonds are paying
Basis rate	The rate on which interest under a loan or bond is based, e.g. LIBOR, EURIBOR
Bear	An investor who thinks the market will fall
Bells and whistles	*Swaps* and *options* attached to a bond issue
Beta	Correlation between a share and the index
Bid/Offer	Brokers quote two prices for securities – the price at which they will buy from you (bid) and the price at which they will sell (offer) to you. The difference or '*spread*' is their 'turn' (profit) since they will bid for less than they will offer
Bilateral loans	Two-party loans (that is, between a single bank and a single borrower)
Bill of exchange	A corporate IOU under which a company agrees to make payment on a specified future date (like a post-dated cheque)
Block trade	Where a bank buys or sells an entire portfolio of *securities*, usually on behalf of an *institutional investor*
Bond	An IOU issued by a corporate or bank (the terms 'bond' and 'note' are virtually interchangeable)
Book building	A means of syndicating a financing by soliciting indicative bids from prospective syndicate participants (*banks*)
Book runner	In a *syndicated loan*, the bank appointed by the arranger to pull together the syndicate of banks that will participate in providing the loan
Bought funding	Where a bank buys the entirety of a proposed issue or loan
BRICs	Brazil, Russia, India and China
Bridge financing	Temporary financing used before the long-term funding is put in place – for instance, a loan taken out by a bidder in an *M&A* transaction which will then be refinanced by a share or bond issue once the takeover has been completed

Broken funding	Where a bank receives a payment from the borrower earlier or later than expected which it cannot therefore use towards a matching borrowing it has obtained on the inter-bank market
Broker	Intermediaries that buy and sell *securities* as agents for institutions or on their own account, including 'broker-dealers' (market makers) and 'inter-dealer brokers' (brokers that specialise in intermediating between dealers that want anonymity when trading in the markets)
Broker company	An insurance term for an intermediary that passes insurance risk to reinsurers that aren't *direct writers*
Bull	An investor who thinks the market will rise
Bullet	Bank loan, the principal of which is repayable in one *tranche* on its maturity (i.e. no *amortisation*)
Buy side	That part of the market that buys *securities* – i.e. *institutional investors*
Cable	The $/£ trade in the foreign exchange market
Call option	Option that allows the holder to buy at a specific price (locks in a maximum price)
Cap	An upper limit or ceiling on the interest payable under a loan
Capital adequacy	A minimum amount of money (capital) that a bank is required to maintain as a ratio to the loans it has made (assets), for prudential reasons to ensure it is able to repay depositors; it is now based on an internationally accepted framework (the Basel Accord) that assigns risk weightings to bank assets and minimum capital ratios
Carry trade	Borrowing at a low rate to buy high-yielding investments, so ensuring a profit
Cashflow	The strength of revenue or income flowing through a business; a business can be very profitable (i.e. make a large margin between its sales and its cost of production) but still go bust because its income lags its cost of sales; equally a business can have strong cashflow but only marginal profitability and still go on year after year
Catastrophe (CAT) bonds	Bonds that pay an above-average return but which are triggered by a specified type of catastrophe (such as an earthquake) in which case investors forgo interest and sometimes some or all of the principal invested
CDOs	Collateralised debt obligations – loans or bonds from a variety of borrowers that are pooled and new securities issued that pay according to the performance of the pool
Cede/cession	The act of passing on (part of) an insurance risk (cession) from the primary market to the secondary (reinsurance) market
Central bank	A government entity that may have a regulatory function (regulating local banks) or an economic policy function (e.g. controlling inflation) or both
CFDs or contracts for difference	Retail versions of *futures* where the *broker* and investor agree to exchange the difference between the price of an asset at the beginning and end of the contract

Chapter 11	Named after the US legislation that allows an insolvent company to seek protection from its creditors, so enabling it to restructure and resume trading on a solvent basis
Chartists	Colloquial name for technical analysts who plot past market moves to detect patterns likely to occur in and shape the future
Churning	Excessive buying and selling of *securities* to generate commission
Clearing house	Usually used in the context of a *derivatives* market (*futures* and *options*), this provides the offsetting trade which ensures market participants are not exposed to their *counterparty* credit risk
CLOs	Collateralised loan obligations - like *CDOs*; but can also mean bond issues backed by *leveraged* loans
Closed-ended	An investment fund structured like a company so that investors buy shares in the market which means that at any given moment the number of shares in issue is fixed (compare with *open-ended*)
Collateral	The *security* provided by a borrower for repayment of a loan
Collective investment scheme	A pooled fund that enables investors to invest in shares and bonds indirectly
Commercial bank	A bank that takes in deposits and borrows in the wholesale market in order to make loans. The difference between the interest it receives and the interest it pays is the bank's *margin*. High street clearing banks are commercial banks
Commercial paper	A type of bond with a very short maturity – usually three months (called '90-day paper')
Commitment	The amount of a loan agreed to be lent by a bank
Committed facility	A loan that a bank is obliged to make up to an agreed maximum and that is available to a borrower for a specified period
Contrarian	An investor or analyst who advocates a market view completely at odds with the current accepted wisdom
Convertible	A bond that gives the holder the right to switch it into equity (shares)
Corporate finance	The banking activity of advising a company on how to raise money and/or an *M&A* deal
Counterparty	The other side in a *securities* or *derivatives* trade
Countertrade	A part of *trade finance* involving the barter of goods and services, often in emerging markets that lack hard currency. For example, a New York law firm was once paid by a government in turkeys and denim. Countertrade specialists act as *brokers* in such deals
Coupon	The rate of interest paid on a bond – traditionally bonds (other than debentures) were bearer so the issuer would pay interest only to the person bearing the coupon
Covered option	Where the *option writer* owns the underlying asset to which the option relates

Cov-lite	Used to describe a loan agreement or bond which imposes obligations (covenants) on the borrower that are less onerous than usual (this occurs in a toppy bull market where banks are chasing borrowers or issuers)
Credit agreement	The main document under which a loan or other debt-based funding is made
Credit crunch	The term used to describe the collapse in lending from 2007 onwards (especially in the US home loan market) that prompted a global recession from mid-2008 onwards
Credit default swap (CDS)	A *derivative* that makes good the lender's loss if a borrower *defaults* (or a credit event occurs)
Credit easing	Increasing the ability to borrow by increasing the money supply (*liquidity*) in the market
Credit-linked notes	A bond combined with a *credit default swap* that provides protection against a default or credit rating downgrade
Credit risk	The risk that a borrower or *counterparty* may default
Cross-margin	A single margin position across more than one *derivatives* market
Cost-plus basis	Where the fee is explicitly broken down into the cost to the supplier or provider plus their expected profit margin - used in the inter-bank and corporate lending market
Cram down	See *deleveraging*
Currency market(s)	The virtual market where currencies are traded in which the principal players are major banks and financial institutions
Currency swap	A *derivative* that enables each party to exchange its currency of borrowing with that of the other party
Custodian	A bank that holds *securities* on behalf of an *institutional investor*
Dark market	A private market where cross-trading occurs without traders or prices being revealed
Dark pools	Off-exchange markets where banks, *brokers* and *institutional investors* trade with each other privately (see also *ECNs*)
Dawn raid	*M&A* term where a bidder builds up an unexpected stake in a target by scooping up shares quickly in the market
Day traders	Market players that aim to make a return from intra day (during the day) changes in the market
Debenture	A corporate bond listed on the London Stock Exchange, often secured on the issuer's assets
Debt	Any form of finance where the borrower agrees to repay the principal amount of the debt and in the meantime to pay interest on it (also known as 'servicing' the debt) which is generally tax-deductible; the only other form of money is *equity*
Debtor-in-possession	A company trading out of *Chapter 11* insolvency to which senior-ranking loans can be made

Default	Failure to repay a loan or part of a loan on time – usually because the borrower is bust
Deflation	Decrease in the price of goods with the risk of this leading to reduced economic activity
Deleveraging (aka *cram down*)	Reducing *gearing* (the level of borrowing) – in the case of a bank, reducing its loan book by calling in loans
Delta	Correlation between an *option* and the underlying share
Demand side	In economics, those fiscal policies that affect *aggregate demand*
Demateriali-sation	The electronic record of *securities* ownership, replacing paper or hard-copy certificates
Depository receipts	Where *securities* are held on deposit by a bank, acting as depository, which issues other tradable securities (depository receipts) in respect of them
Derivatives	Instruments that are derived from shares or bonds and are either *OTC* or exchange traded, such as *futures* and *options*
Direct writer	A reinsurer that obtains its business by dealing directly with primary insurers
Disinter-mediation	Borrowers (companies and governments) tapping the capital markets (investors) directly rather than via banks. Banks loathe this idea – it cuts them out – but whenever banks are less creditworthy than their borrowers the latter may bypass them
Drawdown or drawing down	The point at which a corporate borrower gets the money it is borrowing
Drawer/ drawee	Drawer = company that agrees to pay Drawee = the recipient of the promised payment
Drop-dead	Deadline by which a project must come onstream complete
Due diligence	A detailed review of a borrower's financial position, made by a bank or lead manager in a bond or share issue, to satisfy lenders or investors of the borrower's credit standing
DVP	Delivery Versus Payment – an immediate transaction by each party simultaneously fulfilling its side of the bargain (see also *spot market*)
ECNs	Electronic communication networks: off-exchange markets where banks, *brokers* and *institutional investors* trade with each other privately (see also *dark pools*)
Embedded option	Where an instrument behaves as if it contains or is attached to an *option*, such as a convertible bond (bond which allows the holder to convert it into shares in the issuer)
Emerging markets	Countries which are under-developed economically
Equity	The form of finance where shareholders put up risk capital in return for the prospect of dividend payments and capital growth on their shares; dividends are paid out of the company's taxed income

Equity cure	Injection of further equity to prevent a debt default by a *leveraged buy-out*
Escrow accounts	An offshore account (used in *project finance* to divert funds generated by a project to the banks in order to service and redeem the project loan)
ETFs or exchange-traded funds	Funds in which a unit represents an entire stock index or *portfolio* of shares
EURIBOR	Like LIBOR: the interbank offered rate for the euro sponsored by the European Banking Federation
Eurobond	The traditional name for an international bond – i.e. issued by a corporate or *sovereign* outside its domestic jurisdiction in a currency other than its domestic currency (note: here, 'euro' has nothing do with the euro currency)
Event of default	One of the events entitling a lender to terminate a credit agreement and ask for the borrowing to be repaid immediately
Excess	An insurance term where cover takes the form of a share of the claim above a fixed level
Excess treaty	Reinsurance that covers a portion of each claim in excess of an agreed figure and up to an agreed limit, which provides the insurer with stability and allows it to take on more and larger business
Exit route	The way in which an investment is realised – e.g. in *venture capital*
F9 model monkey	Slang for a trader who, before doing a trade, consults a spreadsheet using the F9 key
Face/par/ nominal value	The face value of a bond at which it will be redeemed
Factoring	A financial service that allows a business to improve its cashflow by selling to a bank for immediate money what it is owed by customers (its receivables)
Facultative automatic agreement	Reinsurance which covers many primary policies of the same type on a *proportional* or *excess* basis
Facultative certificate	Where a reinsurer covers a single risk and cover is either proportional or excess
Fannie Mae	Federal National Mortgage Association (FNMA) – originally a government agency that guarantees and securitises US real estate loans to low-income borrowers to provide more *liquidity* to that market
FATF	Financial Action Task Force, an inter-governmental body that tackles money laundering and terrorism
Feeder fund	A fund that channels investment money into another fund (the master fund) that does the actual investing
Finance lease	See *Asset finance*
Financial covenants	Promises made in a loan agreement by the borrower about how it will run its business

Financial Services Authority	The UK's financial watchdog or regulator responsible for supervising banks, fund managers, insurance companies and for the rules governing listings on the London Stock Exchange
Finite or non-traditional	Reinsurance that enables the primary insurer to smooth its financial performance through tax benefits
Flotation	The point at which a private company is listed on a stock exchange and offers its shares to the public; also known as 'listing' or 'going public' or an 'initial public offering' (*IPO*)
Flow monster	An *investment bank* that gains market insight from the volume and size of trades it executes with and on behalf of customers
Following reinsurers	Reinsurers that reinsure part of a primary insurance risk on terms set by the lead reinsurer
Forex (aka currency)	Foreign exchange – the largest money market in the world
Foreign direct investment (FDI)	Where foreign companies establish distribution or manufacturing businesses by setting up operations in a (usually emerging) market
Forward	An *OTC future*, that is, a contract for delivery in the future at today's price which is not an exchange-traded instrument
Freddie Mac	Federal Home Loan Mortgage Company (FHLMC) - originally a government agency that buys and securitises US real estate loans to provide more *liquidity* to the home loan market
Front running	Trading ahead of a customer's order in order to benefit from the consequential market upswing (usually unlawful)
FRN	A 'floating-rate note' – i.e. a bond whose *coupon* varies in line with a benchmark interest rate (as opposed to fixed-rate bonds)
Fund-of-funds	A fund that invests in other funds rather than in the underlying markets
Fungible	Two or more *securities* that in terms of issuer, interest rate, par value and maturity are interchangeable
Future	A *derivative* that allows the holder to command a market position without actually holding the underlying *security*, by putting up a *margin* (a small percentage of the total exposure) and which is settled on expiry by payment or receipt of the difference between the future price and the underlying. Unlike an *option* which gives the holder the right but not the obligation, a future imposes the obligation which – together with the ability to trade on *margin* – is what makes futures so dangerous to novices
Gamma	The rate of change of *delta* in relation to the underlying share
Gearing (aka leverage)	The ratio of a company's *debt* to its *equity* capital
Gilts	UK government bonds
Global bond	Nowadays *issuers* issue just one paper bond, the global bond, which is deposited with a securities *custodian* which then keeps electronic records of individual bond holdings

Global custody A service offered by banks to *institutional investors* to hold their *securities*, receive any income in respect of them, reclaim any tax rebate and conduct any associated foreign exchange transactions

Growth stocks Shares of companies that are fast-growing so may not produce much dividend income but should increase in value over time

Heating degree days Measures of energy used when trading weather *derivatives*

Hedge fund A *collective investment scheme* that takes high-risk positions in *derivatives* and currencies and uses short positions to generate high returns; the manager is usually on a performance-related fee

Hedging The use of *derivatives* to protect an investment or market position against market fluctuations

High-net-worth individuals (HNWIs) Rich or wealthy people (strictly speaking: people who are rich once their borrowings are deducted from their assets to arrive at a net figure for their wealth)

High-yield bonds See *Junk*

Hung bridge Short-term *acquisition finance* that cannot be refinanced

Ijara *Islamic banking* equivalent of *asset finance*

Illiquid investments Investments than cannot be readily sold or realised

Index-tracking Matching a *portfolio's* return to that of an index by replicating or mimicking the index's constituent stocks in the *portfolio* (aka *passive management*)

Inflation Increase in the price of goods leading to a fall in the real value of money

Institution or institutional investor The ultimate buyers of *securities* (equities and bonds) – insurance companies, pension funds and investment managers (who run *unit trusts, investment trusts* and *OIECs*)

Interest rate swap An agreement to exchange a floating-rate liability for a fixed rate or vice versa – the two parties notionally swap an underlying principal amount then pay each other interest as if they had made the swap; in practice the amounts are netted so that only one payment passes from one to the other; the effect is to give each party a *synthetic* position as if it had borrowed at the swapped rate

In-the-money An *option* that, if exercised, would produce a profit as opposed to one that is out-of-the-money ('under water'), which would normally be allowed to expire without being exercised

Intra-day Within the trading day

Investment bank An institution that at heart underwrites the issue of *securities*, makes a market in them and trades them for its own account. Mostly American

Investment trust A listed company that invests in the shares of other companies. Also called a *closed-ended* fund because (being a company) it has a set number of shares in issue

Investment grade	*Securities* that are rated as such by rating agencies (BAA and above by Moody's or BBB and above by Standard & Poor's), enabling pension funds to buy them
IPO	Initial public offering – same as listing, floating and going public: when a private company lists its *shares* on an exchange
ISDA	The International Swaps and Derivatives Association, a trade body representing market users that provides standard legal documentation for these trades
Islamic banking	Forms of financing in accordance with Sharia law which forbids interest (*riba*) and gambling (maisir) but allows participation in profit
Issuer	A company, bank or government that issues bonds or equities
Istisna-ijara	*Islamic banking* equivalent of *project finance*
Junior debt	Debt that ranks behind senior debt so is the last to be paid out on a borrower's insolvency
Junk	Below-investment grade bonds which most pension funds are not permitted to buy. Also called *high-yield bonds*
Late trading/ market timing	Trading in and out of mutual funds to exploit valuations that are no longer current (usually unlawful)
LBO	Leveraged buyout – like an *MBO* but where the ratio of debt funding to equity is high
Lead manager	The bank that leads a syndicated bond issue, liaises with the *issuer* and puts together the *syndicate* of other underwriters
Lead reinsurer	The reinsurer that sets the terms when a primary insurer lays off risk to more than one reinsurer
Letter of credit or L/C	Used extensively in *trade finance*, a document issued by a bank at the instructions of the buyer in a transaction to pay the seller (called the beneficiary) a stated sum within a prescribed time limit – by being drawn on a bank, the L/C becomes a tradable instrument that the beneficiary can sell in the market, usually at a discount to its face value
Leverage	*Gearing* or borrowing
Liar loan	A *sub-prime* loan where the borrower self-certifies their income
LIBOR	London Interbank Offered Rate – the rate at which creditworthy banks will lend to each other in the wholesale market
Life assurance	Insurance that provides a lump sum on death or disability
Limited recourse	Used in *project finance* where the lenders do not look principally to the borrowing entity for repayment but to the cash-generation of the project itself
Liquidity	A measure of the tradability of a company's *shares* – affected by free-float of shares held by outside investors – and of the ease with which a *security* can be traded on the market
LLP	Limited liability partnership – an investment vehicle used in private equity deals aimed at pension fund participation (LLPs have tax and regulatory benefits)

Loan book	A *commercial bank's* portfolio of corporate loans
Local	A member of a *futures* or *derivatives* exchange (also a speculator)
Lock-in	A ban for a specified period on redeeming or selling a holding (usually of an investment in a *hedge fund*)
Long	To have a position in the market – i.e. to have bought a share or bond (compare *short*)
Long-stop date	Deadline by which a project should be completed
M&A	'Mergers and acquisitions' – i.e. the activity where companies take each other over
Macro-economics	Economics at a global level
Macro-prudential	High level regulation that focuses on *systemic risk* to the financial system as a whole
Mandate	The appointment by a borrower or issuer of a bank to arrange a *syndicated loan* or bond issue
Margin	The deposit required by a *derivatives* market to hold a *futures* position; also the profit on a loan or trade
Market risk	The risk that general market movements – for instance in interest rates, shares or currencies – will affect a particular investment
Mark-to-market	The daily requirement to recalculate the current value and increase margin as a *futures* position deteriorates
Market value	What a purchaser will pay for a *security* - may not be its *par/nominal* value but the two are likely to converge as the security nears maturity (assuming the issuer's credit rating doesn't change)
Matched funding	Where a bank borrows short-term in the inter-bank market to lend long-term to a borrower and the payments of interest and principal it receives from the borrower exactly meet its inter-bank obligations as they fall due
MBO	Management buyout where the managers of a business (usually a division or subsidiary of a large public company) agree to buy it from the company, usually using *venture capital* to pay for the bulk of the purchase price
MBS	Mortgage-backed securities - bonds issued off a pool of mortgages
Merchant bank	A UK term for a bank that traditionally provided *corporate finance* advice to companies raising money and/or involved in *M&A*. Some also provided investment advice through a fund management arm. Most have been absorbed into *commercial* or *investment* banks. Called 'merchant' because they assisted UK exporters/importers by providing letters of credit when Britain was a trading empire
Mezzanine finance	Found in *venture capital* deals (e.g. *MBOs* and *LBOs*) where the capital is part-equity, part-debt, and ranks behind *senior debt* but ahead of *junior debt* and *equity*. Also used to describe debt that can flip into equity (e.g. convertible bond or loan)

Microcredit	Providing small loans to poor people in third world countries to stimulate economic activity
Microfinance institutions (MFIs)	Banks that offer microcredit by extending tiny loans (microloans) to the very poor
Micro-prudential	A detailed level of regulation that addresses the risks carried by individual institutions
Money markets	Market for short-term instruments from overnight to a year in duration
Monoline	Specialist insurer that back-stops complex securitisations and *project financings* by providing a credit guarantee or completion bond
Mortality bonds	Bonds issued by insurance companies to offset the risk of a high incidence of death (which would trigger large insurance pay-outs)
Mortgage-backed	A bond issue collateralised by a pool of mortgages
MTN	Medium term note – a bond; usually part of an 'MTN programme' where a panel of banks provide a wide range of financings to a corporate, ranging from loans to bond issuance
Munis/ municipal bonds	US term for bonds issued by municipalities - which includes cities, towns, schools, hospitals and similar civic or public organisations
Murabaha	*Islamic banking* mark-up transaction which avoids the payment of interest (banned in Islamic banking)
Naked option	Where the *option writer* does not own the underlying asset to which the option relates
Negative pledge	A financial covenant in which the borrower promises not to pledge its assets as security for other loans
Netting off	Where two parties owe each other a number of payments and only a single net amount passes from one to the other in settlement
Ninja loan	A *sub-prime* loan extended to a borrower said to have 'no income, no job, no assets'
Non-recourse finance	An absolute version of *limited recourse*, where the lenders do not look to the borrower for repayment but to the income generated by the assets being financed
OECD	Organisation for Economic Cooperation and Development, a club of 30 developed economies
OEIC	Open-ended investment company – a type of investment fund
OFC	Offshore financial centre - usually an island or archipelago with a no or low tax regime
Ofex	An off-exchange share matching and trading facility for companies that do not want to join the London Stock Exchange or AIM. Appeals to illiquid or family stocks
Office	Part of a bank or institution: front office is the client-facing, fee-

	earning part; back office is the administrative part (e.g. settlement of trades); middle office means those parts that are not fee-earning but are crucial to a bank's well-being such as IT, compliance and legal
Offtake or take-or-pay	A contract under which the output from a project is bought (critical to project financings in order to ensure a flow of money out of which the financing can be repaid)
Open architecture	Where a financial institution offers (or advises on) investment products that are not restricted to its own
Open-ended	An investment fund structured like a unit trust or mutual fund where investors buy units from the fund manager which means that new units can be issued at any time (compare with *closed-ended*)
Option	A *derivative* that gives the holder the right to buy (call) or sell (put) an underlying *security*, but not the obligation. 'American' options are exercisable at any time up to expiry; 'European' options are only exercisable immediately prior to expiry
Option writer	The party selling the option (whether a put or call) to the option buyer
Order driven	Where buy and sell orders are matched through an order book, usually electronic (compare *auction*)
Origination	The *investment bank* activity of advising borrowers on the issue of bonds
Originate-to-distribute	A form of *securitisation* where loans (especially home loans in the US) are made specifically to be sold on (a principal cause of the sub-prime credit crunch)
OTC	Over-the-counter: a *security* or transaction that is not traded on an exchange but is bought bespoke from a bank. Also used to refer to virtual markets where trading is between participants without the structure of a regulated market, such as the foreign exchange market
Pari passu	A financial covenant in which the borrower promises not to pledge its assets as security for other loans
Passive management	See *index-tracking*
Peer-to-peer	A system that connects individuals to individuals (used in this book in the context of *microfinance*)
Pension holiday	Where a plan sponsor (a company) is able to cease temporarily from contributing to a pension fund because it is overfunded
Peppercorn	A nominal amount (for instance for extending a finance lease beyond the primary term)
Piggyback loan	A sub-prime loan where a second mortgage is taken out to provide the deposit for the first
PIKS	Payment in kind securities, used in an *M&A* where the return accrues over their term and is often guaranteed by the target
Placing	Where a broker or *investment bank* places an issue of shares or bonds with a small group of institutions – this means the issue is not public and less disclosure is required. Also known as a 'private placement'

Plain vanilla	A financing that is straightforward, e.g. a bond issue without any 'bells and whistles'
Poison pill	An *M&A* term meaning a defensive tactic employed by a company to prevent itself from being taken over – generally frowned upon as protecting the incumbent management
Portfolio	A holding of different investments
Portfolio equity investment	Gaining indirect exposure to (usually emerging) markets by investing in the shares of companies that have made direct investments in those markets (aka *foreign indirect investment*)
Precipice bonds	Bonds linked to equity market returns that offered some protection in declining markets but huge exposures if shares 'fell off a cliff', that is, collapsed
Premiums	Periodic payment (for instance for insurance)
Pre-pack	A business pre-packaged to be sold on insolvency (that is, where a business is bought as soon as it becomes insolvent)
Price/earnings ratio	A measure of a company's rating by the stock market – calculated by dividing the share price by the last published annual earnings per share (net profit divided by the number of ordinary shares in issue)
Price/pricing	The interest rate at which a loan is made
Primary market	The market in which a loan or bond is launched or a risk insured (compare with *secondary market*)
Prime brokerage	The range of services provided by *investment banks* to *hedge funds*
Principal finance	The activity of an *investment bank* in buying and selling businesses for its own account, using its own capital, to generate a profit for itself
Principle-based regulation	Financial markets regulation where basic overarching principles are set out and participants are required to respect them in spirit and not just by the letter (contrast with *rule-based*)
Privatisation	The term covering the many ways in which public sector activities are transferred to the private sector
Program trade	A computer-driven trading activity that is triggered by discrepancies between the price of bonds or shares and their related *derivatives*
Project finance	Also known as 'limited recourse' or 'non-recourse' finance because the lenders have recourse only to the project itself; often used to finance third-world infrastructure projects where the state buys the output (e.g. hydro-electricity) which funds the lending, and the lenders have rights of 'step in' if the borrower (the project company) *defaults*
Property investement fund	A *collective investment scheme* that holds a pool of underlying property investments, allowing investors to move in and out of property more quickly (by buying and selling units in the fund) than if they held the underlying assets directly
Proportional	An insurance term where cover takes the form of a proportion of the claim

Pump and dump	Using rumours to drive up a stock's price in order to offload shares (usually unlawful)
Put option	Option that allows the holder to sell at a specific price (locks in a minimum the holder will receive)
Quantitative easing	Provision by a *central bank* of a sharp increase of *liquidity* to the economy through buying financial assets (aka printing money)
Quants or quantitative analysts	Analysts who use complex computer-driven models to help them predict future market moves
Quota-share treaty	Reinsurance which covers a fixed percentage of each policy – used to help a primary insurer smooth its financial performance
Quick flip	The re-listing of a business taken private (usually by a private equity fund)
Rating	The rating conferred on a bond issue by a *rating agency* that indicates the likelihood that the issuer will repay it
Rating agency	Independent agencies (Standard & Poor's, Fitch and Moody's are the best known) that assess an issuer's ability to service and repay a bond and provide a credit rating (triple A is the highest) to enable institutions and *brokers* to assess a bond's creditworthiness quickly
REIT	Real estate investment trust: a type of *property investment fund*
Regulatory capital	The capital cushion a bank is required to set aside (as a percentage of its loan book) under the Basel rules
Reserve currency	Market term for a national currency that, because of the home country's global economic dominance, is also the currency of international trade
Repo	Repurchase agreement – a method of providing a secured loan, usually for a three-month period, where institution A sells a bond to institution B for price X and in the same agreement agrees to buy the bond back from B for price Y: the difference between X and Y is the carry-cost or implied interest rate; the loan is secured since if A *defaults*, B has legal title to the bond and can sell it. Repos are one of the techniques used by *central banks* to control *liquidity* in the markets
Rescheduling	Where the banks agree to spread the repayment of a loan over a longer term to enable the borrower to repay it at all
Retail	Where the customer is an individual (contrast *wholesale*)
Retiring debt	Paying off a loan or other debt funding
Retro-cessionaire	A reinsurer or re-reinsurer
Revolver	Revolving credit facility – i.e. a bank loan that works like an overdraft: any principal repaid can be drawn again
Riba	Interest – banned by *Islamic banking*
Rights issue	A further issue of shares by a listed company – called a 'rights' issue because in some markets existing shareholders have a right to the new shares in proportion to their existing holdings so that their stake in the company is not diluted

Rule-based regulation	Financial services regulation where rules are set out in detail which, although rigorous, lacks flexibility, can be voluminous and may lead to a tick-box mentality (contrast with *principle-based*)
Search for yield	Attempts by investors to seek higher-yielding instruments when interest rates are low
Secondary market	The market in which an existing loan, bond or risk is passed on
Secular trends	Major trends that mark a fundamental shift in the economic environment
Securitisation	Financial engineering that turns an income stream (for instance from a book of loans) into tradable *securities*, by selling the income stream to an *SPV* which then issues bonds. Also described as repackaging predictable cashflows from an asset class (such as mortgages) and refinancing them by issuing securities in transferable form
Security	Lawyers use this term to mean security for a loan but markets use it to mean an *equity* or a bond
Sell side	That part of the market that sells *securities* – i.e. bond issuers such as companies and governments, as well as *investment banks* and *brokers* that underwrite, distribute, sell and trade them
Senior debt	Loans that rank ahead of *junior debt* and shareholders on a company's insolvency
Settlement	Following clearing, where a *clearing house* arranges for payment (by the buyer) in return for delivery of the *securities* (by the seller)
Share	Evidence of *equity* ownership in a company
Sharia banking	The provision of finance in accordance with Islamic rules, avoiding interest, gambling and speculation (aka *Islamic banking*)
Short	To have sold a share or bond without owning it (in the expectation that the price will go down so that the broker can buy it in at a cheaper price when required to deliver the security) – hence 'shorting the market'
SIF (stock index future)	A *derivative* that enables an *institutional investor* to obtain exposure to the constituent stocks of a market index through a single instrument
SIV	Structured investment vehicle – a fund dedicated to investing in *securitisations* such as *CDOs* and *ABSs*
Soft-closed	A fund that says it is not accepting any new investors
Sovereign	A bond issuer which is a country or government
Sovereign wealth fund	An investment fund owned by the country whose assets it invests (aka SWF)
Special drawing right (SDR)	A unit of account of the *International Monetary Fund*
Specific risk	Risk particular to a bond or share. The opposite of *systemic risk*

Spot market	A transaction for immediate payment and delivery (as opposed to a *forward* or *future*) - usually associated with the currency market
Spread	The difference between a broker's *bid* and *offer* for a security – i.e. its turn or margin; the less liquid a market, the wider the spread
SPV	Special purpose vehicle – a shelf company used to make a bond issue, usually incorporated in a low-tax jurisdiction to reduce fiscal drag on the deal
Square book	A term used by *brokers* and *investment banks* to mean that their positions in the market are completely offsetting
Step-in rights	The rights of banks in a *project financing* to take the project over if it fails to meet milestones or the project company becomes insolvent
Stock pickers	Fund managers that specialise in identifying and investing in undervalued shares
Stock ramping	See *pump and dump*
Stretch loan	A *sub-prime* loan where more than half the borrower's gross income will be required to service the loan
Structured finance	A loose term that covers various activities from the repackaging of *securities* to the linking of *derivatives* to securities, preferably with a degree of complexity
Sub-prime lending	A fancy term for lending to poor *credit risks*
Sukuk	An *Islamic banking* securitisation
Supply side	In economics, those policies that drive competitive advantage such as investment, technology and education
Surplus-share treaty	Reinsurance which covers a variable percentage of each policy based on the limit of the policy and the treaty's agreed net line retention, so providing the insurer with greater capacity – the reverse of the *quota-share treaty*
Swap	A way of changing a floating-rate loan into a fixed-rate and vice versa; also a way of changing a loan into a different currency by swapping interest streams but not the underlying principal, enabling each of the two *counterparties* to obtain a better rate or currency position than they would in their respective markets
Swaption	An option to enter into a *swap*
Syndicate	A group of *commercial banks* (lending to a single borrower) or *investment banks* (underwriting a bond issue)
Syndicated loan	A loan made by a syndicate of banks to a borrower using a single loan agreement
Syndication	The banking activity of creating a syndicate for a loan or bond issue; usually done by the lead manager
Synthetic	The use of *derivatives* to replicate a market position
Systemic risk	Market risk – i.e. not risk that is specific to a particular *security*

Teaser loan	A *sub-prime* loan at an artificially low rate of interest, designed to be refinanced at a later date
Technical analysis	Using historic data about market movements to predict the future – practitioners are also known as *chartists* because they plot such movements on graphs
Term loan	A loan with a fixed *drawdown* period, schedule of repayments and specified end-date
Tick	Technically, the smallest price movement by which a *future* can go up or down; usually used to describe a bond, share or general market movement – it 'ticked up' or 'down'
TIEAs	Tax information exchange agreements entered into between developed economies and *OFCs* under which the latter make depositor information available to discourage capital flight and tax evasion
Tombstone	The rectangular advert or lucite ornament announcing the successful *syndication* of a loan or bond issue, listing the borrower/issuer and syndicate members (so called because it looks like one)
Toxic tranche	The riskiest slice of repackaged *debt*, often left with the bank originating the repackaging
Trade compression	Reducing banks' exposures to each other by netting off transactions - used especially in *derivatives*
Trade finance	A method of ensuring that exporters get paid and buyers pay only when they have the goods; uses *letters of credit* (drawn on creditworthy banks) that are then discounted in the '*à forfait*' market
Tranche	A slice of a loan or bond – may apply to a particular part-repayment
Treasuries	US government bonds – the US government is the largest borrower in the world and is regarded as the safest (if it goes bust we might as well all pack up) so it commands the finest pricing of its bonds, which is the benchmark off which all international bond issues are priced
Treaty	Reinsurance which covers a particular set of insurance policies (within agreed limits) over a set period
Triple witching hour	The occasional convergence of expiry dates on *options*, *futures* and options-on-futures which can cause enormous volatility in the run-up
Trustee	Some bonds are issued with a trust structure allowing a corporate trustee to act on behalf of bondholders
Turn-key basis	A project that is ready to come onstream as soon as it is completed and handed over by the builders
UCITS	The name of the EU directive that regulates investment funds, often applied to the funds themselves (unincorporated collective investment schemes)
Underlying (aka cash market)	The instrument(s) from which *derivatives* are derived
Underwriting	Most issues of bonds or *equities* are underwritten by *investment banks*, which guarantee that the *issuer* will raise the intended amount

	of money even if, on the day of issue, market sentiment means that take-up of the issue is less than expected
Unit trust	An *open-ended collective investment scheme*, i.e. where the investment manager can issue as many units as necessary to meet demand
Upper quartile	The top twenty-five percent of fund managers ranked by investment performance
Upstream/ downstream	In private equity, upstream is raising the money (from *institutional investors*) and downstream is spending it (for instance on takeovers)
Value-at-risk (VAR)	Computer-based risk analysis that enables a bank to gauge and manage its aggregate exposure to markets — done by devising models based on historic data of market movements, price volatility and correlations between markets
Value investing	Investment style that seeks out shares that are undervalued on the fundamentals (for instance, in a growth industry) regardless of market sentiment
Vendor placing	Linked to *M&A*, where the target's shareholders are paid in the bidder's shares which are then sold in the market to give them what they really want — cash
Venture capital	Equity finance provided by specialist 'venture capitalists' in return for a shareholding in the business (usually a relatively new and small one); they realise their investment when the company floats or is sold in a 'trade sale'; note that they also finance *MBOs*
Visibles and invisibles	Economic term for exports: visibles = goods; invisibles = services
Vulture funds	Think of these as investment funds run by *arbitrageurs*
Warrant	A bond or *derivative* that allows the holder to buy shares in a company
Weighting	Mathematical adjustments to an index to counter dominance by one or more large shares
White knight	An *M&A* term for a third company that comes to the target's rescue in a bid — usually by bidding for the target itself
Whole business securitisation	A *securitisation* where the entire income of a business is securitised
Wholesale	Where the customer is a business or government
Yield	The income from an asset expressed as a percentage of its market value

Index

If you can't find what you want here, try the Jargon Buster

LONGTAIL